Even Dawkins Has a God

Probing and exposing the weaknesses in Richard
Dawkins' arguments in The God Delusion

NEIL LAING

WESTBOW
PRESS
A DIVISION OF THOMAS NELSON
& ZONDERVAN

Cover photo by Rupert Sanford-Scutt
Front cover: Doubtful Sound, New Zealand.

WestBow Press books may be ordered through booksellers or by contacting:

WestBow Press
A Division of Thomas Nelson & Zondervan
1663 Liberty Drive
Bloomington, IN 47403
www.westbowpress.com
1 (866) 928-1240

ISBN: 978-1-4908-4789-4 (sc)
ISBN: 978-1-4908-4790-0 (hc)
ISBN: 978-1-4908-4791-7 (e)

Library of Congress Control Number: 2014914242

Printed in the United States of America.

WestBow Press rev. date: 08/27/2014

CONTENTS

FOREWORD

Christina Biggs

Most UK Christians of my acquaintance have a personal relationship with Richard Dawkins even when they don't have a particular favourite Christian leader. Church sermons often contain the phrase "people like Richard Dawkins ..." with no additional name (perhaps sometimes Sam Harris and Christopher Hitchens to hide their lack of knowledge of atheists other than Dawkins!). Yet very few Christians I know have actually read Dawkins' books. Rather like with Chesterton, most Christians rely on anecdotes and quotations in the press. Certainly I never read *The Selfish Gene*, and from some superstitious terror have still never read it, despite (or perhaps because) being quoted to from it by atheist friends at university, and I freely admit my motive was fear. The power of words can be very strong and, until someone has a faith that is independent of the words of preachers and Christian books and builds their faith on experience, it's very hard to avoid the feeling that by letting words pass through your eyes into your brain you may become infected against your will, rather like Dawkins' idea of memes and mental viruses.

What changed the game for me was coming across Richard Dawkins in person when I was living in Oxford. The first time was at a prize-giving ceremony in 2001 where I had just won the annual

Oxfordshire Science Writing contest sponsored by the "Oxford Times". I had attended with an atheist friend who pointed Dawkins out to me. Rather blithely, I went straight over to Dawkins and said, "Are you Professor Dawkins? I'm one of the prize winners." I introduced my atheist friend and said he had given me the idea for the story I had written ("Life on Mars?") before I was whisked away by the photographer for the official photo. I bumped into Dawkins a couple of times more that week – I went to one of his talks which he gave with his wife Lalla Ward and then a week later met him again at the bar at Linacre College, where I was studying. We had a chat then, and I asked what I thought was a suitably clever question, namely "Which are more important, genes or memes?"; and that, apart from a couple of letters a few months later, was it.

I'm not trying to make any grand claim to understanding Dawkins any better, but what did come across was his very polite and charming demeanour, which certainly in his public talk with Lalla appeared every bit as sincere as many good Christian preachers. And so I started to read Dawkins' next books as they came out: first *Climbing Mount Improbable*, then that huge tome, *The Ancestors' Tale* (which I read over three months in a church bookshop where I was working) and finally *The God Delusion*. What I found in *The Ancestor's Tale* was a deep appreciation of the grandeur of the natural world, beside which the religious account was (in Dawkins' words) "miserably inadequate" and the creationist or Intelligent Design account "lazy". By the time I read *The God Delusion*, I found myself able to acknowledge the points Dawkins made against Christianity; but rather than throwing me into confusion, they made me see clearly the necessity for Christians to live out the Christian faith authentically.

If you read Dawkins' argument in *The God Delusion*, he is only knocking down arguments (such as the proofs for God) that should never have been advanced in God's defence, since God is not a mathematical idea but a living Person. In addition, Dawkins shows up the hypocrisy of Christians and the Church down the ages that should never have been perpetuated so repeatedly and so embarrassingly; and most of all Dawkins shows up the lack of faith in Christians that leads them to attempt to teach children a childish Christianity out of fear of the "world", and to display a fear of death quite incompatible with belief in the life everlasting. In short, what Dawkins does in *The God Delusion* (should more Christians dare to read it honestly) is to issue a wake-up call to Christians to get real about their faith. It certainly did this for me. This is why, out of all Dawkins' books, it is *The God Delusion*, in the comprehensiveness of its attack on Christianity and in Dawkins' passion against the perceived evil of Abrahamic religion, that I would recommend the beginner to start with. And this is borne out by the way that so many authors have felt the need to put pen to paper to ward off this important book, still the strongest attack on religion in recent years.

Having met Dawkins, I have felt distressed by the public reactions from Christians to *The God Delusion* in particular. Everyone will have heard about the hate mail Dawkins has received, but I have also been embarrassed about the superior and dismissive tone of some of the big names in Christian leadership. A scientist who makes many (to me) valid points about the weaknesses in Christianity, including the really nasty bits in both Old and New Testaments, deserves more respect, honesty and thoughtful response. And this is what Neil Laing attempts in this book.

I first came across Neil when he emailed me in January 2012, after I had left Oxford for Bristol and become secretary of the Bristol local group of Christians in Science (www.cis.org.uk). A science teacher and elder in his local church, Neil came to our next local group meeting, a talk by Bob White, Professor of Geophysics at Cambridge, on why a good God would allow natural disasters to happen. Neil wanted to discuss Dawkins' views, with the aim of refuting them for the benefit of his teenage church members. I advised him to read *The God Delusion* before further discussion. What impressed me was that Neil read it almost immediately, and then wanted to discuss his reactions to the book with me. Neil has a good voice on paper and I admire him for his honesty in wanting to tackle the challenges put up by Dawkins himself, rather than follow others' potted arguments. I encouraged Neil to try and log his thoughts and work out his own arguments in refutation, as I thought that would be more instructive for his youth audience. When Neil produced a lengthy work for me to comment on, I found it very easy to read: Neil has a gentle and ingenuous tone that is lacking in some other Christian authors.

Being familiar with many of the arguments Neil puts forward, having attended many Christians in Science conferences over the years, I don't feel qualified to comment on whether or not Neil's arguments will surprise or persuade the average atheist (or maybe more likely, Christian) reader. What Neil does is to lay out, in a systematic and comprehensive way, without hectoring or lecturing, the general arguments from science put forward by many mainstream Christians working in academic science. Neil does this in an informal and approachable way that many conscientious academic Christians find hard to do while remaining credible as academics. Thus Neil explains why Dawkins is indeed right to call the creationist/Intelligent Design movement "lazy"; but he also challenges Dawkins on most of the straw men that Dawkins knocks down and which I indeed hope are mostly fictional. Neil also adds a personal perspective from his experience of answered prayer as a charismatic Christian.

But my original advice to Neil is also my advice to readers of his book. Please read *The God Delusion* at the first opportunity (preferably before you read Neil's book) – you will find it will challenge and strengthen your faith! If you do that, you may then find yourself wanting to discuss the challenge Dawkins issues to all Christendom with others who are like-minded in their thoughtful response. You will then be interested to read the thoughts of Neil, gently set out in this book, as a way to develop your own authentic response to *The God Delusion*.

CMBB
Bristol, 2014

AUTHOR

An elder (leader) in a small non-denominational church in Glastonbury, Somerset, England, Neil Laing was born in what was then Salisbury, Southern Rhodesia to Jack and Helen and brought up on a tobacco, maize and cattle farm in the north of the country with siblings Rob, Andrew and Margaret. His school education was almost entirely in country boarding schools where he grew to develop a love of wildlife and at first intended to become involved in wildlife conservation as a game ranger.

After obtaining a BSc in Zoology and Botany at the University of Natal in Pietermaritzburg, South Africa, however, he went on to do a post grad certificate in education at the same university. He married Lizzie in between these two qualifications. This was followed by teaching science at a boys' secondary school in Rhodesia for a few years.

After that, he went to the Elim Bible College, in Capel, Surrey, England where he obtained a college certificate (2 years) with honours at the same time as leading a small Elim Pentecostal church in Dorking, a town near the college.

Leaving Capel, he ministered at two Elim churches in North London as an assistant pastor and a supervisor in a school being run on the premises of one of the churches.

With Lizzie's mother in Glastonbury becoming ill, they headed back to Somerset to help care for her and have been involved in the town ever since, being in the leadership of the church in various capacities from when it was first formed in 1983.

Neil has produced a series of teaching modules for church education which are available for the Amazon Kindle. He produced interactive science teaching modules for 11–12 year old children in the UK following part of the key stage 3 science curriculum a few years ago. He is still involved in schools education, teaching Science, Information & Communication Technology and Maths, having been involved in the IT industry for 17 years. He is also, at the time of writing, a moderator in ICT for the OCR (Oxford, Cambridge & RSA) exam board in the UK and continues to write software applications for businesses.

Neil and Lizzie have three adult children: Hannah, Adam and Ruth.

PREFACE

I never wanted to buy *The God Delusion*. I knew that Richard
Dawkins' attitude was proselytising as far as atheism was concerned
and I suppose I found it a bit off-putting.

However, I found an article in the Evangelical Alliance magazine
"IDEA" by someone in "Christians in Science" (www.cis.org.uk)
and, having a degree in Zoology and Botany, I am clearly interested
in science. As a committed Christian I also have an interest in
theology. I made contact with the Bristol-based branch of this society
and came into contact with Dr Christina Biggs who heads up the
branch and she challenged me to read Professor Dawkins' book.
I'm glad that I agreed. She later challenged me to write a refutation
of Dawkins' arguments, thinking particularly of a young audience.
As I started, I realised that dealing with this subject for teenagers
is far more difficult than for adults so decided to aim it at an adult
audience and that quickly developed into this book. However, I
hope I have still kept it accessible for anyone with a reasonable level
of school understanding of science.

I do enjoy debate and have entered into discussions with numerous
people with whom I disagree radically. I have argued with adherents
of the Watchtower Society (Jehovah's Witnesses), with Hindus and
with Muslims. Sometimes it is friendly – as with a leading Hindu
in Brentwood, with whom I stayed in B&B accommodation for

nine months – and we became very good friends although we never agreed. Sometimes I have had to stop the discussion as with a highly intelligent Muslim whose single idea in the discussion was to convert me and who became abusive when he could not convince me that he was right.

However, I am glad I did read *The God Delusion*. Dawkins' style is pretty easy (apart from the aggravations of some of his arguments) and he does write well. It was challenging in places which is good. I always find a challenge sharpens my understanding. That has certainly been the case with *The God Delusion*.

I have to say that I did agree with many of Dawkins' points and felt he made some very well. Many of his criticisms of the church and its attitudes are, I feel, quite justified. I can also quite understand much of what he says and how he reads the Bible in the way he does. His reactions to much of the Bible are logical for someone reading it at face value. It has, let's face it, some very difficult passages which can lead to some painful conclusions for Christians and Jews if not properly understood. I also found many statements in *The God Delusion* that I felt to be unfair. I shall try to deal with these in this book.

I would advise anyone reading this small contribution to the debate to read Dawkins' book first if you want to follow my arguments properly. For many Christians, his book will actually deepen their faith. I know that sounds extraordinary, but it is true. For some, it may disturb their faith. That is not necessarily a negative thing. If it can be disturbed, it needs to be! True faith cannot be destroyed but it can be modified. Whatever your reaction to his book, I hope mine will equip you to think about this debate properly without any fear or head-in-the-sand mentality.

I would advise any atheist or agnostic to read his book first, too. You will probably be quite convinced by his arguments, but I hope you will then have the open-mindedness to look at my counter-arguments and fairly make up your own mind as to what you believe. You could find the odd surprise in this book.

Whoever you are, I hope you find this enjoyable and beneficial, no matter what conclusion you draw from it.

ACKNOWLEDGMENTS

No book is the work of one person and I cannot begin to think how many people have added to my understanding of both science and faith – and all of that has contributed to what you will find in this book.

I want to thank Dr Christina Biggs of Christians in Science, Bristol, who challenged me to read Richard Dawkins' book and then to write a reply. This would not have happened otherwise. In the latter stages of my writing the book, Tina has spent hours critiquing it. I made numerous changes as a result of her hard work. She suggested many of C.S. Lewis' arguments and I have learned much from her over some of the science, too. We have had considerable email correspondence discussing scientific and theological issues, not always agreeing (I am glad to say) but thrashing out conundrums over how God relates to nature and natural law. As always, I have benefited from these debates and have learned a tremendous amount.

Tina's enthusiasm and work in her role in CiS is an inspiration to many people. Her expertise in science (PhD from Cambridge and undertaking private tuition for GCSE and A level students, with a range of pupils including many Somali students in Bristol) together with her determination to approach both science and faith in a ruthlessly honest way qualifies her to speak with authority on these subjects and I feel confident discussing them with her. Many thanks, Tina; I really do appreciate your massive contribution to this book.

I would like to thank Richard Dawkins, too. Although I disagree with him on most essential points mentioned in this book, his book has caused me to think and examine my faith and understanding of God and his nature. It has also made me think clearly about how to explain things to people whose frame of reference is so different from my own. I hope I have at least succeeded in part in doing that. I had the privilege of hearing him when he presented his autobiography *An Appetite for Wonder* in Bath on 22nd November 2013. I discovered then that one of the schools he attended was my primary school. We had a quick chat at the end of the meeting after he signed my copy of his book. I asked him if he would be able to have a look at what I had written and he agreed to look at specific passages. I sent him a copy with two passages highlighted and he replied within about 15 minutes which, I have to say, impressed me. I have included comments he made at appropriate places in the book. Since then, a few emails have passed between us and he has always proved to be nothing but personable, pleasant and friendly. Indeed, he is so different from the persona often portrayed by those who vehemently oppose him and from what you might gather reading *The God Delusion* that you almost wonder if you are dealing with the same man. Thank you, Richard. I have learned a lot as a result of reading your book.

A few members of my old school, Falcon College, some of whom disagree with my views, said they would take a look at the manuscript. As one of these, Charles Nelson, is an atheist, I value his opinion. Charlie, I appreciated the debate we had on the Falcon Old Boys email forum a couple of years ago. It was extremely good-natured even though we disagreed and many members commented on how good the debate was. You are an example of how we can disagree without being disagreeable. You have gone through what I have said without bias and with extremely helpful comments and criticisms. I really do appreciate your time spent. I owe you a few Shumbas or suitable equivalent!

Hugh Thompson (whom I first met in our Covenant Ministries days) was involved at the cutting edge of the very beginnings of the charismatic movement in the UK and has plenty of editorial experience within the publications put out by those early ministries. He has checked my manuscript at least four times and examined it in minute detail. His suggestions and corrections (including every comma) have made a huge difference to the book. His past experience has been invaluable and has increased my confidence in this work enormously. Hugh, thank you so much. I appreciate what you have done more than I can express.

I want to thank my three children, Hannah, Adam and Ruth, too. They each read early drafts of the book and made several suggestions. They were not afraid to criticize what I had said – and knowing that is a great encouragement to me.

Lastly, I want to thank Lizzie, my wife. I am not the easiest of husbands. I spend hours away from you working on all sorts of projects when you want me to be with you. You serve me more than I serve you. You care for me and love me and we have had nearly forty years of being one. I am so thankful to you and to God for your patience, your faithfulness and your love. You demonstrate the truth of the scripture that says whoever finds a wife finds a good thing! *Ine kutanda iwe kakulu.* I love you dearly.

NOTES ON USE OF TERMS

In order to simplify my writing, I shall refer to God as "he". I stress that this does not mean I regard him as male. He is neither male nor female. Both men and women express certain attributes of God's nature. I find "it" detracts from thinking of him in personal terms and the Bible refers to God with masculine pronouns, so I am simply using the same idea.

I will use "it" when referring to other ideas of gods and that will simply emphasise that I do not regard any other "god" as having any validity or actual existence. A "god" can be almost anything – physical, spiritual or conceptual. It is simply whatever is the over-riding principle in anyone's life. I use the word "god" in its widest sense, therefore. Richard Dawkins agrees with this, quoting Steven Weinberg who said, "*like any other word, the word 'God' can be given any meaning we like.*"[1] He does, however, point out quite rightly that if it is used too widely it becomes a useless word and that he means it to indicate some supernatural creator that it is appropriate for us to worship. I include the meaning that if someone attributes god-like functions to something, that something becomes like a god to that person, whether it is living or dead, personal or impersonal, material or immaterial. I do NOT mean that that person necessarily worships that something or that it is an idol in the mind, but simply that there are attributes of that something, say

---

[1]   "The God Delusion" page 33

a process or theory which others would consider god-like. It could, conceivably, also mean an overall idea for the creation of the universe.

The word "Trinity" is very familiar to most people but its meaning is perhaps less clear. It is derived from "Tri" (three) and "unity" (joined in one). Contrary to what some understand from the word, that means the three Persons of the "Godhead" are only One God, not three Gods of the same nature. In order to emphasise this, I have used "Triunity" where appropriate – i.e. when I am speaking about it and not when I am quoting anyone else. "Triunity" means exactly the same as "Trinity".

When I use the term "religion" or "religious", it is quite loose. It can refer to specific systems or to an attitude of mind. Someone who has very strongly held views could be called "religious", whether or not they believe in any kind of "god". Although I describe Christianity here as a religion and Christians as religious, I do not actually regard true Christianity as a religion. I believe it is a real relationship with God and has nothing essentially to do with ritual. However, for convenience and because most people regard Christianity as a religion, I refer to it as such.

Almost exclusively, when I use the word "church" it is referring to groups of Christian believers. I never mean any kind of building. There is no building anywhere in the world that is a church in spite of the way the majority of people use the word. I do not mean the church hierarchy either. They are only part of the church along with all believers. Nor do I mean the gathering of people on a Sunday or any other day. That is not the church – it is a meeting of the church. I am not referring to any denomination or non-denomination or any other grouping. The church consists of genuine Christian believers of all persuasions.

As far as translations of the Bible are concerned, I have used quite a number. I have tried to use whatever version I think expresses a verse in the best way. I do not think any translation is necessarily the best. Where I have given a version, I have used ESV for English Standard Version, NASB for New American Standard Bible and BBE for Bible in Basic English. I have also used the Authorised (King James) version, International Standard, Contemporary English, Young's Literal Translation, Lexham English Bible, Easy-to-Read and Modern King James versions on occasion.

I am totally convinced that every Christian should be a "creationist". By that I mean it is necessary to believe that God created all things from absolutely nothing[2]. However, the term "creationist" is more normally associated with a particular interpretation of the biblical text that insists on a highly literalistic view of the first few chapters of Genesis, resulting in a belief that the universe is approximately six thousand years old (usually up to a maximum of ten thousand years); that the Earth was created first (in substantially the same state as we now find it) and that this was followed by the Sun, Moon and stars; that all animal life was created at least by families (using the modern classification of "families") and that all the above happened within six days; that there is a possibility of "micro-evolution" – i.e. minor changes within species (or possibly families) but no macro-evolution – i.e. one species (or family) arising from another. Almost without exception, I use the term to refer to people with that particular belief.

There are a number of different "creation theories". The above view is a "young earth" theory; most of the others are "old earth" theories. I do

---

[2] I will attempt to show, in chapter 2, that the singularity of the Big Bang is actually nothing.

not discuss these here (you can view my short booklet on "Creation" available as a Kindle e-book if you want to see what I have to say on some others[3]). However, I mention "theistic evolution". This is a broad term covering a fairly wide range of belief, but basically means believing in the process of evolution as put forward by evolutionary biologists in much the same way as atheistic evolutionists would believe. However, a theistic evolutionist (some people call themselves "evolutionary creationists") would say that God is behind the entire process and that he created all things through an evolutionary process. This is my current understanding and it is shared by many individual Christians, churches and organisations such as Christians in Science, Biologos, the Faraday Institute, the American Scientific Affiliation (ASA), Reason to Believe, and the Science and Religion Forum. See Appendix A for web addresses.

Footnote references:

All references and notes are given on a page-by-page basis. I have not given traditionally full references (giving author, title, publisher, date etc.) as I thought this too cumbersome. Apart from references to *The God Delusion*, where I simply refer to it by title as I assume you know it is written by Richard Dawkins, I have given author, book title, page number where possible. The bibliography contains references to publisher and date for all books quoted or used.

Online references are given as footnotes and are not included in the bibliography.

---

3   Go to either amazon.com or amazon.co.uk and type in "Laying Deep Foundations Creation"

INTRODUCTION

I was home from university once and stood in the middle of the large lawn on my parents' farm in the north of Rhodesia (now Zimbabwe) one night staring up at the heavens. I had seen this spectacular sight countless times but suddenly I was awed at my own insignificance in comparison with the unimaginable vastness of the universe. At the time I had no particular religious commitment, though I was interested vaguely in Zen Buddhism as I had been training in karate at university – later to achieve my 2nd Dan black belt. But this experience was a kind of spiritual realisation that, if there was a god, it was totally different from what I had imagined as I grew up. It made me feel that existence was pretty awe-inspiring.

My father was a Scotsman and Presbyterian; my mother was brought up in Surrey and was Anglican. They were more than nominal Christians. They firmly believed in God, taught us to pray (though I remember our nightly prayers were always exactly the same) and gave us a high moral code – which was reflected in their own conduct. As we lived 25 miles from the nearest village, our visits "to church"[4] were fairly infrequent, though far more frequent than the vast majority of people in the district. I never really looked forward to those visits, however.

---

[4]   I say "to church" because, as I explained in my Use of Terms, church is not a building.

From the age of seven, I went to boarding schools and, apart from my very first local government school, the others were church-based. I spent most of my primary school years at Eagle School in the eastern highlands of Southern Rhodesia – a school that Richard Dawkins attended a few years before my time. We were given fairly clear religious instruction there from a very Church of England doctrinal stance. It was an idyllic place in many ways, though I did not appreciate it at the time – school was school!

As I went through my early childhood, I never thought to question my belief in this unseen God. Going to senior school at thirteen, I began to question how he could exist. When I was about five years old, I remember wondering how Father Christmas could get around the entire world in one night. Was this the first stirrings of an enquiring scientific mind? As a teenager I tried to fathom out the existence of a God who had no physical substance and lived in a heaven that had no fixed place. I never gave up praying but didn't really believe it had any effect whatsoever. I still thought of myself as a Christian and was confirmed as a Presbyterian at the age of seventeen.

Dawkins has the opinion that belief in a God is a natural thing for a child but that, once we are grown up the mature mind will reject such fairy stories along with the Tooth Fairy and Father Christmas. I came to that place in my late teenage/early adult life. However, I believe that coming to a proper adult type of belief in God means progressing beyond the "teenage" rejection of the existence of God. That teenage rejection is, of course, more grown-up than the childish belief in a concept of a gigantic person "up there" living in a place called heaven smiling down on the inhabitants of this planet. But that teenage rejection has failed to see that the childish concept was necessary for children but that there is a mature belief that appreciates far more than the scepticism of teenage years. It fails to see that just around the corner a coherent view awaits that makes sense of our existence. Could it be that an adult appreciation of an infinite God is more mature than atheistic disbelief? I shall discuss more on what I mean by this in chapter 14 – "Morality, Ethics and Righteousness".

As I grew up at school, my interest in wildlife increased. My secondary school, Falcon College, was in the west of Zimbabwe near Bulawayo and we were blessed with two thousand acres of "bush" that was a nature-lover's dream. I kept snakes and took up falconry, training small goshawks and did quite a lot of work checking bird's nests, recording incubation periods and fledgling development and sending the records to the Rhodesian Ornithological Society, for which I received a letter of commendation. My friends and I used to spend hours and hours over weekends traversing the bush looking for nests of eagles, hawks and other raptors. A teacher, Peter Steyn, would film and photograph them and later published books on birds of prey in Southern Africa. We were also involved in capturing White-fronted Bee-eaters and Horus Swifts which nested on old slag heaps, as the school was built on a collapsed gold mine. We would ring these birds and release them to help in the study of their migration patterns.

My increasing interest in wildlife meant that, by the age of about fifteen, I had decided I wanted to be involved in wildlife conservation and become a game ranger. So, I took Biology and Geography at A level, although I had not taken either of them at Cambridge School Certificate (GCSE). However, I got through, did my National Service in the army and then worked for the Veterinary Research

Department for a few months in the south-east of the country based at Chipinda Pools on the Lundi River, living in a hut. The game was being shot out in a ten-mile wide corridor to try and protect cattle from the danger of trypanosomiasis (sleeping sickness) carried by tsetse fly. Dr John Condy, a wildlife research vet, was carrying out research on parasites and diseases found in and on the game and I worked for him in the area, shooting and collecting samples as well as supervising a few people who lived in the hunter camps and collected samples from the animals shot by the hunters.

At the end of this time, I went on to university in Pietermaritzburg, South Africa, to study zoology and botany. Unfortunately I did not apply myself enough to my studies, having become intensely interested in karate. I passed my first year but not my second and, after a further year that was not quite as disastrous, I left with no qualification, doing various jobs but becoming increasingly frustrated with my lack of direction. However, I had managed to excel at karate – small comfort!

My scientific studies had shown me quite clearly, though, that life had evolved from simple forms hundreds of millions of years ago to the complexity of living things we see today. The fact that this might conflict with the teaching of the Bible did not bother me. It was the truth and that was that. I still held on to a belief in God but would have regarded him as the summation of all the laws of the universe – probably something similar to the "theory of everything" sought by scientists like Stephen Hawking. Although I would not have put it in those terms, I had essentially ceased to believe in God's existence. Christianity seemed pretty boring.

After three years of going from job to job, I felt I needed to return to university and get my degree. The only way I could see of funding this was to become a teacher and get government grants. Before returning, however, I spent a year in London broadening my limited horizons. During this time I met my future wife, Lizzie, but I also began to wonder about the meaning of my life. I saw it stretching ahead with the prospect of getting a degree, marrying, having children and settling down, working for forty-odd years, retiring, growing old and dying. I have to say, it did not look incredibly meaningful or exciting and I sensed a whole lot of conflicting emotions over the prospect.

In February 1973 I returned to university with a determination to get my degree. Before starting, I was staying with my old landlady while looking for student digs. She lent me a book called "Beyond Ourselves" by Catherine Marshall and I found I could not put it down. Catherine Marshall related a lot of her own experiences with God plus those of many of her friends. It spoke to me of an aspect of God that I had never dreamed was possible. They seemed to actually know him. God had always been a theory to my mind and it was just a matter of whether you believed in his existence or not and then trying to live a moral life – something I knew I had not done too well. On Thursday 1st March I was reading near the end of the book, where she had a prayer of commitment. I felt I should pray it but decided against because life was a lot of fun just then and I didn't want to have to be good or at least not until I was a lot older. It was then that God spoke to me!

I know many people reading this are liable to imagine I suddenly went delusional or was hallucinating. However, it wasn't an audible voice and I can guarantee it was nothing like you are thinking. I was not expecting it, I was not seeking it, I didn't particularly want it and I had never experienced anything remotely like that before. I was stone-cold sober and I know it was no delusion. He simply said, "Whose terms are you coming on? Yours or Mine?" Nothing more. Just that. I knew I had to make a decision and I chose his terms. Although I didn't at that time have any understanding of the gospel, I turned myself over to him that night by responding "Ok, Lord, I give up!"

I did not personally arrive at that point after having worked out his existence intellectually or checking through evidence and probability. The story of how each human being comes to faith is very individual – some look at all the evidence (e.g. C.S. Lewis in *Mere Christianity* and Frank Morison in *Who Moved the Stone*), but many feel a supernatural encounter with God as God reveals himself to them personally – this is called "conviction". Most famously the apostle Paul heard an audible voice and a light on the road to Damascus (as recorded in Acts chapter 9 verses 1–31). If God "fills heaven and earth" as the Bible tells us[5], should one not expect him to reveal himself to individuals?

However, much of the time God feels frustratingly far from us, believer and non-believer alike. Various thinkers have pondered this problem: Iranaeus back in AD 202, argued that for humans to have free will, God must be at an "*epistemic distance*" (or intellectual distance) from humans, far enough that belief in God remains a free choice.[6] In Romans chapter 1 verse 20, Paul says that mankind has evidence for God from "what is made" and that leaves us without

---

[5]   Jeremiah chapter 23, verse 24.

[6]   http://en.wikipedia.org/wiki/Irenaean_theodicy

excuse for not believing in God's existence. But there is a sense in which God does not usually force belief, but wants us to seek after Him first, and most of all to want to submit to him as Lord and not go our own stubborn way.

God reveals himself first to the simple (e.g. to the shepherds at the time of Jesus' birth) and wants the "wise" to become open-hearted, so that instead of congratulating ourselves on our cleverness in "proving" God, we are all sat together at Christ's feet: Matthew reports Jesus' words: "*Truly I say to you, unless you will be converted and become like **children**, you will not enter the Kingdom of Heaven*"[7] The apostle Paul said, "*we preach Christ crucified – a stumbling block to the Jews and foolishness to the Greeks*"[8] – the Greeks were those who relied on reason for everything. Thus the Bible does warn that intellectual people in particular may find Christianity – at least, the central story of the way in which God has chosen to rescue mankind through Jesus Christ – foolish. But it doesn't mean that there is no evidence for God from what we see around us.

C.S. Lewis explains, however, that faith does not believe against the evidence, but in fact makes sense of what we see of the universe once we have accepted the premise (or working hypothesis) that God does exist. In *Pilgrim's Regress*, C.S. Lewis says, "*I believe in Christianity as I believe that the sun has risen: not only because I see it, but because by it I see everything else.*" Other writers have testified about the sense of the hypothesis of God "fitting" the evidence in a holistic way, most recently, for example, *Big Bang Big God* by Rodney Holder.

---

[7]   Matthew chapter 18, verse 3

[8]   1st Corinthians chapter 1, verse 23

However, faith that believes *against* all the evidence is not faith. It is plain stupidity. I don't know how atheists have come to the conclusion that faith means believing either against or in spite of the evidence. Perhaps it's because they cannot understand faith or perhaps it's because that is what some Christians do. The fact is belief is no less reasonable than unbelief. I would maintain not only is it as reasonable but that it also makes better sense of existence.

For myself, having come to this point of commitment via a route that did not include intellectual reasoning but being prepared to face my short-comings and make a decision to have my life turned around, I was then confronted with intellectual questions. Being totally convinced of the truth of evolution from all available evidence and also assuming that the Bible taught a six-day creation approximately six thousand years ago, I had a problem. I had heard that Billy Graham, for whom I had great admiration, had made a decision that no matter what science had found, he would believe God and if the Bible said the world had been created in six days, he believed it. I had also known people who had become Christians and completely abandoned a belief in evolution. Was I going to do the same? If I were to be honest, I could not deny the theory of evolution; if I were to be true to God, I needed to believe the Genesis account. So, I prayed.

As I read the Genesis account in the Authorised Version, I noticed, "*God said, **let the earth bring forth**"*... and "***let the seas bring forth**"*... and "***the earth brought forth**"*... or "*God created great whales*"..."*which **the seas brought forth**.*" In a poetic way, this was actually describing what I understood had happened. The non-living world was involved in the creation of life. In addition, the first couple of verses could be said to be a poetic account of the formation of planets from gaseous masses slowly solidifying and forming gradually cooling rocky planets. What's more, in a very rough sense, the order of creation reflected the dependency of plants on the non-living world and of animals on plants. Animal life is portrayed as starting in the seas and then on land. Was this in some way reflecting a natural process that could include the invasion of the land and the evolution of land species from forms that emerged from the seas? I shall examine this in more detail in chapter 18 on the compatibility of faith and science.

Interestingly, a book came out in 2009 by Andrew Parker called *The Genesis Enigma* where he had noticed something similar. I felt that, while I could not necessarily say this was the answer, at least God did not want me to be dishonest intellectually and I could still accept the Bible as the word of God, even though I may not accept every part of it literally. Some things helped me in this – books like C A Coulson's *Science and Christian Belief* – and I knew that the sense I had of science and faith being complementary rather than confrontational was not an isolated one, as a professor of science and maths at Oxford University thought in some way like I did. Now I know that this view is gaining the consent of such individuals as the Pope and numerous professors at prestigious universities, as well as the organisations named earlier and listed in Appendix A.

From then on the dilemma ceased to bother me, but in recent years I have found this debate coming to the fore again with emotional responses on both sides, and I don't believe this is necessary. I have become interested, not because it worries me but because it worries others, and I find such ignorance of the true nature of this dilemma.

On one side, we have the likes of Richard Dawkins and other New Atheists such as Sam Harris and the late Christopher Hitchens insisting that a Darwinian belief necessarily leads to atheism as the only honest view, derived from evidence-based reason. Dawkins says, *"like nothing else, evolution really does provide an explanation for the existence of entities whose improbability would otherwise, for practical purposes, rule them out. And the conclusion to the argument, as I shall show in Chapter 4, is close to being terminally fatal to the God Hypothesis."*[9] On the other side, the creationists such as James Le Fanu in *Why Us?* or Edgar Andrews in *Who Made God?* agree with them but totally reject evolution and try to disprove it on scientific grounds.

Along with what I have discovered to be a large minority, generally in the scientific fraternity (like the organisations named earlier – CiS, ASA, Biologos, Faraday Institute, Reason to Believe and the Science and Religion Forum) who tend to accept evolution as understood by scientists (random mutation plus natural selection), I drop between the two. It's not always an easy position in which to find yourself.

Dawkins is pretty sure that the reason most people believe is because of the way they were brought up and that many are trapped in that belief system. He says:

> *If you feel trapped in the religion of your upbringing, it would be worth asking yourself how this came about. The answer is usually some form of childhood indoctrination. If you were born in Arkansas and you think Christianity is true and Islam false, knowing full*

---

[9]   "The God Delusion" page 85

well that you would think the opposite if you had been
born in Afghanistan, you are the victim of childhood
indoctrination.[10]

Rather than being indoctrinated by parents who made me believe some sort of fairy-tale, as he may imagine, I ended up coming to a faith that was different from that of my parents. They had a very rudimentary belief but taught us as well as they could. They encouraged us to think for ourselves, although my mother was quite upset when I committed my life to Christ because it seemed to her to be so different from the quiet serious Anglican kind of belief she had taught us. It certainly wasn't my parents who forced me into belief. While I agree that parental belief has a large bearing on what their children believe, there are countless instances of people, whose parents are total unbelievers, becoming Christians. And the opposite is also true.

As I said earlier, I had come to a place of peace about the whole creation-evolution issue, though I knew it bothered a lot of people. I found the ostrich-like attitude of some Christians a bit upsetting. I have no problem with someone disagreeing with me over how to interpret Genesis. If my view turns out to be exactly right I will be absolutely amazed, so I feel we need to listen to and learn from each other. What I find aggravating is the attitude of those who believe only they have the correct biblical interpretation and that anyone who disagrees has to be wrong.

However, having read Dawkins' *The God Delusion*, I feel many of Dawkins' statements to be incompatible with historical and personal

---

[10] Ibid. page 25

evidence. I know some excellent books in rebuttal of *The God Delusion* have been written by Professor Alister McGrath and others like Richard Swinburne, John Lennox, John Polkinghorne, Michael Poole, Andrew Sims, T J Nelson, Tom Gilson, Madeleine Bunting, Jim Holt, Peter Williams, Nick Pollard, Robert Slane, Thomas Cream, Keith Ward, Karen Armstrong, Ian Markham, Scott Han and, probably, many others, in which they not only counter Dawkins but demonstrate his lack of evidence-based argument. However, I have felt moved to write this book with a different approach. I shall be touching on science quite a bit but want to spend some time in Chapters 7 to 9 explaining the nature of faith and therefore how I think Dawkins has misunderstood what most Christians mean by faith, and then look at Dawkins' other charges against Christianity and comment on what Christians should learn from him about how Christianity is (mis)perceived by many atheists and what we should do about this.

I shall tackle the following topics by chapter:

Chapter 1: Dawkins – "a deeply religious non-believer". A potted history of the conflict between science and faith and how Dawkins and other atheists actually have a religious fervour.

Chapter 2: Looking at Faith in Science and Religion. Is faith exercised in science and how does this differ from religious belief?

Chapter 3: The Problem of Attitudes. Attitudes of some atheists toward Dawkins and vice versa plus some wrong attitudes on the part of Christians toward Dawkins. A look at presuppositions.

Chapter 4: Different Viewing Angles. Examining our tendency to interpret things only in the light of what we already know. Why it is necessary to appreciate different views on a subject.

Chapter 5: "The God Hypothesis". An examination of Dawkins' main arguments against the existence of God, where I hope to show that he has based them on a completely false premise.

Chapter 6: Trying to find the "mysterious" God. A further look at the fact that science is inadequate in trying to discover God; what is meant by "mystery" and other aspects of God - how can there be a Triunity, etc?

Chapter 7: Is faith really delusion? Looking at the meaning of delusion and of faith rather than the parody presented by Dawkins.

Chapter 8: Faith as belief in certain doctrines. Examining faith as it is usually meant.

Chapter 9: Faith as trust. What does the Bible usually mean by faith - trusting in God and seeing him work in our lives; prayer, healing and provision; how about miracles?

Chapter 10: The Character of God. Is God really the ogre Dawkins makes him out to be? I examine some of the difficult areas of the Bible.

Chapter 11: Is Monotheism the "Great Unmentionable Evil". Are the major monotheistic religions evil at base? I face some of the terrible things done in the name of religion and try to find what it is that is responsible. We start in this chapter to look at morality which is one of Dawkins' bugbears against religion.

Chapter 12: Atheism, Ethics and Evil. An honest look at atheism and the massive evils carried out by atheists in history. But does atheism itself cause evil? How about the similarities in ethics between atheists and Christians?

Chapter 13: Morality, Ethics and Righteousness. An examination of Dawkins' arguments about morality where he states that *we do not need God in order to be good*.[11] I hope to show that he has actually mainly discussed ethics and has completely ignored righteousness which is where God is needed.

Chapter 14: Sin and that Offensive Transforming Cross. Is the cross of Christ really an "engine of grief"? We take a look at the real meaning of the cross in dealing with sin rather than Dawkins' misunderstanding of this central doctrine of Christianity. How does it transform our lives?

Chapter 15: Is faith bad for you? Dawkins' claim is that faith is detrimental to humans. We examine evidence to see whether he is correct or not.

Chapter 16: Purpose in science and faith. Looking at the difference in the approach to "purpose" from a scientific and a theological perspective. I try to show that while science is a purposeful pursuit, it cannot include purpose in its conclusions, especially when applied

---

[11] Ibid. page 258

to evolutionary theory, whereas Judaeo-Christian theology is very much concerned with purpose.

Chapter 17: Awe and Wonder and the Purpose of the Universe. The scientific enterprise can give us sheer wonder when we start to delve into this universe. Although faith should share this wonder, it can go beyond it as we begin to see it in the light of God's creation and the purpose he ordained for it. Atheists accuse believers of having a "small god". I try to show that this is a total misunderstanding

Chapter 18: Are Science and Faith compatible? A look at the apparent incompatibility of science and faith, and critiquing some of the approaches taken which are definitely incompatible.

Chapter 19: Can we find any Compatibility? Looking at the bare essentials of Christian belief, where I hope to show that science and faith do have points of contact in dealing with creation and that each legitimately looks at the same thing from a different angle.

Chapter 20: Concluding thoughts. Faith and science are not opposed to each other. Each can and should enhance the other. I challenge believers to drop their fear of and embrace science rather than seeing it as a threat. I challenge atheists to be humble enough to admit they don't have all the answers and to look around the corner to see something they never imagined was possible.

CHAPTER 1

Dawkins – "A Deeply Religious Non-believer"

Before we start: a glance backwards to how we got here

Over the centuries, naturalists and religious naturalists in particular have struggled to work out exactly how God fits in with nature. The history of this struggle goes back millennia but it is especially the battles of the past few hundred years that affect our current understanding.

In some ways, these struggles have led people to atheism. Charles Darwin himself had originally intended to become an Anglican clergyman and attended the University of Cambridge to prepare himself for ordination. He was, however, a zealous follower of science as defined by John Herschel, who himself followed William Paley's idea of natural theology. Paley argued that nature had a divine design and used that to show that God acted through the laws of nature to produce adaptation of species to their environment. After his voyage on the *Beagle*, Darwin grew increasingly sceptical of the

1

Bible as history. Formulating his principle of natural selection, he regarded that as removing the need for design in nature.

There is a need in those of a scientific mind to have an explanation for everything. Any scientist who is also a believer naturally wonders about how God relates to the creation. Hence, the theories that emerged over time. According to John Hedley Brooke (Andreas Idreos Professor of Science and Religion at The University of Oxford from 1999–2006), *"there was no consensus among 17th-century natural philosophers about the significance of nature's laws. They could be understood, as they were by Galileo, as mathematically expressed idealisations against which the real world could be compared. They could be understood as divine commands, as they were by Descartes; or merely as the 'rules' by which nature operated according to the divine will."*[12] The extent to which these theories agreed with biblical doctrine ranged from pure deism to ideas that were closely allied with the Bible. It must be said, however, that there was and is considerable disagreement among Christians as to what it means to be close to biblical doctrine.

Revd. William Whewell (1794–1866) was Master of Trinity College, Cambridge and, as well as being an Anglican priest, he was a highly respected man of science in his day. In 1830, he was selected to be one of the authors of *The Bridgewater Treatises* – a work subtitled "The Power, Goodness and Wisdom of God in the works of Creation."

According to J R Topham, Whewell argued that *"the idea of divine purpose and providence is not endangered by the explanation of natural*

---

[12] Brooke, John Hedley "Natural law in the natural sciences: the origins of modern atheism?" taken from "Science & Christian Belief", vol 4. No. 2 p 87 (April 1990)

phenomena in terms of natural law. Indeed, the existence of order in nature speaks of purpose, and law of intelligence. The existence of natural law, he supposed, could never be explained in any ultimate way by science. Its implication was, in fact, that there must exist a powerful legislator who created the physical universe."[13]

Whewell represents a more theistic approach while Newton, who considered that design in nature pointed to a designer, represents a more deistic approach although he did believe God would sometimes nudge the planets back into their correct orbits and had a high view of the Bible unlike pure deism.

Deism is happy with a God who created all things, designing the creation in such a way that his subsequent intervention becomes more of a refereeing role. This is reflected in Islam which is more a deistic than a theistic religion.[14] The recent Intelligent Design movement on the other hand proposes a "two-tier" system where some things happen as an outworking of impersonal natural law, but other features of the biological world, such as the eye and the bacterial flagella are said to be evidence of God intervening to design a particular marvel and are then used as evidence for God's existence and activity. Theistic evolution tends to shy away from giving God any role in design that would not have happened in accordance with the observed laws of nature, and instead proposes that even miracles can be understood as miracles of timing and therefore foresight, and not actually breaking the laws of physics. Most recently, Simon Conway Morris in *Life's Solution* speculates that God has designed

---

[13] Topham, J R "Teleology and the concept of Natural Law" taken from "Science & Christian Belief" vol 1. No. 2 p 151 (October 1989)

[14] Islam accepts the transcendence (separate nature from creation) but not the immanence (intimate involvement in creation) of God

the laws of the universe in such a way that were evolution to be re-run, something very like human beings would emerge again. There is a sense that God does not need to "tweak" the laws of physics as he is the perfect designer, and that we should resist the temptation to hail certain scientific discoveries as knock-down "proofs of God", such as the nuclear resonance in stars that even Fred Hoyle, an agnostic astrophysicist, felt that the evidence indicated the universe to be a "put-up job". There is a current antipathy in theistic circles that we should at all costs avoid a "God of the Gaps" scenario where a new finding is used as evidence for God only for a scientific explanation to be found later which then "pushes God out" from that "gap" and discredits Christian belief. This could even apply to the origin of life!

As early as A.D. 354–430) in his work *The Literal Meaning of Genesis (De Genesi ad litteram libri duodecim)*, the monk Augustine warned against Christians *"speaking nonsense"* on matters about the natural world that others know are *"certain from reason and experience .. not so much that an ignorant individual is derided, but that people outside the household of faith think our sacred writers held such opinions, and, to the great loss of those for whose salvation we toil, the writers of our Scripture are criticized and rejected as unlearned men"*.

When trying to reconcile a creator God with a universe that works very well according to a multitude of scientifically explained laws, deism provides a fairly neat solution. Having a God who designed and created all things in the beginning and then sat back and watched the whole thing develop according to the laws he had constructed gets around a number of issues. You no longer have to explain how God could be intimately involved in every aspect of creation while it is blatantly obvious that natural law can ultimately account for and explain the universe.

A large number of natural philosophers, like Descartes (God was a mere mathematical abstraction), John Locke and Copernicus as well scientists like Rutherford seem to have had a somewhat deistic approach to this problem. But the thing is, if design can be shown to be a mere interpretation or a mechanism can be found by which the design of the universe developed, then it does away with the need for a designer. As recently as Jan 2013, Nicky Campbell in *The Big Question Show* on BBC1[15] expressed this view as "God twiddling his thumbs". So, it is not a huge leap from deism to atheism or agnosticism and, while deism is still current, it led inevitably to the atheism we see so widely among scientists and philosophers today.

Theism, on the other hand, contends that God is immanent as well as transcendent, i.e. that he is intimately involved in every aspect of creation all the time, while at the same time being completely separate from it. Trying to reconcile this type of God with a universe where everything has, potentially, a scientific explanation is not easy. Creationists make a great effort to match science with the actions of God. However, I am sure that such efforts are fruitless as I hope to explain. That does not mean I don't accept that God is involved. I am totally a theist!

Richard Dawkins, who is far better versed in the history of science and the works of these and many other scientists than I could ever hope to be, appears to follow on from these philosophies, becoming convinced that there can be no supernatural being because there is,

---

[15] BBC is the British Broadcasting Corporation

at least potentially, a perfectly good explanation for everything. God has simply been pushed out of the way by the advances of science (*"evolution provides an explanation that is close to being terminally fatal to the God Hypothesis"*).[16]

Similarities between atheists and creationists

It's interesting how similar we can be to each other, even when we disagree fundamentally on an issue. There are certain similarities between atheists and creationists. While Dawkins totally opposes creationism, he says, *"I do have one thing in common with the creationists. Like me, but unlike the 'Chamberlain school', they will have no truck with NOMA and its separate magisteria."*[17]

Dawkins' book starts with an immediate attack on those of a religious conviction whom he labels as faith-heads immune to argument[18]. He is presumably trying to give the subliminal impression that they are people who do not really use their brains but just believe against all evidence. He also attacks fellow atheists who share his convictions but dislike his approach, labelling them as *vicarious second-order believers*[19]. An example is Michael Ruse, an atheist and a renowned British scientist working in America who is concerned to promote

---

[16] "The God Delusion" page 85
[17] Ibid. page 92. NOMA means "non-overlapping magisteria" – basically the idea that science and religion are dealing with totally different "magisteria" or areas of authority – science covers the empirical, while religion covers ultimate meaning and moral value.
[18] Ibid. page 28
[19] Ibid. page 13

a scientific approach to the creationism vs. evolution debate[20]. Ruse stresses that evolutionists should regard believers who also accept the theory of evolution as allies rather than enemies in the fight to have evolutionary biology accepted as science by all. Dawkins regards him as an appeaser, describing him by saying *"another prominent luminary of what we might call the Neville Chamberlain school of evolutionists is the philosopher Michael Ruse."*[21]

Dogmatism in science

Most recently in 2012, the eminent psychiatrist Professor Andrew Sims, in his *Is Faith Delusion?* says, *"the man in the street comes into contact with science in three guises: science as fact; science as hypothesis; and, science as dogma."* He rightly points out that science has progressed by forming hypotheses and that most hypotheses turn out to be wrong. But even if that is so, hypotheses need to be made in order to test them and find which ones are right. He explains (as a psychiatrist) that there used to be conflict between science and faith, between psychiatry and faith and between psychiatry and science and insists that the reason for the conflict is when experts in one field begin to pontificate on other fields. He classes most scientific teaching as dogmatic – i.e. laws are learned by rote as established fact and suggests this is why many students are switched off.[22]

---

[20] Michael Ruse: "Why I think the New Atheists are a bloody disaster" http://blog.beliefnet.com/scienceandthesacred/2009/08/why-i-think-the-new-atheists-are-a-bloody-disaster.html

[21] "The God Delusion" page 91

[22] Andrew Sims: "Is Faith Delusion?" pages 84 & 85

Commenting on science becoming dogma, he says, *"As an example of dogma, when every last detail of natural selection is put forward as something that has to be accepted as literal truth with 'religious' fervour, it has stepped outside science, it is no longer falsifiable in Popper's sense, and therefore it cannot be a scientific hypothesis."*[23] (Popper formulated the principle that every hypothesis must have a means of falsifying it – i.e. there is some way it can be tested to see if it is false. This is the basis of "empiricism". I shall comment more on this in chapter 6).

Dawkins describes himself as being a "deeply religious non-believer".[24] I would agree with his description as he is nothing if not vehement in his beliefs. However, he cannot be described fairly as being dogmatic in the way Sims defines scientific dogmatism as he does not portray his beliefs as totally established fact. The one thing I would say is that he is unable to see the other side of the argument. But dogmatism is easily ascribed to some religious believers.

Dogmatism in religion

Ardent creationists can very dogmatic. The conclusion of an article on the dangers of theistic evolution found on the *Answers in Genesis* website says, *"The doctrines of creation and evolution are so strongly divergent that reconciliation is totally impossible. Theistic evolutionists attempt to integrate the two doctrines, however such syncretism reduces the message of the Bible to insignificance. The conclusion is inevitable: There is no support for theistic evolution in the Bible."*[25]

---

[23] "The God Delusion" page 86
[24] Ibid, chapter 1
[25] http://www.answersingenesis.org/articles/cm/v17/n4/theistic-evolution

They lump all those believing in evolution together. The *Answers in Genesis* site speaks of fundamental principles of the doctrine (itself an emotive word) of evolution[26]. To some creationists there is only one possible Christian belief about creation: that the universe is approximately 6,000 years old and was created more or less in its present form in six days. Other views are compromise.[27] For example, John Otis of "Triumphant Publications Ministries" has published a book called *Theistic Evolution: A Sinful Compromise*.[28] In addition, they believe every living thing was created very close to its present state by God and that virtually no change has taken place although there can be change within "kinds". Otis discusses this on page 100 of his book where he defines a kind like this:

We can talk about the dog kind, or the cat kind, or the fish kind, or the amphibian kind, or the reptile kind, or the bird kind, or the mammal kind. While there is a certain speciation among the same kind, there is no modification of descent among the different kinds, commonly known as macroevolution. In other words, there is no type of change that can transform an amphibian into a reptile.

Unfortunately this well demonstrates the misunderstandings on the part of creationists. For a start, imagining that evolutionists think an amphibian gets transformed into a reptile is nonsense. Evolutionary change normally takes place over hundreds or thousands of generations as Dawkins explains in his *Climbing Mount*

---

[26] http://www.answersingenesis.org/articles/dgue/basic-assumptions-of-evolution

[27] Jason Lyle & Tim Chaffey, "Old Earth Creationism on Trial", Master Books 2008

[28] http://www.triumphantpublications.com/TheisticEvolution.pdf

Improbable and the changes from one generation to the next are hardly discernable.

In addition, Otis appears not to realise that dogs and cats are mammals so has a dog kind, a cat kind and a mammal kind! He is happy to classify animals emotionally close to us in sub-groups of kinds (according to "families") but then puts all fish, amphibians, reptiles and birds in single kinds ("classes" in taxonomical terms). I wonder if there is a "bird of prey kind" and "seed-eater kind" or do we just have "bird kind"? Among the mammals, would we have an "ungulate kind" (all hoofed mammals) or do we split them up into "horse kind", "bovine kind", "deer kind", "antelope kind" and so on? How specific do "kinds" become? What criteria do we use to decide?

I really cannot imagine the writer of Genesis had the slightest idea of Linnaeus' classification system or anything like it. It is obvious to me what he was saying – "like begets like". No one would argue with that. It's a genetic law. And I really do not think the apostle Paul had anything like that in mind either when he wrote about the different kinds of flesh different animals had. It's obvious that they do have different kinds of flesh – anyone can see that. When he says, "*for not all flesh is the same, but there is one kind for humans, another for animals, another for birds, and another for fish*"[29], was he making a scientific point? Apart from the fact that birds and fish are animals anyway, we could note that chimpanzee flesh is much closer to human flesh than it is to dog flesh. To suggest that all mammalian flesh apart from human flesh is "one kind" is also untrue, so if he was being scientific, he was clearly wrong. Trying to use this to prove that the Bible is against evolution is, to my mind,

---

[29] 1 Corinthians chapter 15, verse 39

stretching credibility beyond breaking point. He was not trying to make a point about origins or about biology.

In creationist science, Tectonic Plate theory (Continental drift) and geological epochs over millennia are evidence of a "uniformitarian" view – i.e. that it takes a very long time to happen. Instead, continental drift is seen as a possible explanation of flood geology and it would have happened extremely quickly (catastrophic plate tectonics)[30]. Henry Morris (founder of Institute for Creation Research[31]), in the foreword to his son's book, argues from the apostle Peter's words[32] that "uniformitarianism" is claiming *"that all things continue as they were from the beginning of creation"*[33] when evolutionary theory actually argues for a gradual change. I find that a strange conclusion when you think that he rejects evolution. He says those who, therefore, believe in evolution are the scoffers referred to by the apostle. Clearly, anyone having a different view of origins cannot be a genuine Christian. To me, that indicates a very strange and dubious method of biblical interpretation.

Of course there are variations amongst the different creationist groups. British creationists, on the whole, tend to be a little less dogmatic than their American counterparts. The *Earth History* website[34] adopts more of a "gap theory" approach but it is still unashamedly creationist.

---

[30] http://www.answersingenesis.org/articles/nab/catastrophic-plate-tectonics

[31] http://www.icr.org

[32] 2 Peter, chapter 3, verses 3 - 4

[33] John Morris, "The Young Earth: The Real History of the Earth - Past, Present, and Future", Master Books 2007

[34] http://www.earthhistory.org.uk/

Creationists agree with atheists that evolution means God becomes redundant, but instead of rejecting God, they reject evolution. I really think creationists who have such a condemnatory attitude toward anyone with a different interpretation need to examine their hearts. They do not have exclusivity on correct biblical interpretation. One thing I have learned (and it has taken me some time, I have to admit) is that it is very difficult to judge another person's motives. We make assumptions based on our previous experience and our prejudices and are sure we are right. I have often found that, when I think I know why someone does or believes something, I turn out to be wrong.

Dawkins and his understanding of faith.

While Dawkins is not scientifically dogmatic (though a little monocular in his viewpoint), he can be quite scathing in his approach to people and their motives. He describes conversion from atheism as a "trick" used by such people as C.S. Lewis, claiming that *"I used to be an atheist but… is one of the oldest tricks in the book."*[35] He employs mockery, saying, *"Most of us happily disavow fairies, astrology and the Flying Spaghetti Monster, without first immersing ourselves in books of Pastafarian theology."*[36] Dawkins likens Christianity to such unrealistic belief propositions throughout *The God Delusion* as he argues that it similarly has little evidence to support it. This infers that a deep study of the Bible is unnecessary in order to dismiss its teachings. And is he right in interpreting Lewis as exercising a "trick"?

---

[35] "The God Delusion" page 13

[36] Ibid. page 15

I am convinced that Richard Dawkins has misunderstood what faith is because he has, as always, only seen it from one angle - interpreting it according to what he can understand rather than how it is seen by those who have real faith. An inability to see the other side of the argument is an indication of religiosity, whether as a believer or a non-believer. We need to understand that faith is exercised in different ways and is involved in many aspects of life. In the next chapter, I shall try to examine the differences (and similarities) between faith as exercised in science and in religion.

CHAPTER 2

Looking at Faith in Science and Religion

I shall discuss faith specifically in chapters 7 to 9 but it is worth looking at the differences between belief in science and belief in religions.

According to the Penguin English Dictionary, faith is, *"1. complete confidence or belief in something, esp. without objective proof. 2a. a particular system of religious beliefs. 2b. belief in the traditional doctrines of a religion."*[37] The Oxford online dictionary defines it similarly: *"1. complete trust in someone or something; 2. strong beliefs in the doctrines of a religion, based on spiritual conviction rather than proof."*[38] I will discuss in chapters 8 and 9 what the Bible describes as the essence of faith in Hebrews chapter 11. This has a long list of examples of faith which is *"the assurance of things hoped for, the conviction of things not seen"* (verse 1) – a list of people recorded in the Bible as having believed what they knew of God to endure suffering,

---

[37] Penguin Books Ltd. Penguin English Dictionary page 310

[38] http://oxforddictionaries.com/definition/english/faith?q=faith

in order to gain *"the city that has foundations, whose designer and builder is God."*[39]

Belief in Science

I think we can say with a great degree of confidence that evolution is the best explanation we have for the origin of species in the light of all current evidence, but it cannot be subjected to empirical tests in the same way as can, say, a physics hypothesis. Similarly, Cell Theory[40] cannot be subjected to final proof. We can legitimately say that some living thing *not* composed of cells could conceivably be discovered, but all the current evidence we have is that Cell Theory is true. Now, the processes (random mutation and natural selection[41]) of evolution have been proved beyond reasonable doubt. The fossil evidence gives us a high degree of certainty that these processes have occurred over hundreds of millions of years to create the massive variety of species we see today. Simply because the course of evolution over that time cannot be subjected to a similar process of empirical testing as can a physics hypothesis, it could be said that it has not been proved and has to be taken on some sort of "faith", but then we would have to say the same for all scientific theories. This kind of faith cannot be fairly compared with religious faith.

---

[39] Hebrews chapter 11, verse 10

[40] Cell Theory states that (1) all living organisms are composed of cells; (2) the cell is the basic unit of life and (3) cells arise from pre-existing cells

[41] There could, quite conceivably be other processes involved as well – these may not be all there is to evolution

Christian faith

"Irrational" and "without objective proof" are two somewhat different concepts, which I feel that Dawkins has conflated (knowingly or unknowingly) in his argument to discredit faith. The point I want to make is, faith *is* based on evidence but the evidence can be from many sources and could be subjective, rather than exclusively based on scientifically reproducible experiments. I and many other Christians in the "charismatic" arm of the church have seen people healed immediately after prayer – not once but on numerous occasions. Although some "faith-healers" have been discredited when their claims are examined in a scientific way, many other healings remain permanent. I will discuss the evidence on this in Chapter 9. And healings are reported to happen every day in numerous places all over the world.

Are these miracles? I don't know but the fact that these healings are so often linked with prayer gives me the faith, without objective proof, to say that God is at work. And healings are not the only evidence that believers receive throughout their lives as confirmation of God's presence – George Muller's Ashley Down orphanage in Bristol received enough anonymous and unsolicited donations to keep the orphanage thriving in the nineteenth century. Even now the George Muller Foundation[42] relies entirely on prayer – praying for God to supply their needs – and have an explicit policy never to try to fundraise. Books such as Joni Eareckson's autobiography "Joni" and Jackie Pullinger's "Chasing the Dragon" tell the stories of Christians living in dependence on God and finding their needs

---

[42] http://www.mullers.org

met as they continue their morally courageous work (more on Jackie later).

Is faith "believing what you know ain't so"?

The other point is that the expressions "God did it" and "there is a scientific explanation" are not necessarily logically or philosophically mutually exclusive.

So where does this idea that faith is irrational come from? I can only think it has come from the atheist lobby, from people who agree with Mark Twain's quote that it means "*believing what you know ain't so*."[43] But who gave atheists the authority to change the definition of words in the English language arbitrarily? Why should I give them or Richard Dawkins any credence in this at all? He is perfectly entitled to make up his own words like "meme" and invest them with a certain meaning but he cannot redefine perfectly good words without explaining that he is using them in a different sense to the normally accepted meaning.[44] Otherwise, it gives the reader a wrong impression. The sad thing is that some people seem to think that if Richard Dawkins says it, it must be true.

In a similar vein, according to online *The Skeptic's Dictionary*, "*Faith is a non-rational belief in some proposition. A non-rational belief is one that is contrary to the sum of the evidence for that belief. A belief*

---

[43]   Austin Cline: "Comment of the Week: Faith is Believing What You Know Ain't So" http://atheism.about.com/b/2010/01/19/comment-of-the-week-faith-is-believing-what-you-know-aint-so.htm

[44]   That is why, for example, I felt it necessary to state what I meant by the word "god" at the beginning of the book

is contrary to the sum of evidence if there is overwhelming evidence against the belief, e.g., that the earth is flat, hollow, or is the centre of the universe."[45]

Now that kind of faith *is* irrational, because it is a matter that can be clearly proved or disproved scientifically. I would suggest that faith could be said to have elements of "non-rationality" (rather than "irrationality" which is *against* the evidence), since it is hard to get absolute incontrovertible, scientifically reproducible evidence, for or against the existence of God, simply because God is proposed by the Bible writers to be a sentient being not subject to the laws of the material universe and who decides whether and when to reveal himself to us humans. This could sound like "special pleading" or "moving the goalposts", but surely if this amazing universe was created by a being, that being could well have the freedom to either draw close or remain distant, in a way that humans (Christian or atheist) do not have the right to prescribe. As King Solomon puts it. *"God is in heaven and you are on earth. So let your words be few."*[46] But neither is God deliberately trying to make it hard for us to find him – in Isaiah chapter 1 verse 2, Israel is described as having rebelled against God and Jeremiah promises that if we seek after God we will find him[47].

---

[45] http://www.skepdic.com/faith.html

[46] Ecclesiastes chapter 5, verse 2

[47] Jeremiah chapter 29, verse13

Fundamentalism and reason

Dawkins admits that not all believers are completely bonkers and that some are quite reasonable but says:

> *If only such subtle, nuanced religion predominated, the world would surely be a better place, and I would have written a different book. The melancholy truth is that this kind of understated, decent, revisionist religion is numerically negligible. To the vast majority of believers around the world, religion all too closely resembles what you hear from the likes of Robertson, Falwell or Haggard, Osama bin Laden or the Ayatollah Khomeini.*[48]

What does he mean by "numerically negligible" and what categories did he mean?

I was not sure whether he meant that the vast majority of believers were rabble-rousers or violent or that the vast majority of believers had an unthinking, uncritical irrational kind of faith. I specifically asked him, when I finally made contact and sent him a draft of this book, which of these he meant. He replied as follows:

> *Unlike you, I was including Islam, which means a huge population at least officially committed to the literal truth of the Koran, i.e. fundamentalist. Christianity is rife in Africa and it is mostly fundamentalist. USA Christians are at least 40% fundamentalist. European*

---

[48] "The God Delusion" page 15

Christians are a dwindling band. Adding all this up, it is surely true that an absolute majority of religious people in the world are fundamentalist. However, I may have been exaggerating when I said the VAST majority of believers. It is arguable that I should have cut the word 'vast', but I think it safe to leave the word 'majority'.

It is good to understand what he means, but, just in case anyone thinks the vast majority are violent, let me say this:

The issue of fundamentalism in other religions, particularly Islam, has not been well researched. Certainly Islamic extremists hit the news very often, but could this just be from the nature of the violence and inhumanity rather than any numerical dominance? Certainly Muslim community leaders in the UK are constantly distancing themselves from the militants, and in Bristol there is a large Muslim Somali immigrant community who, Dr Christina Biggs reports, are both "very religious" by their own description and also peace-loving and very determined to contribute to British society. And I think we can say with certainty that among the millions of Muslims world-wide, the vast majority are not suicide bombers or jihadists. I shall discuss this further when dealing with the question of morality.

As regards the fundamentalist question, I felt it fair to use some sort of measure as to what we mean by "fundamentalist" because one person's fundamentalism may be another's reasonable belief. In light of Dawkins' view of those he would regard as having an unreasoning faith, I thought I would look at proportions of those who would believe "creation science" or Intelligent Design (ID) especially as evolution is his main area of expertise.

The USA has less acceptance of evolution than other Western countries according to a study done in 2010 and reported by "National Geographic"[49]. It is where the Christian Right is most vociferous and strident; where there is a strong lobby for teaching ID or "creation science" in schools alongside evolution as equally valid scientific views, so it is where you would expect to find a very high proportion of Christians against evolution. In looking at figures, I found that about a third of believers in the USA would accept a theistic evolutionary view while two thirds were creationist or ID supporters (see Appendix B for further details).

A survey in the UK conducted by "Theos" indicates that about thirty percent of people felt a belief in evolution and creation was possible although eighty percent believe in evolution. As Christians are a minority in the UK, this would seem to indicate that the majority of believers would accept some form of theistic evolution (again see Appendix B).

I could hardly call this a "study" but during the process of writing this book, I attended the "New Wine" event at Shepton Mallet, Somerset in 2013, where thousands of evangelical Christians gather for teaching and worship each year[50]. I was one of the people manning the "Christians in Science"[51] stand and had the privilege of chatting to numerous people about science and faith. I was very surprised to find that only a tiny minority of those people would

---

49   http://news.nationalgeographic.co.uk/news/2006/08/060810-evolution.html

50   I heard a lady attending this event explain that she had been completely blind but had her sight totally restored within minutes after people prayed on the stage for her the day before.

51   http://www.cis.org.uk

accept a creationist interpretation of Genesis chapters 1 & 2. One lady said she had been gob-smacked when she discovered a friend who held a creationist stance. Of course, many of the people who approached us had a science background and so would be more likely to have an understanding and acceptance of evolutionary theory, so this is hardly reliable but it certainly to me confirmed the findings of the Theos study.

I think Dawkins is probably right, therefore, to say that the majority of believers are fundamentalist. He has, if my figures above are correct, even underestimated the proportion of fundamentalist Christians in the USA. However, he suggests that the number of non-fundamentalists is "numerically negligible". I would not consider figures around 30% anything like numerically negligible. Checking through the figures I found, I feel confident to say that he is clearly not correct in that estimation.

Getting back to the evolution question, it is interesting that faith schools in Britain teach evolution. It is, of course, law that they do so, but they are entitled to teach about alternative theories as well if they so wish. There are a few that teach evolution alongside creationism and tell their students to answer exam questions **as if** they believe in evolution but I visit many schools through my work as a supply teacher and ICT moderator and a number are faith schools. Every one that I know will simply teach their students evolution. I cannot comment on what happens in non-Christian faith schools but I would imagine the story would be similar there.

According to charts I saw in a very good children's book "Information is Beautiful" by David McCandless, where they gave proportions of people holding different beliefs on the origins of life in the world, the largest proportion of all believed in some kind of theistic evolution. The literal creationist proportion was far smaller, ID was even smaller, while the proportion of atheistic evolutionists was a little smaller than the proportion of believers in theistic evolution.[52] His sources were Wikipedia, BBC.com and Skeptic.com (an atheist website).

What can we conclude from Richard Dawkins' statement about a "reasoned, nuanced" Christian faith being "numerically negligible"? The problem is that there is not very much data about this in parts of the world other than the USA and UK – whether the rest of Europe, or the Middle East where the church is very much underground, or Africa (which does have many evangelicals and charismatics), or even Asia where the Christian church is growing and some say is numerically stronger than the rest of the world put together. I think it is probably going to be too difficult to bandy statistics, but would want to challenge Dawkins' statement as being too imprecise to have the evidence or public perception to support it!

---

[52]   McCandless, "Information is Beautiful" pages 20 & 21

CHAPTER 3

The Problem of Attitudes

Dawkins' attitude to atheists

There are many atheists who find Dawkins embarrassing. For example, Michael Ruse says that Richard's *The God Delusion* makes him embarrassed to be an atheist and that it is simplistic[53]. Peter Higgs, the theoretical physicist who postulated the "Higgs' boson" which has since been discovered at Cern in Switzerland, says he agrees with some of Dawkins' thoughts over the unfortunate consequences that have resulted from religious belief but that he was unhappy with his approach to believers and agreed with those who found his approach embarrassing[54]. I don't know that many who disagree with his atheism but they find his strident attitude to religious belief unacceptable and some describe him as a "liability" while conversely some creationists regard him as an "asset".

In answer to this, he quotes a hypothetical criticism: *"I'm an atheist, but I wish to dissociate myself from your shrill, strident, intemperate,*

[53]   http://www.youtube.com/watch?v=UaQgWl-HtYA

[54]   http://www.theguardian.com/science/2012/dec/26/peter-higgs-richard-dawkins-fundamentalism

intolerant, ranting language." And then says, *"Actually, if you look at the language of **The God Delusion**, it is rather less shrill or intemperate than we regularly take in our stride – when listening to political commentators for example, or theatre, art or book critics. Here are some samples of recent restaurant criticism from leading London newspapers:"* He then selects a few extreme examples of comments about restaurants and adds this assessment, *"the strongest language to be found in **The God Delusion** is tame and measured by comparison. If it sounds intemperate, it is only because of the weird convention, almost universally accepted..., that religious faith is uniquely privileged: above and beyond criticism. Insulting a restaurant might seem trivial compared to insulting God. But restaurateurs and chefs really exist and they have feelings to be hurt, whereas blasphemy, as the witty bumper sticker puts it, is a victimless crime."*[55]

I can understand how threats from Islamic extremists can lead someone to claim that religious faith is above and beyond criticism but he seems to be including all faiths here. From what I see, the church is ridiculed in sitcoms, its standards are attacked fiercely and regularly in parliament; it is made to look variously pathetic and wishy-washy or domineering and intolerant. Yes, there are some programmes on television that uphold "churchianity" and there is a regular five minute religious slot on BBC Radio 4 called "Thought for the Day" but by and large the BBC could hardly be accused of having a religious slant and I find very few people afraid of criticising Christianity. There is a difference, however, between criticism and ridicule.

---

[55] "The God Delusion" page 16

Today, Christians are portrayed as being eccentric, anti-sex, anti-fun, bigoted and ridiculous in their outmoded attitudes. Television shows like "Father Ted" and "The Vicar of Dibley" on British TV channels, which, I have to say, I find thoroughly amusing, poke fun at aspects of church life that are sometimes painfully close to the truth. That hardly backs up Dawkins' assertions above.

I have to say though, in his defence, that I was horrified to read some of the things some "Christians" had written to him and other atheists, such as this one addressed to Brian Flemming, author of *The God Who Wasn't There*:

> *You've definitely got some nerve. I'd love to take a knife, gut you fools, and scream with joy as your insides spill out in front of you. You are attempting to ignite a holy war in which some day I, and others like me, may have the pleasure of taking action like the above mentioned. However, GOD teaches us not to seek vengeance, but to pray for those like you all. I'll get comfort in knowing that the punishment GOD will bring to you will be 1000 times worse than anything I can inflict. The best part is that you WILL suffer for eternity for these sins that you're completely ignorant about. The Wrath of GOD will show no mercy. For your sake, I hope the truth is revealed to you before the knife connects with your flesh. Merry CHRISTMAS!!! PS You people really don't have a clue as to what is in store for you ... I thank GOD I'm not you.*[56]

---

[56]   Ibid. pages 242-243

I share with him a condemnation of and shock at such behaviour. Not only is that totally against the spirit of Christ, it is abhorrent by any human standards. No matter how much you disagree with someone, that person is a human being with the same rights and feelings as you have. To attack them with such spiteful venom is the opposite of what you would expect from a Christian. I can only think those people felt desperately threatened in their beliefs (I was going to say "faith" but it was not faith being threatened; it was their particular interpretation). Richard Dawkins' own language is certainly very temperate in comparison with that. I will not say more about this at this stage as I will discuss the question of behaviour among Christians in chapter 11 but I do not want to leave my reader with any impression that glossing over this in one paragraph indicates that I do not take it seriously.

I would also agree with him on fundamentalist attitudes among Christians. When I first became a Christian, I would have called myself a fundamentalist. I thought that it simply meant you believed in the fundamentals of Christian doctrine; not that you could not listen to reason or that you were not prepared to change your mind on an issue. I felt it meant that you believed the Bible but was not confined to a particular narrow interpretation. In my early naïveté, I didn't realise that it was more a particular slant on Scripture that represented a highly literal interpretation with a huge intolerance of any deviation.

I think Dawkins has a point in labelling the American Christian extreme as the "American Taliban". I would hope they are nothing like as bad as the actual Taliban but they have some tendencies in that direction. Attacking abortion clinics and women who use them as well as nurses and doctors has nothing to do with faith and does nothing to stop abortion. How can you say you love life and people and then attack them, however much you may detest what they are doing?

While this type of behaviour does occur among Christians (who really should know better), to label the vast majority of believers in the same way is being dishonest. Christians who label scientists as having an ulterior motive in teaching evolution are being equally dishonest.

Surprisingly, the Bible has a lot to say about people who are outwardly religious but do not have a heart commitment. For example, Jesus spoke of the Pharisees being like *whitewashed tombs*[57] (tombs were whitewashed to warn people not to touch them in case they became ritually "unclean" so he was saying the Pharisees should be avoided). The Pharisees used religious traditions, for example, to excuse themselves from having to care for and love their parents. James, the half-brother of Jesus, says in his letter, "*if a brother or sister is poorly clothed and lacking in daily food, and one of you says to them, 'Go in peace, be warmed and filled,' without giving them the things needed for the body, what good is that?*"[58] The apostle Paul, in 2 Timothy chapter 3 verse 5, speaks of those who have an appearance of godliness but deny its power and says they should be avoided. They are people who love the shadow but not the substance. If believers feel offended when they are criticized then they are not secure in their faith.

Jesus did not come as a "super-human" because he was God incarnate; He showed us what it is like to be truly human without

---

[57] Matthew chapter 23, verse 27
[58] James chapter 2, verse 15

all the baggage and rubbish that the rest of us drag around. He didn't perform miracles of healing because he was the Son of God but because he was the Son of Man totally relying on his Father. Those who follow him, as C S Lewis pointed out, should be the most normal and human people there are and not in any way "super-spiritual". Dressing up in religious garb does absolutely nothing to a person. In fact, Lewis said Christians should not wear religious garb at all as that implied that it was more their business to serve God than those in "normal" clothing. I would add that it creates a false and unhelpful separation between them and other people.

Dawkins questions the rights of such people to special treatment. I agree. I don't see why I should have any special treatment as a believer. If you are confident in what you believe, you welcome challenge. If it results in your changing or adjusting your belief, then that is positive, not negative. You have no need to hide from facts that would challenge you; you seek out contrary opinion, knowing that you will either be more convinced of what you believe or will have to adjust – both of which are positive.

If I still believe exactly the same things next year as I do now, I will not have progressed at all. Richard Dawkins, of course, tries to paint a picture of religious belief being static and science being dynamic ("*theology, which – unlike science or most other branches of human scholarship – has not moved on in eighteen centuries*"[59]). I would challenge that. The mere presence of so many different groups within the church speaks of the way that the church itself has had to evolve as it grapples with different issues arising in history and with different interpretations of biblical theology.

---

[59]   "The God Delusion" page 54

Coupled with our attitudes to the arguments of others is the matter of our attitude to our own arguments. We all have the tendency to believe we are right. Of course, we do; there would be no point in believing anything otherwise. However, we often tend to be unaware that we assume certain things to be self-evidently true and do not question them. Then, our beliefs arise from those assumptions.

Rainbows and presuppositions

When reading any book promoting a particular viewpoint, including this one, it's very important to gauge the writer's slant and understand their presuppositions.

Dawkins does state his presuppositions by saying what an atheist is. He says:

> *An atheist in this sense of philosophical naturalist is somebody who believes there is nothing beyond the natural, physical world, no supernatural creative intelligence lurking behind the observable universe, no soul that outlasts the body and no miracles – except in the sense of natural phenomena that we don't yet understand. If there is something that appears to lie beyond the natural world as it is now imperfectly understood, we hope eventually to understand it and embrace it within the natural. As ever when we unweave a rainbow, it will not become less wonderful.*[60]

---

[60] Ibid. page 35

Of course it is true that a rainbow will not become less wonderful if we unweave it. I should imagine virtually every scientist is able to appreciate beauty while seeking to understand the mechanisms behind it. However, a few points need to be made about beauty:

1. You do not need to unweave a rainbow to appreciate its wonder. In fact the majority of people don't.
2. Understanding refraction and appreciating beauty are not mutually exclusive (as Dawkins points out). They are simply looking at the same thing from a different perspective – a different dimension – and neither invalidates the other.
3. Seeing the wonder of a rainbow and understanding the science behind it can give an increased appreciation, but **we should not confuse** the two dimensions.
4. If we think the "unwoven" rainbow is **all there is** to a rainbow, we will never appreciate its beauty.
5. We cannot say with surety that there is not another way to look at a rainbow – another dimension from which to view it. We were not aware of the scientific view thousands of years ago.

But looking at his presuppositions in the first part of his statement above – he assumes they are correct and it is from that position that he "proves" his thesis. If, however, his presuppositions are not correct, his whole argument falls apart. I believe that science can "unweave" every rainbow but it still does not prove that his presuppositions are correct. Science does not have exclusivity to all dimensions of knowledge.

He quotes Jefferson who says that to talk of immaterials is to talk of nothings.[61] So, if something is not composed of matter (or energy, presumably) then we are talking about nothing, and so by extension, God is nothing. Now, Jefferson may have been a very intelligent man, but this is quite a statement, based purely on an *a priori* argument that if science cannot measure it, it does not exist. Well, on that arrogant assumption, God does not exist, but how can it honestly be possible to assume Jefferson is right? It is simply not good enough to dismiss possibilities that are outside your presuppositions without giving any argument or evidence.

Let's go on to examine Dawkins' arguments on the existence of God in greater detail. Has he understood the biblical theology of God and his nature?

---

[61] Ibid. page 62

CHAPTER 4

Different Viewing Angles

I would defend Richard Dawkins' right to comment on theological issues even though he has not been trained in theology. The apostle Peter had not been trained in theology but he developed an incredible insight into God's nature over time. Granted, he made some pretty monumental blunders and Paul had to reprimand him over some distinctly racist attitudes but he was a fisherman who led the early disciples – a bit of a go-getter who tried (and failed) to walk on water. He was convinced he would never deny Jesus; then did so when confronted by a servant girl. And yet the writings and life of this untrained fisherman have been studied by theologians, Christian believers and unbelievers over the past two thousand years.

No, there is no reason why Richard Dawkins (or anyone else) should not comment on theology. But just as we would tend to trust a scientist more than a non-scientist when speaking on scientific matters, so in theology there are many deep thinkers who have a good knowledge of the Bible and other ancient texts as well as a grasp of the language of the Bible and the extent to which it is self-consistent and consistent with the thinking and knowledge of the ancient civilisations of that time. Dawkins has made it clear that he does not consider theology to be a serious academic discipline. Can I then take him seriously?

Attacking a straw man

The point is not whether Richard Dawkins is entitled to discuss theology or not but whether or not his view on theology has any validity? It has nothing to do with his academic qualifications. Is his view on God (or the lack of a god) a valid view? He spends a considerable part of his book disproving God although he does point out that it is impossible to do so conclusively, saying that it is, rather, a case of massive improbability. But what kind of God is he talking about? He defends himself against the charge that he is attacking a straw man but has he any idea of the actual doctrine of the nature of God?

To defuse the straw man charge, he says that he is not attacking a bearded man in the sky. He may not attack that childish concept, but he still attacks a straw man. He says:

> *Any creative intelligence, of sufficient complexity to design anything, comes into existence only as the end product of an extended process of gradual evolution. Creative intelligences, being evolved, necessarily arrive late in the universe, and therefore cannot be responsible for designing it. God, in the sense defined, is a delusion.*[62]

---

[62]   Ibid. page 52

In a similar vein, he says:

> *Seen clearly, intelligent design will turn out to be a redoubling of the problem. Once again, this is because the designer himself (herself/itself) immediately raises the bigger problem of his own origin. Any entity capable of designing something as improbable as a Dutchman's Pipe (or a universe) would have to be even more improbable than a Dutchman's Pipe. Far from terminating the vicious regress, God aggravates it with a vengeance.*[63]

Neither of these raise any charge against the real Christian belief in an eternal God; they only attack a made-up idea of some deity that has evolved or arisen somehow, generally within the universe. What's the point? Why does he bother?

The concept he puts forward is not found anywhere in the Bible or held by any Christian believer I have come across: the Bible simply starts *"In the beginning, God created the heavens and the earth."*[64] Dawkins' idea is of course based on his presupposition that there can be nothing outside the universe that can interfere in it and on the observation that human beings, the most complex of organisms, emerged after four and a half billion years of evolution.

But in what way is a transcendent God necessarily an evolved being? How can Dawkins defend his assertion that although biological life increases in complexity with time, this must be true of everything in

---

[63] Ibid. page 145
[64] Genesis chapter 1, verse 1

the universe? More than this, how can he defend this assertion when he applies it to something Christians insist is transcendent? Indeed, Dawkins' *"God, in the sense defined"* certainly is a delusion, but his problem is that he has wrongly defined God in the first place and secondly, it is actually impossible to define God ("define" has the concept of limits – putting something within specific parameters).

A biblical perspective on "unbelievers"

However, let us look at a biblical principle here before we continue. There are a number of passages that indicate it is impossible for those who are not "in the kingdom" to understand it at all. The New Testament writers were totally against an "enlightened elite" as occurred in the mystery religions of the time but, nevertheless, it is quite clear that you cannot understand much at all unless you are "born again" – that widely misunderstood term which I will now attempt to explain.

In John chapter 3, there is the story of a conversation between Jesus and Nicodemus (a ruler of the Jews and someone who knew quite a lot about theology). Nicodemus is wondering about this new teacher who is doing amazing deeds. Just who is he? He approaches Jesus by night and obliquely says, *"we know you must be from God because no one does the things you do unless they are from God."*[65] Jesus replies: *"Truly I say to you, unless a man is born again, he cannot see the kingdom of God."*[66] He is saying the kingdom is out of sight to those not born again. It's around the corner and they don't even know

---

[65] John chapter 3, verse 2
[66] John chapter 3, verse 3

there is a corner anyway. They can no more understand it than a foetus can understand the outside world into which it is yet to be born. Once someone is born again, this "kingdom of God" begins to come into focus.

The apostle Paul puts it another way. He says "*the natural person does not accept the things of the Spirit of God, for they are folly to him, and he is not able to understand them because they are spiritually discerned*"[67] and earlier, he says, "*the preaching of the cross is folly to those who are perishing.*"[68] Almost as though to confirm the truth of this scripture, Dawkins goes one step further and describes the cross as "*barking mad!*"[69]

How does being "born again" happen? It seems it is something that cannot be explained methodically. It just has to be experienced. When Nicodemus asked Jesus to explain, he told him it was to do with being "born of the Spirit (of God)", not physical birth. Furthermore, he said the Spirit is like the wind "blowing where it wants" and you cannot tell where it comes from or goes (we may know now but the illustration was valid then because they didn't). He said that was what it was like being born of the Spirit - you can't reason it out!

I am sorry I cannot explain it any better but the only way to understand it is to experience it!

---

67   1 Corinthians chapter 2, verse 14
68   1 Corinthians chapter 1, verse 18
69   "The God Delusion" page 287

But is this fair?

This of course would seem to present a moral problem. If God expects us to believe in him and in fact judges us at the resurrection according to our faith in him and acceptance of Jesus' authority and sacrificial death for our sins, then why would God set it up so that unbelievers could not believe in him? I would say that the answer is that it has to be on God's terms, not our own. Jesus himself was angered by the demand of the Pharisees for him to prove himself by a sign. In Matthew chapter 16 verses 2–3, Jesus replies: "*When it is evening, you say, 'It will be fair weather, for the sky is red.' And in the morning, 'It will be stormy today, for the sky is red and threatening.' You know how to interpret the appearance of the sky, but you cannot interpret the signs of the times. An evil and adulterous generation seeks for a sign, but no sign will be given to it except the sign of Jonah.*"

What I think Jesus was saying was that the evidence was there for people who wanted to find it. But Jesus also wants a movement of the will, a relationship of trust, a desire to submit to his authority. It's one thing to say "Okay, you've convinced me; I concede that you exist" and quite another to say "Show yourself to me Lord so I can know and love you better". As a general rule, I think anyone who only wants intellectual proof will be permanently disappointed or they might find they get more than they bargained for! On the other hand, anyone who genuinely seeks the truth, even if it may contradict what they currently believe, is likely to find it. And there is nothing to stop anyone doing that. I'll be looking at this aspect of personal trust (rather than scientific impersonal proof) in Chapter 9.

Everyone has presuppositions and it is important to acknowledge them. It is a sign of maturity and security when you are able to do so. Christians need to acknowledge their presuppositions as much as anyone else. I suppose the problem is that we often fail to recognise our own.

As I said before, in considering Dawkins' argument about the non-existence of God, we need to appreciate where he is coming from and what his presuppositions are.

A very human tendency

Most people tend to interpret anything new in the light of what they already know. It's a perfectly natural tendency. In the Acts of the Apostles chapter 2 is a record of the first day of Pentecost after Jesus had ascended to heaven. The frightened disciples were in an upper room praying when something pretty dramatic happened. The account speaks of "tongues of fire" resting on each one of them and then they all started speaking in different languages (languages they had apparently not learned) publicly glorifying God. Clearly, everyone who heard this was astonished. But there were two different reactions.

One lot asked, "What does this mean?" The other lot just said they were drunk and mocked. The thing is, what was happening must have had some resemblance to drunkenness. No doubt they were pretty happy. But it must also have been different from drunkenness; otherwise they would all have come to the same conclusion. The first lot, therefore, asked questions; the second could only interpret in the light of the most similar thing they already knew. I believe it is better to be in the first lot. You need to question, look beyond and ask what makes the most sense. The Bible enjoins us to "look beyond".

Many atheists have very similar presuppositions to Richard Dawkins; they assume that if God exists, science can prove it one way or the other and then, from that standpoint, use their human logic to come to a conclusion. Human reason acting upon empirical evidence is assumed to be supreme. But we need to question this. Can we assume that science potentially has *all* the answers? Are atheistic presuppositions unassailably right? Is the universe/multiverse a closed system? Can we definitely say there is no other possible view of existence than that which can be measured in a scientific way?

Dawkins and, I am sure, other New Atheists would have no difficulty in accepting that different scientific theories can be held in tension about one issue – e.g. is character due to nature or nurture or is light particles or waves? In both cases, it depends how you look at it. Taking light, according to Wave-particle duality theory, all matter has wave-like and particle-like properties and it is impossible to describe fully the behaviour of quantum-scale objects by only referring to waves or only to particles. You need both for a full explanation and yet both "sides" can put up a case for light being particles (matter) on the one hand or waves (pure energy) on the other. Theology has disagreements over various issues – e.g. is salvation dependent on the sovereignty of God or the free will of man? Extreme Calvinists would insist that free will is ultimately an illusion – God has already chosen those he will call and those he will not. Jesus said, *"you did not choose me but I chose you."*[70] Extreme Arminians would insist that this is a non-biblical position – otherwise there is no point in preaching the gospel. Jesus said, ***"whoever** will come after me; let him deny himself"*[71] and the apostle Peter said ***"whoever** shall call on the*

---

[70]   John chapter 15, verse 16
[71]   Mark chapter 8, verse 34

name of the Lord shall be saved,"[72] both of which speak of the will of humankind. Extremes on both sides insist the other side is wrong. I believe the truth is that the two views, apparently contradictory, need to be held in tension – they are both right – it depends how you look at it.

Why is it not possible to hold in tension a totally scientific explanation for origins and at the same time an acceptance that God is entirely responsible? Granted this is not a direct comparison with either of the above cases (the former is a scientific tension and the latter a theological one), but I do not see why some people are incapable of seeing this possibility. The point I am trying to make is that it is quite possible to hold two apparently contradictory positions in tension; the answer is not somewhere in the middle as a compromise position but recognising the truth of both positions.

Of course, that in no way indicates that God therefore exists, so we need now to look at that conundrum. I shall try to assess Dawkins' arguments disproving God's existence.

72   Acts chapter 2, verse 21

CHAPTER 5

"The God Hypothesis"

Arguments for the existence of God

In my first year at Bible College we were given the various "proofs" for the existence of God that Dawkins covers in his book. We looked through what they said and it was then shown quite clearly that they all failed. I am not going to go into them here. It is pointless as none of them prove his existence anyway. And, if you have read Richard Dawkins' book, he adequately shows their deficiencies – if they are used as "proofs".

The point is that no-one has become a Christian from following such arguments – the different "arguments" all come from people who already believed in God, who were just trying to disprove the charge that Christian belief is irrational. Clearly if these "proofs" were the only way to God then Dawkins would be right to attack them, but I have already tried to show that belief in God is about personal trust in a living God who freely chooses whether or not to reveal himself to us, and is not a dry intellectual mind-game, This is definitely a straw man! It sounds convincing but it's a bit like trying to make someone homeless by smashing up a house they don't live in! Easy to do and it may make your fans cheer, but it is quite pointless!

However, belief in God is not so obscure that it is inaccessible to anyone who wants to find him.

Understanding the arguments

Dawkins complains of the obscurantist flavour of theology, quoting St Gregory the Miracle Worker, who said: *"There is therefore nothing created, nothing subject to another in the Trinity: nor is there anything that has been added as though it once had not existed but had entered afterwards: therefore the Father has never been without the Son, nor the Son without the Spirit: and this same Trinity is immutable and unalterable forever."*[73]

He comments: *"Whatever miracles may have earned St Gregory his nickname, they were not miracles of honest lucidity. His words convey the characteristically obscurantist flavour of theology, which – unlike science or most other branches of human scholarship – has not moved on in eighteen centuries."*[74]

Many believers find St Gregory's statement about the Triunity quite easy to understand, since we have already accepted that God is a transcendent being and that he has revealed himself and relates to us in three ways – the creator of the universe, the God born as a human and the Spirit who lives in each believer. The fact that Dawkins

---

[73] "The God Delusion" page 54
[74] Ibid. page 55

could not understand it probably relates to what I mentioned above about the inability of those who have not been born again to understand the things of the Spirit, but this understanding is nevertheless accessible for people who genuinely want to get to know their Creator on his terms and not their own.

I can well remember reading a paragraph in some Religious Philosophy notes by Julian Ward, our lecturer at Bible College. He was previously an aeronautical engineer and has a fairly formidable intellect. It was a paragraph about the existence of God and talking about how he wills himself to exist (that's putting it in simple terms). I had to read the paragraph about three times before I began to get an inkling of what he was trying to tell me. But I persisted and eventually found it gave me a better appreciation of the Being of God. Many people just could not be bothered.

The other point to make is that theological writings and terms are not the same as scientific writings, so why should he expect them to be the same? Dawkins says, *"I can easily be moved to tears by poetry."*[75] If he can so appreciate poetry which is written very differently from science and seeks to provoke the reader to see beyond the actual words, why can he not see that theology may be in a similar category? The proverb "There are none so blind as those who will not see" comes readily to mind. The general sense I get from his book is: "You prove to me, on terms I dictate, that God exists. I decide the conditions; if you can't prove it, then it means he does not exist." Why should I accept Dawkins' terms of argument if I don't consider them valid anyway? My main aim is not to convince Richard Dawkins or anyone else for that matter although I would be

---

[75]   Dawkins, Richard, "An Appetite for Wonder" page 46

pleased if anyone did become convinced. I am concerned, though, to show that Richard Dawkins, who makes such a strong case for the truth, is being unfair to the evidence in his approach.

The Anthropic Principle

According to many Christians, this is the principle that it should be possible to deduce from the appearance of design in the laws of the universe that the existence of God is at least highly plausible. Data cited are the apparent "fine balance" of the exact values of the physical constants used in physics equations for the four forces of nature (gravitational, electrostatic, strong and weak nuclear forces) and the resulting coincidences that seemed to have been "rigged" to permit the evolution of life, particularly the "carbon resonance" in stars permitting the early production of carbon and therefore all the rest of the elements. There is also the occurrence of dark matter and dark energy which give rise to the expansion of the universe being neither so fast that no interaction between stars were possible, nor collapsing so fast that there is no time to evolve biological life.

Even Dawkins admits the appearance of design, notably in *The Ancestor's Tale*, and has been reported as saying that physics is a "problem" to atheists – that is, until Stephen Hawking published his book *The Grand Design* which appealed to string theory to ensure the balance of these constants and to the multiverse theory to posit that all possible universes in fact exist, and we happen to be in the universe which "worked". Rodney Holder's *Big Bang Big God* looks at the whole story and suggests, using William of Ockham's razor[76], that the simplest, most energetically economical solution is surely a single universe created by a sentient God.

There are other ideas on other aspects of the "fine balance" seen in the universe we inhabit. John Polkinghorne's short paper, *The Anthropic Principle and the Science and Religion Debate* sets out his idea (later elaborated and refined by Arthur Peacocke) based on the balance and interplay between *chance* and *necessity*. There is an enormous number of theoretical possibilities for how the universe could have evolved and chance represents what could happen. However necessity requires some things to happen – for example gravity causes particles to be attracted to each other. If necessity predominates too much, the universe would have been so stable that nothing new could ever have occurred; if too many random happenings occurred with too little stabilising action, then the changes would not have "stuck" and the universe would simply have been so unstable that galaxies, stars and planets could not have evolved.

In organic evolution, this would mean that if there were too few mutations, new variations and species could never be produced because life would be too stable; if too many occurred, the new variations would be so different that they could never survive.

This balance has produced a planet (the Earth) that is entirely suitable for life. Everything about it is just right – its distance from the Sun, its tilt, its size, the fact that it has just the right atmosphere and, of extreme importance, that it has liquid water with its extraordinary

76   For an explanation of Ockham's razor, see http://math.ucr.edu/home/baez/physics/General/occam.html

properties plus a number of other features. The size of the universe and its age is exactly right for the production of *anthropoi* (intelligent life as complex as humans). If its size were any smaller or it had evolved in a shorter time, it would not be stable enough; if it were any larger or older, it would be too stable.

Utterly amazing precision

This precision is staggering. Sir John Houghton[77] puts it like this:

> *To open a combination lock by chance with four dials each with ten digits has a probability of one in ten thousand (10^4, 1 followed by 4 zeros). As the Astronomer Royal, Lord Rees has pointed out in his book* Just six numbers *the balance between the big bang force causing the universe to expand and the force of gravity pulling it together had to be set to one part in 10 to the power of 60 (10^{60}, 1 followed by 60 zeros[78]), the precision required to hit a target one millimetre square at the edge of the universe). If that seems a large number, there is a further number that is far, far bigger. Sir Roger Penrose, an Oxford mathematics professor, has considered the degree of order required*

---

[77] Co-chairman, Scientific Assessment for the IPCC 1988-2002, chairman of Royal Commission on Environmental Pollution 1992-1998, Chief Executive Meteorological Office 1983-1991, Professor of Atmospheric Physics, University of Oxford 1976-1983, Honorary Scientist Hadley Centre, Trustee of Shell Foundation, President of John Ray Initiative, University of Gloucestershire

[78] That's a number that is one trillion trillion trillion trillion trillion

at the universe's start and found that it was set to one part in 10 to the power of 10^{123}. [79] If all the trees on earth were turned into paper and all the paper covered with zeros to follow the 1, that would be nothing like enough zeros to define that number. If a zero could be placed on every atom in the universe, it would still fall far short of the number of zeros required. What precision in that fine tuning![80]

Dawkins considers this principle as an alternative to the design theory put forward by religious apologists. There are literally quadrillions[81] of planets in the universe. The odds of a fair number of those supporting life are extremely high. It is highly probable that there are many other planets within the universe that would be similarly capable of supporting life, though that fact does not require that they do. So the fact that there is at least one (the one we happen to inhabit) that does support life is hardly surprising.

It could also be legitimately argued that some sort of precision would have to arise and it just so happens that it was this precision (mentioned by Penrose) in the same way as it could be argued that the probability of receiving a specific deck of thirteen cards from a pack is less than one in 2.5 $\times 10^{11}$, but you have to receive some sort of deck of cards.

---

[79]   That's a number that is 10 to the power of one thousand trillion trillion trillion trillion trillion trillion trillion trillion trillion trillion (i.e. 1 followed by that many zeros - what that number is, I have no idea)

[80]   Houghton, Sir John "Big Science Big God" page 3

[81]   That is billions of billions

What absolutely amazes me, though, is that a few atheists try to accuse Christians of being cretins for believing that God is responsible for creation, when we are faced with this sort of precision requirement arising from absolutely nothing right at the very start of the universe. How they have the temerity to do this is utterly beyond me. Quite frankly, it says far more about their arrogance than about anyone else. Thankfully, I have not found Dawkins to be so ridiculously judgmental although he does find it amazing that Christians use the Anthropic Principle to back up their arguments. I imagine the vast majority of thinking atheists would not be so judgmental either.

An alternative to the deck of cards argument is that God is somehow responsible. Personally, I think it is a vastly more reasonable alternative. It just puts a whole new meaning for me on that almost simplistic statement *"In the beginning God created the heavens and the earth"*[82] – simplistic if it didn't turn out to be so utterly profound. And if God is responsible for that initial big bang, then I would argue he is responsible for everything since then.

Dawkins is probably right that the Anthropic Principle is an alternative to the design theory because the design theory sees God as just the originator rather than the sustainer of the universe. But he principally looks at the Anthropic Principle in relation to organic life and evolution, not so much on the cosmic scale. And for life to be maintained *anywhere* in the universe, the most amazing number of factors have to come together.

Polkinghorne and Holder argue, after considering all the possible interpretations of the Anthropic Principle, that there are only two

---

[82]   Genesis chapter 1, verse 1

possible conclusions – (1) that there is a multiverse where all possible balances of chance and necessity are found and we happen to live in a universe where the balance is just right; that the other worlds (universes) within the multiverse are pushed out of our sight so we are unaware of them, or (2) that there is one universe *"whose anthropic character simply reflects the endowment of potentiality given it by its Creator."*

In spite of these simply enormous figures quoted above, I don't think we can legitimately use this theory either to prove or disprove the existence of God. Polkinghorne stresses that his conclusion is a metaphysical guess. He believes, however, that it does much to help us understand the wonder of the universe. He ends his paper saying *"the anthropic specificity of our world is not claimed to provide a logically coercive argument for belief in God that no one but a fool could deny, but it makes an insightful contribution to a cumulative case for theism, regarded as the best explanation of the nature of the world that we inhabit."*

I would add that even if there is a multiverse rather than a single universe, it still does not necessarily lead to the conclusion that there is no God. And in addition, if the multiverse contained all possible balances, would there have to be an infinite number of universes within it to accommodate those balances? If the number of universes were infinite, then surely there would have to be an infinite number suitable for life – based purely on the mathematical understanding of infinity. I pose this just as a question to be considered.

Does a possible scientific explanation threaten God?

Dawkins' view is, once again, based on the principle that, if there is a possible scientific explanation for something, it rules out the necessity for God. He rightly accuses creationists of having a "God of the gaps" mentality desperately trying to find gaps, but the implication is that as gaps are filled, it shows that science is the answer. He says *"creationists eagerly seek a gap in present-day knowledge or understanding. If an apparent gap is found, it is assumed that God, by default, must fill it. What worries thoughtful theologians such as Bonhoeffer is that gaps shrink as science advances, and God is threatened with eventually having nothing to do and nowhere to hide."*[83] As there is, potentially, a scientific explanation for everything, God will reach that point!

But that is simply flawed logic. This is surely in the nature of a premise and not a reasoned conclusion from all the evidence for the possible explanations for the nature of the universe, and ignores the way that the same event can have different descriptions right across the different sciences (physics, chemistry, biology, psychology and psychiatry) where a wide variety of models are used with varying degrees of success. How can Dawkins rule out belief in God on grounds of a completely unspecified improbability, given the gigantic improbability of the universe itself?

---

83   "The God Delusion" page 151

China Teapots orbiting the sun

Dawkins argument from improbability follows Bertrand Russell's argument of the likelihood of a china teapot orbiting the sun. I quote from Russell's argument as stated in *The God Delusion*:

> *If I were to suggest that between the Earth and Mars there is a china teapot revolving about the sun in an elliptical orbit, nobody would be able to disprove my assertion provided I were careful to add that the teapot is too small to be revealed even by our most powerful telescopes. But if I were to go on to say that, since my assertion cannot be disproved, it is intolerable presumption on the part of human reason to doubt it, I should rightly be thought to be talking nonsense. If, however, the existence of such a teapot were affirmed in ancient books, taught as the sacred truth every Sunday, and instilled into the minds of children at school, hesitation to believe in its existence would become a mark of eccentricity and entitle the doubter to the attentions of the psychiatrist in an enlightened age or of the Inquisitor in an earlier time.*[84]

Let's examine this argument briefly.

Firstly, while it may be excessively difficult, it is *not* true that nobody would be able to disprove the assertion. It is at least theoretically possible to disprove it. A china teapot is a physical entity and its existence or non-existence is provable. The fact that no one would

---

[84]   Ibid. page 75

bother with the endeavour is irrelevant and actually I would say the fact that Dawkins bothers so much with the endeavour to disprove God shows that the two are totally different categories of argument.

Secondly, it has never been the contention of biblical theology that God is a physical entity (i.e. composed of atoms and molecules). I don't think you can compare the arguments for the existence of a physical entity like a teapot however unlikely and the arguments for the existence of God: God describes himself as "*filling heaven and earth*."[85] But one thing Dawkins has understood: either God exists or He does not. We should only believe in God if we have reason to believe that the propositions in the Bible are "true" in an absolute and verifiable sense. The apostle Paul was the first to acknowledge this: in 1 Corinthians chapter 15 verse 19, he says, "*if in Christ we have hope in this life only, we are of all people most to be pitied.*"

Thirdly, most Christians would not say it is intolerable presumption on the part of human reason to doubt the existence of God, so Russell was talking rubbish there. Even Jesus was gentle with his disciple Thomas, when Thomas doubted (quite understandably) that Jesus had come back from the dead. In Luke chapter 24 verse 39, Jesus invites Thomas to touch his risen body physically to verify its reality: "*See my hands and my feet, that it is I myself. Touch me, and see. For a spirit does not have flesh and bones as you see that I have.*"

Trying to prove or disprove the existence of a china teapot orbiting the sun *is* possible, even though the possibility is extremely close to zero.

---

[85]   Jeremiah chapter 23, verse 24

Did Jesus actually live here?

Proving the existence of Jesus is much more possible: very few would doubt that in Palestine two millennia ago there was a preacher from Galilee who was subjected to that most horrible of executions, crucifixion, by the Romans. Independent historians like Josephus have documented this. The Roman historian Tacitus wrote around AD116:

> *Nero fastened the guilt...on a class hated for their abominations, called Christians by the populace. Christus, from whom the name had its origin, suffered the extreme penalty during the reign of Tiberius at the hands of...Pontius Pilate, and a most mischievous superstition, thus checked for the moment, again broke out not only in Judaea, the first source of the evil, but even in Rome...*[86]

The assertions of some atheists (Dawkins included) that Jesus probably never existed is based on assumptions that there are *no* external records outside Christian writings. This is clearly untrue. In addition, the thought that many of the very early disciples would give their lives for someone they knew never existed is a little strange to say the least.

Bart Ehrman, historian and professor of religious studies at University of North Carolina Chapel Hill, in his book, *Did Jesus Exist? The Historical Argument for Jesus of Nazareth*, examines the evidence as a historian. He argues, among many other points that, if someone

---

[86] Tacitus, Annals 15.4, cited in Strobel, The Case for Christ, p82

invented Jesus, they would not have created a messiah who was so easily overcome, saying, *"The Messiah was supposed to overthrow the enemies – and so if you're going to make up a messiah, you'd make up a powerful messiah... You wouldn't make up somebody who was humiliated, tortured and then killed by the enemies."*[87] However, he does believe that the gospels portray Jesus in ways that are not historical. The fact is that most historians of that period consider him to be an historical figure even though they may differ on specific incidents recorded in the gospels.

And one further point. The teaching of the New Testament is unequivocally calling for complete honesty, integrity, truthfulness and right living. Is it at all logical that the writers were people who would knowingly lie about the entire thing? I can quite accept that they may have got some details wrong, as much of it was written many years after the events (and the slightly differing accounts of the same events would suggest that could be the case) but the overwhelming evidence is that they were, themselves, people of integrity. It seems to me that those who claim that this was all made up are really clutching at straws.

How could Jesus be God and man?

What is of course the sticking point is whether or not Jesus was in fact God born as man: will God so consent himself to be subject to repeatable experiments in the nature of a laboratory animal, without first wanting us to love and obey him on the basis of a more personal

---

[87] http://www.npr.org/2012/04/01/149462376/did-jesus-exist-a-historian-makes-his-case

and subjective experience? This is a big topic and we'll look at this in Chapter 9.

It's significant that the Bible describes God's nature as a "mystery" (1 Timothy chapter 3 verse 16). Dawkins paints a picture of the meaning of mystery in religion that is probably commonly held by many. In discussing "religious memes", he says one of these would be:

> *There are some weird things (such as the Trinity, transubstantiation, incarnation) that we are not meant to understand. Don't even try to understand one of these, for the attempt might destroy it. Learn how to gain fulfilment in calling it a mystery. Remember Martin Luther's virulent condemnations of reason, quoted here, and think how protective of meme survival they would be.*[88]

I am not going to discuss transubstantiation as that is a purely Roman Catholic doctrine with no basis in scripture, but the Triunity and incarnation are biblical doctrines. Is Dawkins right in his assessment of mystery when related to these topics? He is in company with the Watchtower Society in using the word as he does.

What does mystery actually mean? The word occurs twenty one times in the New Testament and is applied to a number of topics – e.g. the "mystery of the gospel". To a Christian, the gospel is fairly easy to understand, though there are always further depths to be explored and discovered; to an unbeliever, it probably is a mystery – in fact, foolishness! Another mystery is the fact that Gentiles are now

---

[88] "The God Delusion" page 232

to be included in the people of God rather than just racial Jews (they had always thought the "people of God" and Jews were synonymous). We would hardly think of that as being a mystery now.

So how about the Triunity of God? What is the mystery over that? Many Christians find it hard to understand and, like other mysteries, there will always be further depths to be discovered. So it is little wonder unbelievers find it impossible to understand. Perhaps we need to have an encounter with God before we can start to understand this amazing being!

CHAPTER 6

Trying to Find the "Mysterious" God

Mystery: is it forever hidden?

The word "mystery" is indeed a mysterious one! We say, "it's a mystery where my keys have got to". We have crime mysteries on television. Both these scenarios have a solution. They are not mysteries in the sense of being completely insoluble and counter to reason. Occasionally, the word may be used in that way but that is not the most common. Christian "mystery" plays are not portraying something which is totally beyond all human grasp. They are designed to make people think beyond the obvious; to stimulate a part of us that we don't usually use – our spirits; to cause us to seek. Jesus said those who seek will find. He never said they would be eternally frustrated in their minds. The word "mystery" is used in that way in the Bible. It is *"that which, being outside the range of unassisted natural apprehension, can be made known only by Divine revelation, and is made known in a manner and at a time appointed by God and only to those who are illuminated by his Spirit.*"[89] That is why Jesus so often asked questions of those who questioned him. He wanted them to think and seek; he avoided giving them an answer that would simply produce the response, "Oh, okay, I see now" and then not bother any further. Questions that lead to more questions produce a seeking spirit in us and set us on an adventure of discovery that will never end.

Now, I can quite understand Dawkins and other atheists including those many atheists who cannot stand him reacting very negatively to Vine's definition of "mystery" above. It smacks of the "enlightened elite" I said the Bible was against. Actually it is quite the opposite. It requires those who are able to swallow their pride and reliance on their own powers of reason and accept that they may not be able to understand everything alone. That does not mean to *abandon* their powers of reason but to acknowledge their severe limitations. Dawkins, on the other hand, has an enormously high opinion of his own intellect and of scientists compared with others. If ever there was an "enlightened elite" in his view it would be the band of atheistic scientists, particularly those who think like he does and, indeed, he refers to them often as an "intellectual elite".

Dawkins compares the attitude of mystics (and I assume he means believers in that) and scientists to mystery: *"Mystics exult in mystery and want it to stay mysterious. Scientists exult in mystery for a different reason: it gives them something to do."*[90] That may be true of some mystics but actually what he says about scientists is true of Christian believers who seek in order to find as Jesus enjoined his disciples to

---

89   Vine, W E, "Vine's Expository Dictionary of New Testament Words"
90   "The God Delusion" page 152

do. They constantly want to understand more – and find that as they increase in understanding, there is more they don't know. It has many parallels with a scientific mindset.

Jefferson says *"ideas must be distinct before reason can act upon them; and no man ever had a distinct idea of the trinity. It is the mere Abracadabra of the mountebanks calling themselves the priests of Jesus."*[91] If God has chosen to make it known by revelation (i.e. God choosing to reveal himself to us personally) and not by reason alone, why should Jefferson or anyone else insist that it should be through reason? Why should God condescend to the demands of Thomas Jefferson and Richard Dawkins if he has decided otherwise?

In fact, I find the Triunity of God quite understandable. I am not saying I fully understand it. That would be impossible. I cannot understand infinity, even though I have a very limited concept of what it is. But, having been a Christian for over 40 years and having wondered about this "mystery", I have come to a reasonable understanding of the nature (if we can call it that) of God.[92] But as with any mystery like this, you never come to the end of understanding it. Trying to understand it further certainly "gives me something to do". I think I could legitimately say there should be a certain agnosticism about Christians. We need to acknowledge that there is much we don't know and much about which we cannot be sure.

---

[91] Ibid. page 55
[92] I have written an essay on the Triunity of God, if you want to read it. It is available as a download at a very low price(!) for the Amazon Kindle under the general heading of "Laying Deep Foundations"

Dawkins appears not to understand the doctrine of the nature of God at all. He says:

> *Arius of Alexandria, in the fourth century AD, denied that Jesus was consubstantial (i.e. of the same substance or essence) with God. What on earth could that possibly mean, you are probably asking? Substance? What substance? What exactly do you mean by 'essence'? Very little seems the only reasonable reply.*[93]

Now Dawkins probably does not know what it means because he is only capable of approaching everything from a scientific viewpoint and 'substance' normally means 'matter' of a particular kind in science. In theology, where concepts of infinity and eternity are being expressed in language that is not fully up to the job, words are sometimes used with a different slant on the meaning. 'Substance' or 'essence' is used to try and express something about God's nature – though that word is also inadequate. I don't blame atheists for misunderstanding this – most people would. But the answer is to try and understand, not to reject it as nonsense.

As far as the Triunity is concerned, if God is infinite as the Bible indicates he is then it is fully possible for him to exist in infinity at the same time as being totally present in the body of a Man. Whether or not I can understand that is beside the point.

---

[93] "The God Delusion" page 53

The existence of God: a scientific question?

In expressing his view of "Permanent Agnosticism in Principle" (PAP), Dawkins makes a statement about the existence or non-existence of God. He says:

> *Either he exists or he doesn't. It is a scientific question; one day we may know the answer, and meanwhile we can say something pretty strong about the probability,*[94] and *the presence or absence of a creative super-intelligence is unequivocally a scientific question, even if it is not in practice – or not yet – a decided one. So also is the truth or falsehood of every one of the miracle stories that religions rely upon to impress multitudes of the faithful.*[95]

I agree he either exists or he doesn't. I would also agree that it is possible to examine the truth or falsehood of miracles, especially those that are claimed today and it is right that we do. But let's examine his assertion that God's existence is unequivocally a scientific question. What is the basis for his assertion?

Over and over again, Dawkins describes the god in whom/which he does not believe as an "entity". And he says:

> *The God Hypothesis suggests that the reality we inhabit also contains a supernatural agent who designed the universe and – in many versions of the*

---

[94] Ibid. page 70
[95] Ibid. page 82

> *hypothesis – maintains it and even intervenes in it*
> *with miracles, which are temporary violations of his*
> *own otherwise grandly immutable laws.*[96]

Actually, that is quite simply untrue. I know he quotes Richard Swinburne (*"one of Britain's leading theologians"*) to back up what he says and Swinburne says God can suspend his laws if he so wishes. Yes, if God is God, he can, but would he and does he need to do so to perform miracles? Biblical belief in no way suggests that the universe contains such an agent (in fact, if anything, Christian belief would say the agent contains the universe and that is still not accurate) and it is highly arguable as to whether miracles are violations of natural law or not. When you really think about it, if God is "wholly other than" creation, he cannot be an entity as we know entities.

An entity is something that has a discrete, definable and separate existence. Every physical thing is an entity; systems can be described as entities, e.g. the justice system of a country, a loving relationship or a marriage. It is something that exists in its own right. It is something to which we can point in some way. A justice system has certain limits. There are places to which its jurisdiction does not extend. But can justice itself be described as an entity? I don't think it can. It finds its expression in entities, in systems or people who act justly or maintain justice. The same can be said for love. It is not in itself an entity; it's something most of us instinctively know and it finds its expression in relationships but does not itself actually exist as an entity. Does that mean that love and justice do not exist? Of course not! We know they do, even though some people may insist they are only constructs of the human mind.

---

[96] Ibid. page 81

Sadly, Dawkins seems to recognise very few different expressions of love – mainly sexual love and that is interpreted purely in terms of selection pressures. Commitment is seen as being advantageous for the successful rearing of children; at base, it is irrational but makes sense. He suggests that religious devotion could be a mis-firing of this same tendency to commit two people to each other to enhance the survival chances of their offspring.[97] I feel sorry for anyone who can only see love in that narrow way, even though of course it is true when looked at in purely evolutionary terms. But does Richard Dawkins not love his friends? And how about Jesus' injunction to love your enemies? There is vastly more to love than Dawkins can see. But, back to entities.

Is God an entity? Well, if we accept Christian doctrine, based on what the Bible teaches, he is infinite; he "*fills heaven and earth*"[98] and infinitely more. King Solomon declared, "*Heaven and the heaven of heavens cannot contain him.*"[99] God's infinity is not a mathematical infinity which is just a number that is larger than any known or possible real number. His infinity is beyond our understanding entirely. I can accept that an atheist will object and say that I have just made a meaningless statement but that is simply because of a mindset that insists on having to explain things in certain terms. "Meaningless" becomes a euphemism for "it's impossible to understand" in some way like a teenager's "it's unfair" can be a euphemism for "I don't want to do that".

God is a being but according to Judaeo-Christian doctrine he is uncreated, so his existence is nothing like anything else. We are

---

[97]   Ibid. page 213 ff.

[98]   Jeremiah chapter 23, verse 24

[99]   2 Chronicles chapter 2, verse 6

talking about the creator of the universe here, so aren't we going to accept that the evidence for His existence might be a matter of God's choice to contact us rather than us being able to somehow corner God into a physical space and pin Him down to scientific scrutiny?

God's infinity

We think of infinity as endlessness. But that is not what we mean by God being infinite. When it comes to space, we ask the question, "Does it go on forever or does it come to an end somewhere?" I find it impossible to conceive of either proposition. However, with God, it's not a matter of whether or not he goes on forever. The concept of his infinity is that he is totally different from anything we can envisage even including infinite space.

If he is infinite, he must be present everywhere infinitely. There is just as much of him in my little finger as in the entire universe. That illustration is inadequate but it's the best I can do. If God were visible or scientifically discoverable, he could not be infinite.

God's eternity, immortality and invisibility

Not only is God infinite; he is also, according to 1 Timothy chapter 1 verse 17, eternal, immortal and invisible. Again, we naturally think of eternity as endless time. Each moment in the universe is a point on that timeline. But that is not what is meant by God's eternity. He is in the eternal present. Polkinghorne describes God as being completely outside time and yet fully able to relate to us within time. God can relate to any point in time all at the same time. It is a concept totally beyond the limited human mind to grasp fully. But just because something is almost impossible to grasp, it does not mean it is not true. Some science concepts are extremely difficult to grasp – e.g. quantum mechanics. Richard Feynman, the brilliant physicist, said, *"I think I can safely say that nobody understands Quantum Mechanics."*[100] And it is what the Bible actually says about God that we have to deal with in this argument, not what Richard Dawkins *thinks* Christians believe.

According to the best current scientific evidence we have, the universe is about 13.8 billion years old. That is a long time but is not eternity. We have no idea how much longer it will go on or if it will ever come to an end. Without understanding how, we could say time began when the universe began but what was there before? The word "before" can only relate to time so how is it possible for there to be a before time began? And yet, if God is eternal, he was there "before" time began. And "from everlasting to everlasting" implies he will still be there for eternity "after" time has gone. "Invisible" also implies he is beyond all attempts to "see" him with our eyes or anything else including any scientific instrument that could ever be devised. I very much doubt that were God himself (for example, the "burning" bush that Moses came across) to stand before us we would be able to measure His characteristic electromagnetic spectrum!

Science and biblical concepts

To try and apply scientific method or understanding to these concepts is, when you really think about it, a bit of a ridiculous

---

[100]   http://en.wikiquote.org/wiki/Quantum_mechanics

notion. Not even the Bible can express this properly. We can only pick up hints of God's nature as we study it. The Old Testament, especially, is written in a very concrete way but is expressing abstract thoughts. Dawkins' attempts to regard God as an entity remind me of Khrushchev saying of Yuri Gagarin, the first cosmonaut in space, that he had been into space and had not seen God, so he could not exist.

The problem with an atheist viewpoint is that it presupposes that nothing exists outside the universe/multiverse; there cannot be any actual existence apart from that which can be measured or sensed in some empirical way. Existence means, on an atheist viewpoint, that which can be investigated scientifically. So, Dawkins says the existence of God is a scientific matter (can be investigated scientifically). On that basis, if he cannot be found or if it is impossible to investigate him, it follows perfectly logically that he does not exist.

Well, as far as that kind of God is concerned, I would agree. On an atheistic presupposition that nothing exists outside the universe, I agree that God does not exist. But I hope I have shown that we are not talking about that type of God at all when we look at the biblical account. And on what basis can it be proved that there is no existence apart from the visible universe (or possibly multiverse); that there is no other possible mode of existence or that infinity and eternity are utterly impossible?

Is empiricism provable?

Empiricism suggests that no knowledge is valid unless it can be proved empirically and that knowledge comes from sensory experience with evidence resting on our human scientific experimentation. An hypothesis that has no possible way of being falsified cannot be accepted as a scientific hypothesis. Proposals that rely solely on *a priori*[101] reasoning, intuition or revelation (God choosing how to reveal himself to mankind) are rejected. And I would agree that, as far as scientific knowledge is concerned, this would seem to be a very reasonable and correct position. So on this basis and on the above presuppositions, then, it is impossible to falsify the existence of a God outside the universe or to prove his existence by experimentation, so (on this basis) it follows logically that no God exists.

But I would contend that to transfer this proposition to every single area of life is going too far. It would have to be applied to the whole of human experience. What about quantifying the beauty of a poem? How do we calibrate the greatness of a composer? We try very hard with our music and skating and dance competitions (most recently with TV "reality" star-manufacturers like Strictly Come Dancing, the X factor and Britain's Got Talent"), but everyone knows that the Eurovision Song Contest comes down to pure politics!

And another thought: how would you prove or falsify empiricism, especially if it is to be applied to these metaphysical concepts?

What do we mean by God's existence anyway?

God's existence does not seem (from the Bible and from the accounts of believers down through history) like the existence of anything

---

[101] knowledge that stems from theoretical deduction rather than observation or experience

else that exists. Although God has a distinct character and will, he cannot be called an entity as discussed above. If love itself is not really an entity but finds its expression in entities, then we can say the same of God – and *"God is love."*[102] God finds his expression (makes himself "visible") through people and through nature.

You may not like the description of God that he is love, but this is not mere cliché – the apostle John, in stressing that "God is love", is trying to express the idea that everything God does is motivated by love and that all true unconditional love is derived from him – but that love that is very hard for mere humans to grasp. C.S. Lewis talks about God's perfectionism in being determined that after this "boot camp" of training on Earth, we humans should be absolutely perfect in every way – above our temporary personal comfort. Jesus said, *"Be perfect, even as your heavenly Father is perfect"*[103], and the mysterious Triunity – the unity of God as creator, God born as man and God within each believer – is described in terms of mutual love – and indeed the motivation of God to send Jesus to save the world was out of love for the world. I hope I don't need to quote John chapter 3 verse 16 to you even if you are a non-believer!

How is it possible to investigate something that is infinite and eternal within the bounds of limited and temporal existence through scientific enquiry when scientific enquiry cannot even investigate the meaning of a poem? You cannot define the infinite.

Alister and Joanna McGrath point out that Dawkins says the existence of God is extremely improbable and yet fails to say *how*

---

[102] 1 John chapter 4, verses 8 &16
[103] Matthew chapter 5, verse 48

improbable. Dawkins also reckons that highly improbable things do happen. Well, does that mean that God could quite conceivably exist or that highly improbable things do *not* actually happen? Is his improbability anything like his statement saying that the people believing a reasonable nuanced kind of religion are numerically negligible? I don't know.

Unless the probability is zero, there is the possibility of the existence of God. The fact that it is impossible to measure such a probability means that to make such a statement is statistically meaningless. Why does Dawkins bother?

So, let's accept the scientific viewpoint for a moment (some Christians call this "scientistic" to distinguish it from the type of scientist who both accepts the reality of God but carries on observing God's universe to find out more about God's character). Let's say God does **not** exist – so nor does justice? You will battle to find an entity called righteousness anywhere in the universe. In spite of the "Passionate Love Scale" set up by Hatfield and Sprecher[104] (which is subjective and depends on the perception of love by the subjects but has some way of measuring *how loving* someone is), I would say you could not set up a proper investigation (complete with controls) to measure the quantity of love (as you can with energy or force) in particular marriages?

Whether evolution as posited by Darwin and later evolutionary biologists (i.e. random, purposeless mutation with natural environmental selection) or creationism (that the variety and apparent design of the biological world is only explainable by

---

[104] http://www.elainehatfield.com/Passionate%20Love%20Scale.pdf

divine intervention or guidance overriding scientific laws) is true *is* a scientific question. That is dealing with things we can observe and measure. Whether or not God exists is *not* a scientific question, simply because the God described in the Bible and by countless Christians ever since is a free, sentient being who can choose whether or not to reveal himself to specific people and because he is, by nature, not part of the universe. God simply does not appear to want to subject himself to our feeble scientific methods and instruments. And why should he?

The problem of infinite regress

One question raised by Hawking in *The Grand Design* is "who made God?" This question is supposed to be unanswerable by Christians and certainly there is no indication in the Bible that God himself is a created being. In Hawking's 1988 book *A Brief History of Time* this conundrum is presented as an anecdote from the life of Bertrand Russell:

> *A well-known scientist (some say it was Bertrand Russell) once gave a public lecture on astronomy. He described how the earth orbits around the sun and how the sun, in turn, orbits around the centre of a vast collection of stars called our galaxy. At the end of the lecture, a little old lady at the back of the room got up and said: 'What you have told us is rubbish. The world is really a flat plate supported on the back of a giant tortoise.' The scientist gave a superior smile before replying, 'What is the tortoise standing on?' 'You're*

very clever, young man, very clever,' said the old lady.
'But it's tortoises all the way down!'

The problem to this (as most recently explained in Rodney Holder's *Big Bang Big God*) is that we are faced with a universe that does actually exist. We Christians think the whole universe was created by a supernatural God, but even Hawking has to concede that the Big Bang did not come from nothing, since the laws to bring it into existence must have already existed.

The Big Bang: a confusing concept

Lawrence Krauss, an atheist, in a debate over his *A Universe from Nothing?*, said that there must have been *"no space, no time, no universe."*[105] And he says nothing is an unstable state. But he contends that we can (potentially?) understand how the universe and the laws that govern it could arise spontaneously. He gives as an example that when an electron jumps from one energy level to another in an atom, light is emitted and the light did not exist beforehand.

Holder, in the debate with Krauss recorded on Youtube referenced above, points out that the potential was still there and that potential is not nothing. As I understand it, in jumping from one energy level to another, energy is involved – either being absorbed or emitted and that energy was contained within the atom, even though it was not light. The law of the conservation of energy states that energy can neither be created nor destroyed. But could it have been a different set of laws in the moment of the Big Bang? To my mind, it would

---

[105]   http://www.youtube.com/watch?v=sD3_6fugvXE

have to be in order to create something from nothing and yet if it was, there must have been some sort of law and that is still not nothing. How can nothing be unstable anyway? Can we say that it is a state at all?

The Big Bang Theory states that the entire universe came from a "singularity", which is something that has zero size and infinite density. So we have got something that, essentially, doesn't really exist but is infinitely dense! Black holes are supposed to have a singularity where there is infinite density. My problem with this is that infinity cannot be divided or multiplied. The result is always infinity. You cannot add or subtract from infinity either. Zero can be multiplied and divided, but the result is always zero.

So, if this universe came from the sudden expansion of a singularity, we have something with zero size being multiplied in size with its infinite density being reduced when infinity can only ever be infinity. So, how can a singularity with infinite density produce a universe with limited density? If something was added to the singularity to change its size, what was added and what was its origin? This is very much delving into the philosophy of physics which I have to confess is pretty well beyond me but you can see the contortions of mind needed to try and fathom these things out.

However, we end up with a scientific view that says the entire universe came from absolutely nothing (the singularity really cannot be any more than a mathematical concept) and suddenly, about 13.8 billion years ago, started expanding into what we have today – an entire universe contained originally in nothing (it certainly puts a new perspective on trying to pack all your clothes into a small suitcase!). What started it and how did it happen? No one really has any idea.

That, of course, does not mean there is no explanation. One day we may be able to find out. If there is no explanation, then we have a similar problem to the old infinite regress.

I find it quite extraordinary that atheists are prepared to say that the universe arose spontaneously from nothing but cannot accept the possibility that God created the universe from nothing – and the reason? God cannot be investigated by science so the existence of God, in the eyes of some atheists, cannot be considered under any circumstance. That really is hardly a reason. I think that for some atheists, God is rejected simply because the possibility of his existence is just unthinkable to their minds. And the New Atheists accuse Christians of being bonkers?! I have to say I find Genesis chapter 1, verse 1 straightforward and elegant – *"In the beginning God created the heavens and the earth."* We will come back to the Big Bang in chapter 18 on the compatibility of science and faith.

Hawking talks about the possibility of subatomic particles self-creating as matter-antimatter pairs and then self-annihilating, and the possibility of this pair being split by the event horizon[106] of a black hole to bring one of the particles into existence as a new, previously non-existent particle, but Holder points out that one would still need a fabric of space time previously existing in which this could happen. Hawking also posits the beginning of time being rather like asking what is south of Earth's South Pole, but Holder ripostes by again saying that you still need to have a space time to put the Earth in.

---

[106] An event horizon is a term used in General Relativity to describe the boundary in spacetime surrounding a black hole beyond which the gravitational pull becomes so great that nothing, not even light, can escape; hence the term "black hole" (see http://en.wikipedia.org/wiki/Event_horizon for more detail)

More recently, in *The Grand Design*, Hawking favours the "multiverse theory" which Holder points out is essentially unverifiable and by Ockham's razor, unnecessarily complex when one creator and one universe is a much more energetically economical solution, Dawkins says that God is essentially an "improbable being" but nevertheless the biblical authors and the rest of Christendom report contact with what atheists may prefer to think of as the ultimate "extraterrestrial being".

Coming back to the question of what we mean by "eternal", the universe is apparently not eternal. Time is not eternal. Even space is not eternal. To believe in a God who causes all things to come into being is most certainly no less reasonable than believing in the eternity of the singularity. And the two are not necessarily mutually exclusive. Even if the universe is a never-ending series of expansions and contractions (which is currently not believed), the concept of the eternity of God is different from the eternity of the universe.

Accepting that something (or Someone) who is totally other than the universe is responsible for it is perfectly reasonable although it is a philosophical/religious proposition rather than a scientific one. If it is possible to believe in a singularity having zero size and infinite density inside the universe, why is it not feasible to accept the possibility of an infinite God totally other than the universe?

How do we determine the start of all things? We can't, though we may do one day. Can you imagine someone writing a meaningful exposition four thousand years ago to explain to the common person a scientific account of origins? That is ludicrous. They didn't even have the vocabulary to express what we can say today. Think about two thousand years from now. What will people say about our explanations? I don't get the impression that the first verse of the Bible is actually speaking so much about time. It is rather speaking of God beginning things. He is always beginning things. He **is** "the beginning and the end". This is not a scientific statement – it is rather trying to give a picture of what the eternity of God means. You cannot interpret it scientifically.

Natural selection, cranes, Dawkins and God

It became quite clear to me, reading Dawkins' book, that he considers natural selection to be the absolute necessary process behind the evolution of all aspects of life, whether organic, social, psychological; in short, everything. Indeed, he goes on to say, "*while natural selection itself is limited to explaining the living world, it raises our consciousness to the likelihood of comparable explanatory 'cranes' that may aid our understanding of the cosmos itself.*"[107] In other words, we can use the idea of natural selection to find comparable processes that show us how the entire universe evolved from simple to complex. Is this the same as the "theory of everything"?

I mentioned in the introduction that I had believed in God as somehow being the summation of all scientific laws. I suppose, although I didn't believe in the same God as I now do, I believed in an over-riding totally impersonal "being" that held all laws together.

In a sense, Dawkins believes something similar. He looks at natural selection as the principle that explains the entire creation of life and it, itself, depends on nothing else and that the creation and evolution

---

[107] "The God Delusion" page 24

of the whole universe can probably be explained by comparable mechanisms. When you consider it, natural selection itself is not an entity, either. It does not have any separate or discrete existence. Really, looked at like that, what is so different between what I believed and what he believes? I called it "god"; he could call it something else. What is in a word apart from what we understand by it?

The God in whom I now believe and the "god" in which he believes are extremely different. My God is not only intensely Personal but infinite and totally "other" than the creation; his is completely impersonal and limited to processes within the universe. I am not, in any way, suggesting he worships these processes or anything stupid like that, nor do I think they are idols in his mind. But he still believes that there is some kind of principle behind the universe that is responsible for its creation.

Hindus believe that the essence of the universe is "god". Could we call the principle behind the universe its essence? That, in no way, makes it anything like the theistic idea of God, but I think we can call it some kind of naturalistic "god".

When I asked Richard Dawkins to comment on a couple of passages I highlighted the paragraphs above (now altered to try and clarify them). He commented: *"Obviously if you can't see the difference between natural selection and God, or if you are redefining God as natural selection, you are not saying anything that is not trivial."* As he was only looking at this passage, it is not surprising that he has such a limited view of what I am saying. Of course I am certainly *not* equating natural selection with God. But I am trying to show that *his* view of natural selection and more particularly of similar as yet unknown processes ('cranes' mentioned above) responsible for the evolution of the universe could be seen as a "theory of everything" and that a "theory of everything" has some similarities with certain views of a god, especially with Hinduism where the essence of the universe is seen as god.

Pantheism (e.g. Hinduism) is, essentially, spiritual atheism (Dawkins describes it as "*sexed-up atheism*"[108]) and there is a gradation of belief between agnosticism and atheism. Buddhism is also atheistic and the same can be said for all the Eastern religions. When you think of it, the Romans and Greeks worshipped various physical objects in their pantheons – e.g. the sun and made them into gods. They worshipped what they could see and understand. Middle Eastern religions in Old Testament times made gods out of stone or wood – again objects that were part of creation.

Judaism, Christianity and Islam are the only major religions that do not accept any created object as god and insist that God is transcendent (not in any way part of creation). They are completely and utterly different from all other religions. Atheism, in a sense, agrees with all the other religions but, in contrast, says that none of these physical objects are gods. However, it is not far from them. Is Richard Dawkins' awe of natural selection bordering on something similar to these religions, however? I have already argued that deism is not very far from atheism either and, in fact, led to atheism among a great many scientists.

---

[108]   Ibid. page 40

The god of the New Atheists

Putting aside the details of these various religions, the major difference between atheism and all of them (particularly the Eastern, Roman and Greek religions) is purely in the use and perceived meaning of the word "god". They see aspects of the universe or the essence of the universe as "god"; atheism, especially the atheism of thinking scientists seeking for a unifying theory of everything is seeking that same essence but would never call it "god".

Dawkins says he is agnostic to some extent – what he calls "Temporary Agnosticism in Practice" – because he cannot with total certainty at present say there is no god in the same way that he cannot say with total certainty that there are no fairies at the bottom of the garden. In addition, there is disagreement amongst atheists over finer points, so while Dawkins regards atheism as being the alternative to the divisions between religions, I would say that the New Atheist view is actually religious.

As with all systems, there is a need to explain creation. How did everything come to be here? This is no less true of atheism than of any religion. Dawkins puts it down to "cranes" in some way related to natural selection. Whatever you attribute as the ultimate cause of creation becomes, in a sense, your "god". I don't care whether you think of god as having a material existence or a super-spirit existence or simply being the theory of everything or having a totally other existence as in the Judaeo-Christian tradition; the massive variation in different people's conceptions of god means that almost anything can become a god. Whatever rules your life and floats your boat could be described as a kind of god, even if it is totally different from YHWH[109].

Moving from a principle to a Person

An atheistic belief in any sort of over-riding principle governing the laws of the universe (a theory of everything) is undoubtedly totally different from the Judaeo-Christian belief in a transcendent and immanent God. I am not in any way trying to equate the two. The God of the Bible is inaccessible in any scientific way. While it is possible for us to understand something of the nature of this God, his fullness is impossible to fathom. We cannot truly grasp infinity; we can only speak in parables that give us glimpses into a reality that is actually beyond us, or as the apostle Paul said, *"now we see only an indistinct image in a mirror but then we will be face to face. Now what I know is incomplete but then I will know fully, even as I have been fully known."*[110]

The God of the Bible, almost tantalisingly, beckons us to dare to discover him; to dare to go beyond what we can safely understand; to launch out in faith without abandoning our reason but recognising that it is limited; to find that there is actually a purpose behind all the sheer wonder of this fascinating universe. I believe he rejoices in our adventurous spirit as we seek to discover how it all works; he delights in our becoming awe-struck in amazement at its wonder.

---

[109] YHWH is the name of God revealed to Moses. Pronounced "Yahweh", it is related to the Hebrew for "I AM" speaking about the total self-existence and eternity of God. Its English transliteration is usually "Jehovah" but it is shown as "LORD" in most bible translations.

[110] 1 Corinthians chapter 13, verse 12 ISV

Scientific enquiry represents, at least to me, one of the highest aspirations of humanity. But it is enhanced immeasurably by an appreciation of Someone behind it all; Someone who is just around the corner waiting to be found but will never be found by those who will not accept that there is even a corner to turn.

Is there any evidence for God, then?

Is belief just a matter of opinion? Well, I don't think that it can be ultimately. There has to be some evidence of God's existence if he is there. It may not be any form of satisfactory scientific proof, but there must be evidence. If he beckons us to discover him, then a "successful discovery" has to have some sort of observable effect. Plainly, many who call themselves Christians seem to have lives that are no different from anyone else, so there would be no observable effect in their lives. But is that always the case?

Emphatically, no! I know many Christians whose lives have been completely turned around by knowing Christ. They have turned from despair to hope, from selfishness to caring about others and from sickness to health to mention just a few effects. Of course, this could be put down to placebo effects or something similar, but how about animals being healed through prayer?

How about the drug addicts from the desperate gangs in Hong Kong living in the highly dangerous back streets, waging gang warfare that would frighten you out of your wits. Countless members of these gangs have been reached by Jackie Pullinger.[111] Jackie is not some sort of fearless woman; she is just somebody who decided God wanted to use her to reach people and so set off in faith that she would end up in the right place. She ended up in the narrow dark alleys of Hong Kong and the work she has done has massively transformed those people's lives. Did she battle? Of course she did. She found it almost impossible to help them stay off drugs until she found that by praying for the Holy Spirit to enter into their situations in what is called the "baptism in the Spirit", it enabled them to overcome the horribly addictive effects of heroin.

Transformed lives like that have to be strong evidence that there is something far more than psychology at work. I have no doubt many atheists will battle to find another explanation, but this is by no means the only bit of evidence. This kind of transformation is repeated over and over again all over the world every single day of every week. If this is not God, then it must something answering closely to his description!

In *The Selfish Gene*, Dawkins believes that free will is an illusion. Everything that happens and all decisions we make are a result of the incredible complexity of all that has happened in the past affecting the genes we have and that those genes govern our behaviour and every decision. There is truth in this as the sciences of psychology and psychiatry attest, as often a particular behaviour can be traced back to an unhappy childhood in that terrible cliché, but it leads us on a linear path backwards in time and is fraught with complexity.

---

[111] Incidentally, my aunt taught Jackie and commented to me once, "I cannot understand why Jacqueline has gone off to Hong Kong and wasted her time" - a common view expressed by unbelievers who fail to see why Christians decide to serve others in this sort of way.

Neurologists are the first to admit that free will is still a difficult area as some people are able to overcome addiction and change their lives while others continue as slaves to their own physiology and emotional past. Interestingly much of the evidence that Christians cite is just in this area – many speak of being liberated from their past to become a stronger and more self-controlled and disciplined person, as Jackie Pullinger found trying to help those drug addicts in Hong Kong.

So maybe there is some evidence for the existence of a God who has a discernible effect on people's lives. This could, though, all be circumstantial evidence. But accepting for now that he might exist and this might be valid evidence (especially because of the extent of the evidence), let's look at another thorny issue and one very difficult to accept or understand.

The deity of Christ

If there is no God, then clearly, this is an irrelevance but as Dawkins challenges his deity and as I believe, with virtually all other Christians, that he is God, I need to deal with this very difficult concept. How is it possible for God to become man or for a man to be God all at the same time? Surely this is not only some made-up nonsense but completely illogical.

I deal with the deity of Christ in my e-book *Trinity*[112] but that is mainly countering other religious views, all of which dispute his

---

[112]   http://www.amazon.co.uk/The-Trinity-Laying-Deep-Foundations-ebook/dp/B005MR4SX6 or http://www.amazon.com/The-Trinity-Laying-Deep-Foundations-ebook/dp/B005MR4SX6

deity rather than trying to tackle it in a way that could in any way answer Dawkins' arguments. He says, *"The historical evidence that Jesus claimed any sort of divine status is minimal."*[113] Apart from a few oblique references by people like Pliny the Younger to Christ being seen as God or a god, virtually all suggestions of his deity are from the Bible. The body of evidence there is colossal and not only from the New Testament. I am not going to go into it here as it is available in my e-book but I do want to deal briefly with Dawkins' assertion above. If by "historical evidence" he means extra-biblical sources, then he is right but if you read the New Testament, you will find massive evidence of these claims as he applies Old Testament passages about YHWH to himself. If Dawkins is referring to biblical evidence, then he is utterly wrong.

It is absolutely true that Jesus never said the words, "I am God" and that he said things like "My Father is greater than I" and "Why do you call me good? No one is good but God". Without going into a massive amount of theological detail (and probably boring you in the process!), I will just say that Jesus had given up his glory as God in becoming man and he was clearly always under the authority of the Father (even before his incarnation) and so, in that sense, the Father is greater than the Son. And in the passage asking why the questioner called him good, it was clear that this man, in calling him "Good Teacher" was not really aware of what he was implying and, as Jesus so often did with questioners, he was challenging the questioner over the implications of what he had said. Neither of these or any other similar passage implies that Jesus was denying his deity.

---

[113] "The God Delusion" page 117

What Christ did say was, *"Before Abraham was, I am."*[114] That was such a direct claim to being YHWH that it is hard to miss it – especially if you were a Jew. And we read that the Jews immediately took up stones to stone him for blasphemy. In the Garden of Gethsemane, when Judas arrived with the soldiers and servants of the high priest to arrest Jesus, Jesus asked them, *"Whom do you seek?"* They answered that they were looking for Jesus of Nazareth and Jesus said to them, *"I am"*, not *"I am he"* as it is usually translated. It then records that when he said that, they drew back and fell to the ground.[115] That is a pretty nonsensical reaction until you realise what he was implying. He was directly claiming the divine name YHWH. I could go into passage after passage demonstrating this but I suggest you read my e-book if you want to pursue it further or check out evidence provided in on-line articles.

But, if it was so important for us to believe Christ was God, why did he not just say it plainly? In a well-known chapter (Matthew 16), Jesus asked the disciples what people were saying about who he is. Then he asked them who they say he is. Peter replied, *"You are the Christ, the Son of the living God."*[116] Jesus responds by saying, *"Blessed are you, Simon Bar-Jonah! For flesh and blood has not revealed this to you, but my Father who is in heaven."*[117]

It seems obvious to me that Christ deliberately did not tell people because he wanted them to come to the conclusion themselves and that he wanted this conviction to be the basis by which people can enter into a life of faith because he goes on to say *"And I tell you, you*

---

[114] John chapter 8, verse 58
[115] John chapter 18, verses 4 - 6
[116] Matthew chapter 16, verse 16
[117] Matthew chapter 16, verse 17

are Peter (Gk. Petros – a little stone) *and on this rock* (Gk. petra – a rock*) I will build my church*."[118] Contrary to common belief, he was not saying the church would be built on Peter the little stone (he was an illustration of receiving revelation) but on the rock of conviction that Jesus is the Christ, the Son of the living God. Faith is not to do with being told to believe certain things; it is a conviction held by that person based on a realisation that prayers do get answered and that belief does make sense.

A further point about this question: it is suggested by many people that his deity was purely a made-up doctrine by the New Testament writers. Of course, anything is possible including this. However, when you think of the Jewish attitude to monotheism and their misunderstanding of Jesus' deity, it would have been an extremely unwise thing for these writers to suggest. And it would also have been a most extraordinary thing to enter their minds in view of their own monotheistic bent – and especially seeing they continued to pursue a strict monotheistic theology. Furthermore, if they were determined to introduce this radical idea, surely they would have gone about it far more directly and had Jesus actually saying he was God. For people who were appealing for absolute honesty, this suggestion that they made it up seems to me ridiculously far-fetched.

And one more aside over the character of Jesus. Dawkins calls him Yahweh's "*insipidly opposite Christian face.*"[119] To be fair he does go on to say that this image owes more to his Victorian followers than to Jesus himself and he is right. "Gentle Jesus, meek and mild" does give a bit of a weak impression. However, if you read some

---

[118] Matthew chapter 16, verse 18
[119] "The God Delusion page 51

descriptions of him in the book of Revelation, you will see that he is, at least on the surface, a pretty terrifying figure[120] – one where you would certainly rather be on his side than the other! I can understand people describing him as Dawkins does, but it is the opposite of the way he is portrayed in the New Testament.

However, nothing I have said above about God or Jesus gives anything like conclusive proof. It still has to be a matter of faith in the end.

Views of faith

In my opinion, one of the big problems in discussing the existence of God is the view people have of what faith is. Listening to programmes like "Songs of Praise", which I don't very often, I sometimes hear the interviewer asking someone, "How did your faith help you to get through …..?" I want to say, "It's not really my faith that helps. It's God!"

Dawkins states that faith is "*belief without evidence.*"[121] In discussing the "Great Prayer Experiment" (page 85 onwards), which he rightly criticizes, it is obvious that he tries to show that prayer does not work. There is considerable misconception about prayer and faith and it is not limited to atheists; it is common among virtually all persuasions and even Christians often misunderstand it.

---

120   e.g. Revelation chapter 1, verses 12-17; chapter 19, verses 11-16
121   "The God Delusion" page 231

Just what is meant by faith? Is it the parody Dawkins describes on page 231 or is it altogether something far more meaningful? In the next chapter, I will examine this and try to offer something coherent as well as I can.

CHAPTER 7

Is "Faith" Really Delusion?

Dawkins says, "*the whole point of religious faith, its strength and chief glory, is that it does not depend on rational justification.*"[122]

He strongly believes that faith is a delusion (hence the title of the book). He uses several definitions of the word "delusion" but one that he quotes is the Penguin dictionary definition: "*a false belief or impression*". On that basis, if God does not exist, then a belief in any sort of god would be a delusion. However, it would mean that *any* belief or impression that was false would also be a delusion. I cannot imagine there is anyone on the planet who is **completely** free of any false belief or impression so everyone would be delusional. That kind of definition is not very helpful, therefore. I would suggest we need to ignore it.

Another definition he uses is the Microsoft Word dictionary which says delusion is "*a persistent false belief held in the face of*

---

[122] "The God Delusion" page 45

strong contradictory evidence, especially as a symptom of psychiatric disorder."[123] That, I believe, is closer to what a delusion is, as we shall see below.

This charge against faith is a serious one and as many atheists believe it, we should examine this seriously, and who better to start with than a scientist who has expertise in the phenomenon of delusion – a psychiatrist?

A recent book, *Is Faith Delusion?* written in 2012 by an eminent psychiatrist, Professor Andrew Sims, agrees that "delusion" is a word that has a psychiatric meaning. As the former president of the Royal College of Psychiatrists, I think I can trust his assessment of delusion better than I can Richard Dawkins'. According to Sims, delusion has certain characteristics:

(1) delusion is out of keeping with the deluded person's cultural or social background,
(2) a delusion is held on delusional grounds,
(3) delusions are held without insight (there is no doubt about their veracity),
(4) delusions involve concrete thinking, e.g. thinking literally about ideas that are meant to be figurative.[124]

He also points out that delusions are held by individuals; groups of people never hold the same delusion. It is inconceivable that vast numbers of people can develop the same delusion independently. As

---

[123]   Ibid. page 28
[124]   Andrew Sims, "Is Faith Delusion?" pages 124, 125

he points out, he could have two patients in the psychiatric ward, both of whom believe they are Jesus Christ –

> *But Joe Bloggs thinks that he, Joe Bloggs, is Christ and Tony Dixon thinks that he, Tony Dixon, is Christ and that Joe Bloggs is not Christ. I have a friend (who does not wish to be identified) who suffers from bipolar disorder and who says that when she was ill she thought herself to be the person of the woman 'clothed in the stars and the sun' described in the Bible book Revelation (chapter 12), but much later, when in her right mind, she met a researcher who had studied religious delusion through history, this researcher told her that there were many other women – the locations of whom she named – who had also had this delusion about themselves. My friend told me about the utter sense of shock she felt – 'But I was convinced I was the only, the real woman in Revelation 12!'*

Sims stresses that religious delusions do occur and most commonly include delusions of persecution, morbid jealousy and delusional infidelity, delusions of love, delusional misidentification, grandiose delusions, delusions of guilt and unworthiness, delusions of poverty and nihilistic delusions, hypochondriacal delusions, delusions of infestation, communicated delusion, delusions of control.[125] He goes on to show that, while people with delusion who are religious will manifest religious delusions, it can in no way be shown that the religious belief causes the delusion – it's the content of the delusion that is religious, not the cause or the form. A schizophrenic who is

---

[125] Ibid. page 126

a believer will have schizophrenic delusions, not because s/he is a believer but because s/he is a schizophrenic. Those delusions will be influenced by his/her faith to give them religious content.

A man we knew in Rhodesia who had been to Eagle School with me had, at one stage in his life, taken the drug LSD. It continued to affect him years later when he became a religious believer. We had great difficulty in trying to help him as he had bizarre delusions – thinking that the pilot of an aeroplane flying overhead was communicating with him "by the Holy Spirit" and similar weird ideas. His damaged mind simply incorporated all sorts of religious ideas as the content of his delusions. We battled (but didn't succeed) to try and steer him onto a reasoning and sensible attitude to life. Normal Christians, who could be certified by psychiatrists to be in good mental health, have no such delusions.

Looking at the list of delusional characteristics, Sims shows that faith cannot be classified as delusion on psychiatric grounds[126]. A person with religious delusions will manifest delusional tendencies in other areas of life apart from their religious beliefs. The vast majority of religious people do no such thing. In fact they show a great deal of maturity in their attitudes to life.

While we may, therefore, be able to dispense with Dawkins' assertion that faith is delusion (while perhaps awaiting his or perhaps an atheistic psychiatrist's response to this very recent book by Andrew Sims), it does not necessarily prove that faith is based on truth. There may be perfectly sensible people who believe something untrue.

---

[126] In addition, the American Psychiatric Association "Diagnostic and Statistical Manual of Mental Disorders" (DSM-IV) specifically excludes religious doctrine from pathology

That, of course, applies to any belief, religious or non-religious and equally applies to atheists as to believers. For an atheist to imagine that being an atheist either makes them immune or less prone to believing falsehood is not only wishful thinking, it indicates a religious and irrational attitude. It could be said that such a belief is one of the delusional manifestations – a belief held without insight, where there is no doubt about its veracity. I am not suggesting that about Dawkins – he admits there is a possibility he may be wrong.

Those strange "memes"

Dawkins believes or suggests that religious faith comes about through "memes". "Memes" are basically ideas that are transmitted between individuals and grow. Dawkins calls religious memes "viruses of the mind". Really this is just a model to explain a normal phenomenon – sharing ideas. Dawkins himself formulated the idea and seems to think of memes in a similar way to genes being passed from generation to generation, so memes are inherited as well as genes though by different mechanisms. Giving a list of "religious memes", he suggests one would be:

> *Faith (belief without evidence) is a virtue. The more your beliefs defy the evidence, the more virtuous you are. Virtuoso believers who can manage to believe something really weird, unsupported and insupportable, in the teeth of evidence and reason, are especially highly rewarded.*[127]

---

[127] "The God Delusion" page 231

Christopher Hitchens put it in a similar way, though a little more sophisticated:

> *Faith is the surrender of the mind; it's the surrender of reason; it's the surrender of the only thing that makes us different from other mammals. It's our need to believe, and to surrender our scepticism and our reason, our yearning to discard that and put all our trust or faith in someone or something; that is the sinister thing to me. Of all the supposed virtues, faith must be the most overrated.*[128]

This does have some truth, as many Christians (myself included) attest to the experience of being asked by God to submit our lives to his lordship, rather than (like C.S. Lewis in *Surprised by Joy*) accepting the existence of God as logically inevitable.

Dawkins is much more mocking, using the "Pastafarian theology"[129] approach. He suggests that people of faith are not even open to reason; that faith is static, whereas science (and, therefore to his mind, atheism) is progressive, always pushing the boundaries. He says, "*as my friend Matt Ridley has written, 'Most scientists are bored by what they have already discovered. It is ignorance that drives them on.' Mystics exult in mystery and want it to stay mysterious. Scientists exult in mystery for a different reason: it gives them something to do. More generally, as I shall repeat in Chapter 8, one of the truly bad effects*

---

[128] http://www.goodreads.com/quotes/503115-faith-is-the-surrender-of-the-mind-it-s-the-surrender

[129] A parody of religion – trying to show that belief in a deity is no better than believing in the Flying Spaghetti Monster

of religion is that it teaches us that it is a virtue to be satisfied with not understanding,"[130]

I have to say, though, that his definition of faith is true of some believers. There are quite a few instances of people believing in the teeth of evidence and reason. I have known some Christian leaders (unnamed) who applaud those who predict that miraculous things are going to happen, even when it is clearly just wishful thinking, and claim it is faith. Dawkins is, I believe, absolutely right to point out the stupidity of such "faith". Unfortunately, that is the "faith" that often gets noticed by unbelievers and I can quite understand them concluding that this is what faith is.

I remember years ago, a lady we knew was suffering badly from back problems. If you asked her husband how she was, he would always say she was healed, and yet she was still suffering. Interestingly, some time later, he "lost his faith". What he had was not faith: He had been reading a lot of material from one of the American "faith preachers" of the "name it; claim it" brigade. Believers need to grow up and find out what faith really is. Wishful thinking is *not* faith.

However, to suggest that religion teaches us that it is a virtue to be satisfied with not understanding is sheer nonsense. Proper Christian teaching does exactly the opposite. The apostle Peter says, *"Do your best to **improve your faith**. You can do this by adding goodness, **understanding**, self-control, patience, devotion to God, concern for others and love."*[131]

---

[130] "The God Delusion" page 151-152
[131] 2 Peter chapter 1, verses 5 to 7 (Contemporary English Version)

Definitions of faith

I hope I have shown that real faith is not a delusion. But before moving on to the next chapter, let's revisit and look in more detail at the online Oxford Dictionary definition of faith:

1 complete trust or confidence in someone or something:

> *this restores one's faith in politicians*

2 strong belief in the doctrines of a religion, based on spiritual conviction rather than proof:

> *bereaved people who have shown supreme faith*
> [count noun] a particular religion: *the Christian faith*
> [count noun] a strongly held belief: *men with strong*
> • *political faiths*

Based on definition 2, I can quite understand Dawkins and others assuming that it is belief in spite of proof to the contrary but that is not what it actually says. It says it is based on conviction *rather than* proof, not against proof. It is also defined as "a strongly held belief", which would include Dawkins' own belief. He does not have absolute proof that God does not exist but has a strongly held belief and conviction that he does not. So Richard Dawkins is in one sense a man of faith – a faith that does not depend on absolute proof but on what he sees as an unspecified lack of probability.

Dawkins' attack on faith is primarily aimed at Christianity. Christians do not read the dictionary in order to see what faith should be. They would, I hope, base it on the Bible (a good starting point is the book of Hebrews, chapter 11). So, it is to the Bible we should be looking for a clue as to what faith means to a Christian. Dawkins fails to do this, relying rather on mockery and in some instances a schoolboy level of understanding. As a result, once again, I would say he attacks something that the majority of Christians do not believe. What is stopping Dawkins from looking at the Bible's definition of faith when he so readily reads the Old Testament with such detail in order to find the (even to Christians) embarrassing passages that seem to indicate that God is "sexist, racist and homophobic"? We need, therefore, to look at what the Bible says about faith.

Faith, of course, is a massive theme in the Bible and I would find it impossible in a book like this to do it justice. But, if we look at the online Oxford Dictionary definition, we see two aspects: 1. complete trust or confidence in someone or something and 2. strong belief in the doctrines of a religion, based on spiritual conviction rather than proof.

The Bible also covers both aspects of faith mentioned in the Oxford Dictionary but majors on the first of the dictionary definitions.

Hebrews chapter 11 verse 6 says *"without faith, it is impossible to please God, for it is necessary for the one approaching God to believe that he is, and that he becomes a rewarder of those who diligently seek him."* I do find it interesting that the Bible uses this kind of expression about the existence of God. It doesn't say "that he exists" but "that he is". When God spoke to Moses out of the "burning" (actually "not-burning"[132]) bush, He said, "*I AM THAT I AM.*" God just IS, and it isn't a temporal thing – it is the eternal Present.

Anyway, the Hebrews 11 verse pretty well sums up the two aspects of faith: (1) belief and (2) trust and seeking. In the following chapters, we will look at these two aspects in that order.

---

[132] Exodus chapter 3, verse 2. Fire needs fuel and oxygen. This bush appeared to be burning but "was not consumed". I have no doubt that there was no oxygen being used either. The message was that God was not in any way dependent on the creation. I don't imagine Moses was aware of the science of combustion and probably didn't fully appreciate the theology – we are better able to appreciate it now with the knowledge we have.

CHAPTER 8

Faith as Belief in Certain Doctrines

The online Oxford Dictionary's second definition of faith is:

strong belief in the doctrines of a religion, based on spiritual conviction rather than proof:

> *bereaved people who have shown supreme faith*
> [count noun] a particular religion: *the Christian faith*
> [count noun] a strongly held belief: *men with strong political faiths.*

Belief in the existence of God is the first definition in the book of Hebrews, where it says, "*for it is necessary for anyone who comes to God to have the belief that God is.*"[133]

---

[133]   Hebrews chapter 11, verse 6 (BBE)

Belief in the existence of God

Dawkins, in a sense, believes in an inanimate, impersonal kind of theory (yet to be discovered and formulated) that is actually a supposed way of explaining how the entire cosmos came into being. As explained in chapter 6, this is similar to the Hindu idea of god being the essence of the universe and is also similar in some ways to deism.

Stoic philosophy believed in the "Logos" as the universal reason. It was a divine principle and was the essence of the universe although seen as material. It was called the intelligent "aether" or primordial fire. In fact Cicero said *the universe itself is god and the universal outpouring of its soul; it is this same world's guiding principle, operating in mind and reason..."* and Marcus Aurelius, in his *Meditations* says that the souls of people and animals are emanations from Fate (or Logos) and *"constantly regard the universe as one living being, having one substance and one soul; and observe how all things have reference to one perception, the perception of this one living being; and how all things act with one movement...."*[134] The popular gods were regarded as manifestations of the universe as God in a similar way to Hindu thought where their millions of gods are illustrations of aspects of the one god which is the universe. There is a similarity between Stoicism and Hinduism.

In Hebrew thought, the Law was not just a set of rules for living. It was regarded as the utterance of God, revealing his very nature. There is a whole psalm (119) of 176 verses extolling the wonder of the Law and how good it is to meditate on it and keep it. It is described

---

[134]   http://en.wikipedia.org/wiki/Stoicism

in various terms, but one common one is the "word" so "word" and "law" are synonymous. It was almost divine. God's name (YHWH) was venerated above everything and in Psalm 138 verse 2, it says *"you have exalted above all things your name and your word."* Philo of Alexandria extended the Stoic philosophy into Hebrew thought as well, seeing a similarity between the biblical concept of the word and the Stoic Logos.

The apostle John, in his gospel, extends the Hebrew concept of the word, perhaps adding something from the Stoic idea and says that the Word was God and that this Word was Christ. He says that this Word, far from being a divine principle, is a divine person.

Logos in Stoic thought and a theory of everything may have a number of differences but there is also an overlap. Both are referring to reason, although the Stoic concept of reason was more connected with ethics. I don't think, however, that they are a million miles apart. An explanation that gives us an understanding of the entire universe is what those philosophers were seeking. The Stoics called it divine; the New Atheists call it science.

We all need some faith. Life could not continue for us without it. We all have some set of beliefs, even if they are principles by which we live. I don't believe there is a person alive who can truthfully say every one of their guiding principles is there as a result of carefully thought-through consideration of empirical evidence-based thinking. Non-scientist air passengers have faith in science! When we get married, we are exercising faith in the good character of the other partner and also faith in ourselves to love "for better or for worse, for richer, for poorer, in sickness and in health, to love and to cherish; from this day forward until death do us part". That takes a lot of faith – indeed Christians would add that they are investing their faith in a God who wants the marriage to hold together. This is an analogy of faith, most famously expounded by C.S. Lewis in *The Four Loves* and we will look at this again.

Evidence for theistic belief

As I have tried to show in earlier chapters, spiritual belief (in the God of the Bible in particular) is not based on scientific proof. But we can now introduce a new analogy, which is used by C.S. Lewis in *Mere Christianity*: that the evidence for God is more like evidence in a court of law than a scientific set of measurements. That can sometimes be absolute proof but is more often "beyond reasonable doubt". The problem is who is judging? Your presuppositions play an enormous part in determining what you believe. Your desires also play a huge part. Dawkins would agree with that for believers but probably not for himself but my challenge to Dawkins is that he simply *does not want* to believe and therefore he (like the Christians he attacks) himself picks and chooses both the premises (the presuppositions or hypotheses) and the type of evidence he considers valid. Are we in a position to determine the rules of the game when it is the creator of the universe whom we are trying to put in the dock? C.S. Lewis puts this question brilliantly in *God in the Dock*, showing at the end that, in fact, it is we who are in the dock!

Some people, however, are more open. Albert Ross (pseudonym Frank Morison) was very sceptical about the resurrection although still having an enormous respect for the person of Jesus. He set out to prove that the resurrection was a myth. As he did his research, he became convinced of the truth of the resurrection story and completely changed his book, writing one called *Who Moved the Stone?* His take on the events was that any jury would have to return a verdict that the resurrection did take place.

Alister McGrath makes a good point when he says a scientific viewpoint and a belief in evolution is entirely consistent with atheism and also with a belief in God. I (and many other Christians with a scientific background) accept that, at least potentially, science can answer every question about how things work, about matter, energy, forces, how living things work as biological machines, how things evolved (or whatever mechanism was used). If something is quantifiable, scientists can study it.

But it cannot go beyond that. The effects of love can be studied and measured however inaccurately but love itself cannot be measured. If a scientist tries to explain a poem in scientific terms, I would say the beauty of the poem is destroyed. There are scientific conferences on jokes and laughter but I very much doubt the participants are still laughing by the end of their paper deadline or even at the conference (though some scientists would disagree with this rather sentimental view, saying that the increased insight should deepen our appreciation of jokes! Dawkins insists in *The Selfish Gene* there is no meaning in existence beyond the figurative "determination" of genes to reproduce themselves. No, from a scientific angle, there may not be. But, maybe there is something beyond science. Understanding the limitations of science is just as important as understanding its strengths.

A multitude of competing religions

Another serious charge raised by Dawkins is why, if Christianity is true, are there so many mutually contradictory religions with no shortage of fervent adherents? If we accept, with Dawkins, that God either exists or He doesn't (something the more mystical religions would disagree with) then we are faced with a huge problem. Who is right? The plethora of religious beliefs means they cannot all be right as Dawkins quite rightly points out. Do we decide based on the most statistically significant religion? Christianity is certainly a contender with an estimated one-third of the planet (2.18 billion people in 2010, according to an admittedly Christian study, Pew Forum[135]) identifying themselves as believing in the Christian God, but what about Islam with 1.6 billion?

Dawkins' argument is often used by the minority cults which claim that the different denominations all disagree but they themselves are united. It's so easy to say, "We are right; everyone else is wrong. Look how divided they all are; we are not". That is an argument that proves precisely nothing. The hard thing to do (and something far more valuable, to my mind) is to realise you disagree with others, recognise that they may have an angle on the truth that you don't have and work toward getting to know them and discuss things with them. Jesus said *"by this it will be clear to all men that you are my disciples, if you have love one for another."*[136] He did not say the test would be doctrinal agreement. Loving people who disagree with you is a far greater test of love than when they agree. Loving your enemy is even more of a test.

---

[135] http://www.pewforum.org/2011/12/19/global-christianity-exec/)
[136] John chapter 13, verse 35 (BBE)

But can we really logically move from saying all the religions disagree with each other to saying that atheism is therefore the answer? It's like saying that as people have different understandings of quantum mechanics then none of the indications that all objects behave both as waves and particles can be right. Maybe no-one living on earth now has a total grasp of the whole of the Christian world-view. That doesn't mean God "vanishes in a puff of logic" as Douglas Adams puts it in his universally beloved work, *The Hitchhiker's Guide to the Galaxy*.

Belief

I don't believe we can ever fully demonstrate (in our pedantic scientific way) that God IS. If we could, faith (belief and trust in God's goodness) would be redundant and the Bible says that without faith it is impossible to please him. But neither does God leave us without any evidence at all. Hebrews chapter 1 verses 1–3 puts it very neatly: "*Long ago, at many times and in many ways, God spoke to our fathers by the prophets, but in these last days he has spoken to us by his Son, whom he appointed the heir of all things, through whom also he created the world. He is the radiance of the glory of God and the exact imprint of his nature, and he upholds the universe by the word of his power.*" The writer to the Hebrews, like the apostle Paul in Romans chapter 1 verse 20, believed that when we come to the end of this physical universe and the beginning of the adventure of the next, that we will be "without excuse".

But I want to make one other point. Dawkins suggests that people believe because they are made to believe, because they are effectively brain-washed by parents. He says "*if you are religious at all it is overwhelmingly probable that your religion is that of your parents*"[137] and "*maybe some children need to be protected from indoctrination by their own parents.*"[138]

He regards belief as a set of (unreasonable) dogmas that depend for detail on what religious persuasion your parents have and not the result of reasoned thinking. There is obviously some truth in this. I have already mentioned that children will tend to take on the beliefs of their parents or of others with a major influence in their lives. But to suggest it is the common thing, especially among Christians, is simply untrue.

The Bible says "*each one should be fully convinced in his own mind;*"[139] it says we are not Christians just because our parents are. Taking on your parental faith just because it is what you have been taught does not really constitute faith. How else did the early Jews and Greeks and Romans come to belief in the godhood of Christ, since their parents presumably still believed that the Messiah was yet to come or that there was a pantheon of gods? And how could Christianity have grown so fast that it is now the major belief system (if not the personal faith) of one-third of the planet? How does the genetics (or the memetics) stack up?

---

[137] "The God Delusion" page 25

[138] Ibid. page 240

[139] Romans chapter 14, verse 5

Belief in other religions

As I said earlier, I do not know enough about other religions to discuss them sufficiently, so what I am saying now is purely my impression.

From what I have seen of Islam, especially in those countries ruled by *Sharia Law*, there is a great deal of intolerance of any belief other than Islam. In Sharia Law, converting from Islam to any other religion is officially apostasy and it is a capital offence. To the Muslim mind, a true Muslim is someone who is "born" as a Muslim - i.e. into a Muslim family. Anyone going against this has totally dishonoured their family and the religion. Being a Muslim is not a matter of individual conviction; it is sticking to the religion before anything else that matters. That is quite the opposite of the Christian view.

In these countries (such as Afghanistan, Iraq and Pakistan), someone converting from Islam could have the death penalty passed on them if they do not repent of their "crime".

I have had discussions with a highly intelligent Muslim in the UK who believed in tolerance. He thought it wrong for an individual Muslim to take it upon him/herself to kill someone for apostasy but it was quite appropriate for the state to pass the death penalty! Faced with this type of attitude, which is, from my limited observation[140], not uncommon, it is quite understandable to conclude that Islam

---

[140] Based very much on what I have read in newspapers which may or may not be reliable

is very forceful and intolerant and insists on strict observance to a rigid belief code.

It is far less understandable to attribute that attitude to all religions. It is, as I hope I have shown, also not true of all Muslims, particularly those living in Britain where the Muslim community leaders are always distancing themselves from the militants and where there have been some heart-warming stories of individual mosques going out of their way to be gracious to, for example, members of the English Defence League[141].

There is considerable disagreement among Muslims about the degree to which they can go in insisting on Islamic observance in others. Just as in Christianity, there is a huge range of "shades" of the moderateness of the expression of Islam in different communities.

In other countries with a Muslim majority, the degree of intolerance varies greatly from country to country and society to society. My elder daughter spent a year in Kosovo and got to know a number of Muslims quite closely. She found them to be lovely people who had no problem whatsoever with her being a Christian. They were hospitable and friendly. I have no idea if this is because they are culturally Islamic and not serious about their religion but the fact is they were very different from the stereotype so many of us have of Muslims. She also spent a short time in Lebanon with a friend. There was a great deal of tolerance between Muslims and Christians and she found it easier to speak about Christ to Muslims there than to the average person in Britain.

---

[141]   The Guardian, May 27, 2013

In addition, there are shining examples of Muslims who work for peace and reconciliation in the face of hostility and persecution. Take the example of Dr. Izzeldin Abuelaish, a Palestinian doctor who works tirelessly in Gaza in the face of blockades and shortages, constantly trying to find ways to serve his patients. He lost his three eldest daughters and niece to an Israeli bomb only three months after his wife died of leukaemia. But he has decided, "I shall not hate" and has written a book of that title. He believes and works for reconciliation, believing it is possible in spite of the fractured politics of Palestinian society and the deep suspicion and hostility between Israelis and Palestinians. He does not despair but constantly works in hope.

I know we have numerous examples of grotesque Islamic terrorism like that carried out by al Qaeda internationally and Boko Haram in Nigeria but in my view, groups like Boko Haram are no more true Muslims than "The Lord's Resistance Army" in Uganda are Christians.

When you think there are 1.6 billion Muslims in the world, there would have to be sixteen million violent jihadists for their proportion to reach just one percent of the total. Can we honestly say there are that many? So we can say with a great degree of certainty that over ninety nine percent of Muslims are not involved in these activities. We get a distorted view because the tiny violent minority appear so prominently in our news.

Hindus tend, traditionally, to be more tolerant than Muslims. After all, their religion says that all roads lead to God, as illustrated by the Hindu picture of a blind man examining different limbs and appendages of an elephant.

Under the surface, though, there can be a lot of intolerance when, say, Christians or Muslims try to convert Hindus and there are many stories of violence between Hindu and Muslim, Hindu and Christian, and Muslim and Christian. However, with an enormous range of different beliefs in Hinduism, there can be little insistence on a particular set of beliefs. A Hindu friend even suggested to me that Hinduism was the best religion because it just included everything else. He regarded all religions as variations of Hinduism.

Gandhi is quoted as saying, when asked if he was a Hindu, *"Yes I am; I am also a Muslim, a Christian, a Buddhist and a Jew."* He was trying to promote tolerance in a particularly difficult time of tension between Hindus and Muslims, but he was able to say that with full conviction because he believed it as a Hindu. While this is a laudable attitude, I do not share it as a Christian, as I believe Jesus' claim to be *"the way, the truth and the life. No one comes to the Father except through me."*[142]

Christian intolerance

I would love to able to say that Christians are all highly tolerant but that would unfortunately be dishonest.

While the church may have a good record of tolerance in recent times, it has not always been true in the past and it is certainly not universally true today. You only have to look at the animosity between Roman Catholics and Protestants in Ireland, Scotland and other parts of the world to realise that lots of Christians are not even

---

[142] John chapter 14, verse 6

tolerant towards each other. While we have, thankfully, left behind the tendency to burn people at the stake for heresy (and heresy was sometimes defined as anything the church authorities didn't like), there is still much intolerance in some cases. The Westboro Baptist Church[143] in America is a "good" illustration of this. I shall discuss this church further in chapter 11. While it may represent one extreme and there are hardly any other Christian groups so filled with hatred, there are plenty of "Christians" who are desperately intolerant.

However, to suggest that, because this occurs, it is general or that belief in God *causes* such intolerance is ridiculous. We must surely all know that anyone, including atheists, can be intolerant. Hate-filled attitudes or actions on the part of anyone (whether religious or atheist) is often a symptom of insecurity in their own beliefs and – it is sin.

There are, admittedly, several passages in the Bible that show an intolerant attitude. An oft-quoted example is the story of the battle against the Amalekites which starts in Exodus chapter 17 verse 8. The Amalekites started the battle at Rephidim, no doubt because they felt threatened by this horde of people that had emerged from the Negev desert and were fighting and conquering other tribes, After an all-day battle, the Israelites won and then God said to Moses: "*Write this as a memorial in a book and recite it in the ears of Joshua, that I will utterly blot out the memory of Amalek from under heaven.*"[144]

---

[143]   N.B. This "church" is not registered with any Baptist Union; they call themselves a "Primitive" Baptist Church

[144]   Exodus chapter 17, verse 14

Later, during the reign of Saul, the prophet Samuel ordered him to finish the job. He tells him:

> The Lord sent me to anoint you king over his people Israel; now therefore listen to the words of the Lord. Thus says the Lord of hosts, 'I have noted what Amalek did to Israel in opposing them on the way when they came up out of Egypt. Now go and strike Amalek and devote to destruction all that they have. Do not spare them, but kill both man and woman, child and infant, ox and sheep, camel and donkey.[145]

This seems insane! What threat do the Amalekites pose to the now prosperous nation of Israel so many centuries later? In fact Saul did not carry through this order but kept the livestock (we might wonder what the poor oxen had done). But this was seen as greed on the part of Saul to take the booty for himself, and as a result of this God is recorded to have rejected Saul as king (in the same chapter, verse 11, Samuel hears God say, "I regret that I have made Saul king, for he has turned back from following me and has not performed my commandments.") And as a result God chose a new king, David the shepherd boy.

This seems not just petty, but downright vicious! How can we possibly claim that YHWH is a God of love in the face of such commands?

It's easy to be wise in hindsight. But it takes hindsight to understand this at all. The Israelites never completely drove out the inhabitants

[145] 1 Samuel chapter 15, verses 1-3

of the land; they were tricked by the Gibeonites into making a treaty that God never intended (but having made it, they remained faithful to it). They lived in the land with the other tribes there and intermarried with them against God's commands. This resulted in them copying the abominable practices of those nations. For example, they indulged in child sacrifice. Ezekiel tells the nation, *"When you present your gifts and offer up your children in fire, you defile yourselves with all your idols to this day."*[146] God, it seems, knew the dangers they faced when he took them out of Egypt. Eventually they ended up in exile in Babylon.

It is difficult to defend such actions. However, we need to understand the kind of society that existed at that time. We are horrified at child sacrifice today (it still occurs) and quite rightly would want anyone who did that kind of thing to be dealt with very severely. I get very angry at hearing about children being sexually exploited. What those nations were practising was far worse. Not long ago, we would consider the death penalty for murder to be entirely appropriate, even though most people see it differently today. The penalty for murder then was death. God was judging those nations for their despicable practices as well as protecting his people.

Understanding the Bible – especially the Old Testament – requires an understanding of the times and of the cultures and the way they thought in those days. Although people are people wherever they are and whenever they lived, those times were radically different from our society today and trying to interpret it completely on our terms is an error and will lead to wrong judgment. But let's get back to belief.

---

[146] Ezekiel chapter 20, verse 31

Basis for belief

Do we understand in order to believe or do we believe in order to understand?

An atheist would insist on the former in all cases or at least that *somebody* could fully understand. So no one may know the exact size of the most distant galaxy but I know the most distant galaxy has a size, and it is at least theoretically possible to investigate its size. I may not understand the methods of astrophysics personally but hopefully all astrophysicists do, so I have no difficulty believing it on the say-so of a scientific paper or textbook (or even newspaper report).

A believer would agree but also say that the former is not necessarily always true. A true believer would not believe in spite of or against the evidence (that is quite another matter). But s/he may believe before the evidence or on very partial evidence.

A flyer advertising "The Believing Brain" by Michael Shermer (founding publisher of *Skeptic* magazine) states:

> *Psychologist and science historian Michael Shermer debunks traditional thinking about how humans form beliefs about the world. He has discovered that beliefs come first and explanations for beliefs then follow. Using data that flow in through the senses, the brain looks for patterns with meaning, forming beliefs. Once formed, our brains subconsciously seek out confirmatory evidence in support of those beliefs, which accelerates the process of reinforcing them, and round and round*

the process goes in a positive-feedback loop. Combining cutting edge science engaging examples and anecdotes, **The Believing Brain** *is an accessible guide to new thinking in neuroscience.*

Shermer has found that "faith comes before evidence" and I would agree. He apparently points out that belief and intelligence are not negatively correlated. He says *"smart people believe weird things because they are skilled at defending beliefs they arrived at for nonsmart reasons."*[147]

One wonders if he includes himself in having a belief in the non-existence of God and then finding reinforcing patterns to back up that belief. Presumably not. He would conclude that his beliefs are all right because they are entirely based on smart reasons. But who is to say that atheistic beliefs are any more smart or reasonable than theistic beliefs?

Having said that, I have to say the very idea of faith means that we do not come to a position of belief based purely on reasoning and working things out. This does *not*, therefore, imply that faith is *un*reasonable. That conclusion is not a logical outcome.

Saying that we believe in order to understand sounds very like Shermer's proposition that smart people basically find evidence to support their belief. And, in a way, it is. Atheists also believe there is no god and then find evidence to support their belief, rather than the other way around. But I would suggest that people who are

---

[147] http://www.michaelshermer.com/2002/09/smart-people-believe-weird-things/

genuinely seeking the truth would be open to look for evidence that may contradict their belief and be prepared to change in the light of it. In that sense, faith is something like a scientific mindset.

If I require scientific proof for something before I am prepared to take any action like praying for the sick, I may never pray. I have to believe that it is possible that my praying could make a difference, be prepared to fail and then act on my belief. Only after trying will I find any evidence to support or negate my belief and that may take a lot of trying. While this kind of evidence may have some vague parallels with scientific testing, it is not the same.

It had been said that it was physically impossible for anyone to run a mile in under four minutes. I imagine this was not based on pure empirical evidence but it was the widely held view of all experts. Roger Bannister chose to believe something different and on 6th May 1954, he ran it in 3 minutes 59.4 seconds. He released the minds of countless athletes after that to do even better. It was less than 2 months later that John Landy beat his record. However, the majority of people will know the name of Roger Bannister rather than anyone who subsequently beat his record because he was the one who proved the experts wrong.

Belief based purely on scientific understanding is easy. It is fine and I am not knocking it but faith is what opens up new horizons. I don't only mean religious faith; I mean the type of faith that refuses to accept that something is impossible and believes there are possibilities beyond that have not yet been seen. This is the sentiment expressed in the Wizard of Oz song *Over the Rainbow* and in certain types of science-fiction film or book where the authors believe that mankind will eventually evolve into being reasonable and decent (and, almost without exception, godless).

Possibly the best known example is in "Star Trek: The Next Generation", in the episode "Who watches the watchers" (1989) where, when encountering a gullible people on a "planet far, away" called Minataka, Jean-Luc Picard, the then captain, reacts with horror to the prospect of reintroducing a type of religion as a form of necessary control. After a discussion between Jean-Luc and Dr Barron, with Dr Barron saying that they have re-kindled the Minatakans' belief in the Overseer and they will have to guide the development of this belief, otherwise it will degenerate into inquisitions, holy wars and chaos, the Captain replies, *"Horrifying. Dr. Barron, your report describes how rational these people are. Millennia ago, they abandoned their belief in the supernatural. Now you are asking me to sabotage that achievement, to send them back into the dark ages of superstition and ignorance and fear? NO!"*

Similar ideas are expressed in some songs like John Lennon's *Imagine there's no heaven*. Incredible though this may seem, this belief that all humankind will evolve into reasonable and decent people is in fact the sentiment shared by many atheists, especially those interested in the possible far future of the universe, speculated on by countless very imaginative people. That is certainly an example of faith if ever there was one, particularly as it often entails populating a new planet. Belief in the God of the Bible is seen as standing in the way of human progression to this state of Nirvana. Personally, I find the vague hope of such perfection staggering in its naïveté.

The Bible: what does it mean?

Surprisingly, the Bible is not a doctrinal book, even though it has been used to formulate Christian doctrine. It is referred to by many Christians as "the word of God". That does not mean that it is a static message from a distant God and we simply read it all, take everything at face value and then, hey presto, we know all we need to know. Calling it the word of God insinuates that it consists of messages from God through people to all generations.

Personally that means that God speaks to me through it. In many ways, it represents God to me. It means life to me. Dawkins caricatures Christian belief as a static set of beliefs going nowhere except to academic idiocy. A thousand times – NO! It is nothing of the sort.

The Bible challenges you to a life of adventure and discovery at the same time as being, surprisingly, utterly honest about the human condition. It challenges your unrealities and pretences. It rejoices in the enquiring mind and encourages you to question. Christianity is not some religious system; it is a dynamic living relationship with a God who is ever new, always exciting, terrifying and loving all at the same time.

In C.S. Lewis' *The Lion, the Witch and the Wardrobe*, Susan asks the Beavers about Aslan, the great Lion ruler of Narnia – "*Is he safe?*" (a very reasonable question to ask about a lion) Mrs Beaver replies, "*If anyone can appear before Aslan without their knees knocking, they're either braver than most or else just silly.*" Lucy responds, "*Then he isn't safe?*" Mr Beaver answers, "*Course he isn't safe. But he's good. He's the king I tell you.*" Faith is dynamic, not static. It goes way beyond a set of beliefs.

In discussing this sort of faith, we are now venturing into the territory of the first definition found in the dictionary – trust. But, for my purpose, I shall again concentrate more on what the Bible says rather than on what the dictionary says.

CHAPTER 9

Faith as Trust

Just to remind you, the first online Oxford Dictionary definition of faith is:

1 complete trust or confidence in someone or something:

this restores one's faith in politicians

Hebrews chapter 11 verse 6 says that those who come to God need to believe that he is and that *he is a rewarder of those that diligently seek him.* It is that last part on which I will concentrate here.

The short passage that is considered to be the biblical description of faith is contained in Hebrews chapter 11 verse 1. This verse, in the English Majority Text version, says, "*Now faith is the substance of things hoped for, the evidence of things not seen.*" That is not speaking of "belief" as we discussed in the last section but of something far more active.

Some of this verse seems to back up a view that it relates to unproved things ("things not seen") but it is to do with evidence, contrary to

Dawkins' assertions. The word for "evidence" here in the Greek is *elenchos* which can be translated as proof, proving or test. This is beginning to sound suspiciously like faith requiring proof to me.

I listened on the internet to some American children trying to define faith and, among the amusing responses, there were some really insightful thoughts. One boy said it was seeing in the future. Roger Bannister probably "saw" himself breaking the four minute mile barrier before it was actually seen on the track. He believed first and provided the evidence later. Scientific discovery is full of examples of such attitudes, notably Rene Descartes who could not believe that God would have to keep tweaking the Newtonian laws to maintain the Earth in its orbit and in fact ended up with a solution which he told Napoleon had "no need of that hypothesis" (i.e. of God needing to intervene constantly).

In order to try and understand what faith is about, we need to look at examples and, from a biblical viewpoint, we should look at Abraham as he is called the "father of faith".

Briefly, Abram and Sarai (as they were originally called) had no children as Sarai was barren. This was a terrible stigma for any woman but worse still for a woman of substance and standing. Abram had no heir and felt it badly. What's more, he was 75 and Sarai was 65. She had reached the menopause (it says, "*it had ceased to be with Sarah after the manner of women*"[148]), so it seemed there was no hope. God then told Abram he would have an heir. I am not going to go into the likelihood or not of this happening; this is about the meaning of faith, but anyone believing in the power of

---

[148]   Genesis chapter 18, verse 11

God to raise his son Jesus from the dead and countless other miracles recorded in the Bible and ever since then to the present day will at least believe that in principle "nothing is impossible for God".

Abram, according to Romans chapter 4 verse 19, looked at the evidence – the fact that his body (and Sarai's) was as good as dead (as far as reproduction was concerned) but he believed God's promise. This, presumably, is what both Hitchens and Dawkins would mean in saying that faith means believing in spite of the evidence. Well, yes, in a way it is. But Abram did look at the evidence. He did not ignore it. However he was convinced that God had spoken to him. It was 25 years after God first promised Abram a son that he (now called "Abraham") and Sarai (now called "Sarah"), at the ages of 100 and 90 respectively, had Isaac.

That was obviously not the result of empirical or scientific evidence-based thinking. If that were the case, they would have given up very quickly. Dawkins, of course, does not believe this couple ever existed but would probably say that if they did, they were stupid faith-heads believing such an outrageous thing against all the evidence – true, but it happened anyway! He would probably say it is an exaggerated account written by someone who wanted to engender faith in others. Miracles don't happen, so it must be nonsense or perhaps they got their ages all wrong; that all the miracles in the Bible are rubbish because they can't happen; that if Abraham is an example of faith then it indicates that so-called faith is nonsense. Nothing like that happens today. People don't get raised from the dead; they don't get healed miraculously and anyway medical science has already achieved what would have been considered miraculous only a century ago. Is this an instance of what Shermer found – that smart people find evidence (or even excuses?) for their beliefs?

If that is true, then we can categorically assert that no miracles will ever happen today and even if they are claimed to take place, there will be a scientific explanation or at least one could be found that will de-bunk the claim. Absolutely no intervention from anything other than something in the universe will ever happen because no such thing exists.

Modern "miracles"

Let me make it clear that I have great admiration for what has been achieved in modern medicine. I am extremely thankful for the advances that have been made and how we can be treated so much more effectively and efficiently today than when I was a child.

I also believe that the vast majority of what people would call miracles may have perfectly reasonable scientific explanations. But one point needs to be made on this. Dawkins seems to take the stance that if something has a scientific explanation, that is the *only* explanation necessary – there is no other. On what basis does he assume this? Only on his own understanding.

Why should it necessarily be true that there can only be one explanation? Being brought up on a farm in Southern Rhodesia, I remember my father "building" a large portion of our house. Did he dig all the foundations, lay all the bricks, put the roof on and so on? No, he didn't but he supervised the work done by others and checked it constantly. He did some of the physical work himself but most of it was done by contract builders and carpenters. But I would still say he built the house. Realising that most of the actual work was done by others does not mean he didn't build it. He was extremely closely involved in all aspects of its construction.

Similarly King Solomon is described, in the 1st. book of Kings chapters 6 and 7, as building the house of the Lord and his own house. Do we imagine he did all the work? Of course not. I imagine he did virtually none of the physical work but he oversaw and ordered the work to be done in detail. So he built the houses.

To say that if we can explain how something happens, it rules out any involvement by God is flawed logic. The two are not mutually exclusive. It may even be possible to explain some aspects of what we call miracles scientifically (or at least it may be possible in the future). But I don't see a problem with saying that we can potentially explain virtually everything scientifically but seeing that God is the unseen King behind it all at the same time.

Suffice it to say that a believer will approach the proposition of miracles with (I would hope) an open mind of how precisely, by what mechanism, God might act to bring about a physically improbable event, or "miracle". Some authors think in terms of miracles being simply ingenious acts of timing only, for example the river Jordan being stopped by a cleverly-timed landslide further upstream at the precise moment (with appropriate time-lag) for the priests carrying the Ark to put their feet in the water (in Joshua chapter 3). Others are more "simplistic" and accept, with the Archangel Gabriel, that nothing is impossible to God – even Christ's virgin birth. I shall discuss some possible explanations for miracles later in this chapter.

Thinking about miracles

If Dawkins and others are right, then we would expect there to be no intervention by God in people's lives. He mentions an "experiment" done by the Templeton Foundation (a Christian scientific group) to determine the effect of prayer on the sick with three groups of patients. Some knew prayers were being said for them; some were being prayed for but didn't know it; the last group were not being prayed for. There was no discernible difference between the last two groups after the allotted time while the first group had, if anything, not improved as much as the others.

A good scientific experiment? I am surprised that the Templeton Foundation even did it. Dawkins says the very idea of doing such experiments is open to ridicule and he is right, but at least they had the honesty to report the results accurately and not try to massage the data. Dawkins comments that if the results had been different, they would have used it to great effect. That may be true, but I hope the Templeton Foundation would have tried to repeat the experiment before releasing the conclusions. One thing I can guess is that Dawkins might *not* have reported a result of this "prayer effectiveness" study indicating external, presumably divine intervention in his book, without suggesting alternative psychological explanations.

I can say, however, I personally have great unease over such "experiments", however the results turn out. How can you possibly "experiment" in that way over faith and by extension, effectively try to pin God down? Dawkins mentions Richard Swinburne, the Oxford theologian who objected on the grounds that God only answers prayer for good reasons and that he would see through this sort of experiment. Of course he would, if he is God! But we cannot try putting God in any sort of scientific box. Personally, I find the whole problem of suffering a very difficult one on which to come to any semblance of a "neat" answer. Why does God seem to answer some prayers and not others? It does not appear to have much relationship, if any, to the worthiness or otherwise of the sufferer. The book of Job, in over forty chapters of discourse, comes to no conclusive answer. That is in contrast to most other religions and it is, strangely, a factor that leads me to believe it is inspired – it is utterly founded in reality.

Faith is a trusting and loving relationship with God, not a scientific exercise or the product of a suspicious and paranoid mind. The Hebrews chapter 11 verse on faith I quoted earlier talks about faith being the evidence of things not seen and that speaks of "proving", "proof" or "testing". But it is not speaking of a kind of obsessive scientific investigation that is permanently sceptical even with positive results. C.S. Lewis draws the parallel with a husband who is insanely suspicious of his wife's fidelity and constantly sends private detectives to spy on her, and distrusts her every protestation of love.

As Christians posit a personal God, the Christian life can indeed be likened to a long-lasting marriage where the trust grows with the shared experiences and setbacks. Abraham was tested ("proved") in his faith for 25 years – and it grew stronger. The late John Wimber decided that if God said we should pray for the sick, he should start doing it. He prayed and, for a few years, nothing happened but he persisted, constantly getting to understand more of the mind and heart of God, until one or two people were healed, then more people, and more and more, until he grew in confidence and found many being healed. I am sure he never reached a one hundred percent "success" rate but it increased all the time. How do you investigate that scientifically?

Having said that, there have been many epidemiological[149] studies done which include the factor of "religiosity" (a term used in this sense to mean a measure of the commitment of people to their particular religion, not, as is often meant, a sort of hyper-religious attitude). According to Andrew Sims, Koenig, McCullough & Larson made a collection of findings (*Handbook of Religion and Health* – Oxford University Press 2001) involving many disparate studies (1200 research studies and 400 reviews mainly from the USA, some from Europe and very few from the rest of the world and covering mainly Christian religiosity but some Jewish and a few from other religions). As the studies were almost all on Christian religiosity, the conclusions they draw can only be applied with any certainty to Christianity. They cautiously draw the following conclusion:

> *In the majority of studies, religious involvement is correlated with well-being, happiness and life satisfaction; hope and optimism; purpose and meaning in life; higher self-esteem; better adaptation to bereavement; greater social support and less loneliness; lower rates of depression; lower rates of suicide and fewer positive attitudes towards suicide; less anxiety; less psychosis and fewer psychotic tendencies; lower rates of alcohol and drug abuse; less delinquency and criminal activity; greater marital stability and satisfaction ...*

---

[149] Epidemiology is a branch of medicine concerned with the incidence and control of disease in whole populations

We concluded that, for the vast majority of people, the apparent benefit of devout religious belief and practice probably outweigh the risks.[150]

Sims comments that, though the authors of this extensive study are very cautious, the results are overwhelming. The benefits in the Jewish communities were not as great as in the Christian communities but there were far fewer Jewish studies undertaken and Sims says there may well be other factors to consider – e.g. genetics, in giving a slightly lower benefit.[151] Although there were very few studies done on Islamic and Hindu effects on health, even there the results showed some small benefit.

However, you will note that Koenig et al say that the "benefit and practice probably outweigh the risks". That implies there are risks and indeed there are. They include "*failure of timely seeking of medical care and replacing medical care, inappropriately, with religion.*"[152] Sims discusses a few causes of these risks but adds that "*the evidence for negative effects of religion on mental health depends upon a few, isolated case reports rather than the larger scale, epidemiological studies, which inform us of the positive effects.*"[153]

Sims' comment on this study and on the many others like it enumerated in his book *Is Faith Delusion?* is that it represents one of "the best kept secrets" of the psychiatric profession – i.e. that faith, particularly as practised by those who participate in a committed

---

[150]   Andrew Sims, "Is Faith Delusion?" page 100

[151]   Sims commented on this in a talk he gave to the Bristol branch of Christians in Science on 25th October 2013

[152]   Andrew Sims, "Is Faith Delusion?" page 102

[153]   Ibid.

sense in worshipping regularly with others, bestows distinctly positive health benefits. He says that if the results had shown the opposite, it would have made headline news in all the media and Dawkins no doubt would have included it in the evidence against the morality of Christians.

This contrasts with Dawkins' claim that *"atheism nearly always indicates a healthy independence of mind and, indeed, a healthy mind."*[154] I am not countering this by saying that there is any indication that atheists have unhealthy minds, but what would be his reason for saying this other than to imply that religious people have less healthy minds than atheists? This is backed up by his recommendation of Shermer's *How We Believe: The Search for God in an Age of Science*, *" for a succinct discussion, which includes the suggestion by Michael Persinger and others that visionary religious experiences are related to temporal lobe epilepsy."*[155] If the evidence of this huge study by Koenig et al has any truth in it (and there is no reason to doubt it) then we can say that Dawkins' implication here is quite simply wrong.

He concedes that there is a *little* (italics mine) evidence that religious belief protects from stress-related diseases.[156] Is this a grudging reference to the above massive report? However, he goes on to say that it would not be surprising if it did – linking it to the placebo effect or with religious memes. I am very much aware of psychosomatic effects and I am sure vast numbers of responsible Christians are, too. Putting this all down to a placebo effect or to memes is really clutching at any slight possibility of explaining away some evidence.

---

154 "The God Delusion" page 25
155 Ibid. page 196
156 Ibid. page 194

And, in addition, it is not a *little* evidence – it is based on many large disparate studies.

It has to be said, though, that Riley, Best and Charlton, in two much smaller studies, report that both religious believers and strong atheists show fewer reported depressive symptoms.[157] I overheard one young lady saying that the advantage of atheism was that you did not fear death because you did not believe in any judgment after death. Sims says, though, that there was less of a benefit for atheists than for committed believers. It seems that being actively involved in a local church, that is, taking part in regular worship and group bible studies had the greatest beneficial impact, and that the least benefit was to Christians who did not feel they needed to be involved in a church.

A cynic might interpret this as evidence for the benefit of community rather than the church per se, and indeed some experimental "atheist churches"[158] have sprung up which share the feature with the church of corporate singing and people developing a sense of "looking out for each other". Perhaps this is a case of imitation being the highest form of praise? Whatever the reality, this new phenomenon is young and it remains to be seen how it will develop – perhaps towards faith in an external "science-fiction being" like the Minatakan "Overseer"? Certainly in Dawkins' home county of Oxfordshire there is currently (at the time of writing) a thriving "Humanist Society"[159], who hold regular talks and social events, with a format rather like the Christians in Science local groups, and certainly enjoying visits from their local deity!

---

157 http://qjmed.oxfordjournals.org/content/98/11/840.1.full
158 The Guardian, Nov 15 2013
159 http://www.oxfordhumanists.org.uk/wordpress/

My personal "case studies"

Let me, however, get down more to some of my own experiences by way of illustration of what I understand by faith. As suggested above, they can only represent examples of faith and so do not enable us to draw any firm conclusions, but I believe they are still important and there are many other Christians who have had similar experiences. Before I continue, I want to state quite clearly that I am a perfectly ordinary Christian. I am no different from the vast majority. I have plenty of weaknesses, plenty of doubts about myself; I have no special power. But I have, at various times experienced "God at work" in my own life and in the lives of people I know and have met. This does not happen on a daily, weekly or even monthly basis. It just sometimes happens. And actually you will see that it is, in some ways, a matter of how I interpret events. My reason for including my own experiences is only that they are first-hand and I know beyond any doubt that these things happened.

I was very militant in "my faith" as a new Christian. I was a proverbial pain in the neck to some people; seeking every opportunity to preach at them. During my second stint at university, I was staying in digs in Pietermaritzburg with my landlady, a Mrs Jacobson (not the lady who lent me the book by Catherine Marshall). She was very kind and put up with me trying to get through to her by singing Christian choruses up in my room loud enough for her to hear me all the time.

•

She looked after me well but became increasingly concerned at the state of my underpants, which were becoming more and more full of holes. She did her best to repair them but it was hopeless and she kept on telling me I should get some new ones. I had no money to spare, so I just said, "The Lord will provide!" She retorted, "You can't think the Lord will provide; you have to buy some." But I seriously could not afford any.

Anyway, one evening another new Christian, also called Neil, and I felt "led by God" to hitch-hike into Pietermaritzburg and speak to someone about God. The first car stopped and took us in, which we interpreted as a good sign – it was pretty unusual. We duly went into a coffee bar but after being there for some time, were unable to engage anyone in conversation. That was probably a blessing to them! So around 10:30 pm we started for the main road to hitch-hike back again. As we walked, a man, obviously very drunk, came towards us and spoke to the night watchman at the Post Office. After a short conversation, the night watchman pointed in our direction and said we would probably be able to help him. We looked at each other, not wanting to get involved but knowing that we now were. After a brief conversation during which he told us he was a psychiatrist who had helped others but couldn't help himself and now "wanted out", we offered to go back to his hotel room with him.

He accepted our invitation. He continued to drink; we tried to pour his drink down the sink but we "shared the Lord" with this sozzled man till about 2 am when he was so far gone, we said we would see him in the morning, put him to bed and hitch-hiked back.

We were up at 6:30; I had breakfast and went across to the university and the two of us hitch-hiked back into town and, by 8 am we were back in his room. He was now sober and as we talked to him, he was attacking what we said and psycho-analysing us. I thought I was making an absolute mess of it but he finally said, "I have attacked you in every way I can; I like what you've got and I want it!" You could have bowled me over.

He was lying on his bed and suddenly said, "Excuse the state of my socks." (they had holes in them). I said, "That's okay; you want to see the state of my underpants." So he said, "Well, I have just bought a pack of new ones; I'll give them to you; they are still in the packet." "I can't take your underpants," I said. He replied, "Why not? You've helped me; I want to help you." So, I accepted the packet gratefully, went back to my digs, put the underpants on the table and announced to Mrs Jacobson, "The Lord has provided!"

Just to finish the story. We were able to enlist the help of a Christian doctor, who confirmed that this man was a psychiatrist, and he was able to help him get over his alcoholism.

Now, was the supply of the underpants a miracle? Of course not! Do I imagine that God somehow stepped into the room and provided me with three pairs of underpants? Don't be silly. I am totally aware that they came from this man. But the two are not mutually exclusive. My interpretation (and I believe it is fully justified in view of what happened) is that God somehow worked in the two of us and in that man for three ends: (1) to provide him with the emergency help he needed, (2) to provide me with underpants when I couldn't afford them and (3) to show Mrs Jacobson that he really did care – years later, she reminded us of the incident. But it wasn't a miracle in the sense that something totally inexplicable happened.

The first "healing"

I was involved then in an Assembly of God Pentecostal church, where there was a high expectation of God healing. It had nothing to do with having done a scientific analysis and discovering that healing was vaguely possible with prayer; we didn't reason it out from biological data. But we did have evidence that sometimes people were healed when we prayed for them – not always, by any means; in fact there were probably a lot more unsuccessful prayers than successful ones. But, it still made sense to ask for healing, so we prayed.

We had a visit from an evangelist who had a healing ministry. Not everyone he prayed for was healed but, every evening, a lot were. A girl I knew well called Helen had a problem in her back and had had an operation to put two metal rods alongside the neural spine of her backbone to partially immobilise it. She asked for prayer and, right in front of my eyes, she bent over and touched her toes! She said she had previously been completely unable to do that. I saw deaf people hearing and blind people seeing. I saw arms and legs that were of unequal length growing. If you say, "I just don't believe that." I will tell you why you just don't believe it. It's because you just don't *want* to believe it. It is knocking your faith too much! But I saw it and I do not knowingly lie. I certainly detected no conjuring tricks.

Shortly after this, a girl stood up in front of the church and said that she had been healed of brain cancer. She had apparently seen various doctors and been for tests in Durban and had, not long after that, been completely healed. A couple of weeks later, the elders of the church had to announce that her entire testimony had been false. They had taken the trouble to check it all out and then, because she had made a public announcement, they had to make a public retraction. They sought the empirical evidence to back up the claim and found there was none. Why had she done it? I don't know but perhaps she thought the way to gain acceptance was to claim some amazing healing. But that will indicate to you that, while there are some Christians who may claim ridiculous things, the vast majority will do their best to ensure honesty. They will not make wild and wacky claims. Dawkins states that the wackier something is, the more it is regarded as faith. That may be true of a few people, but it is *not* faith. In my experience most healings are almost banal in their ordinariness with the majority simply reporting relief from pain.

In that atmosphere of expectation, however, you felt encouraged to pray in spite of the fear of it not working. One evening I was praying with a friend, Pete, who said he was suffering from a splitting headache and asked me to pray for him. Despite my fear of it not working, I prayed. Nothing happened. Without really thinking what I was saying, I then said, "Lord, I am not taking my hands off his head until you heal him". I suddenly thought, "This could be a long wait." But Pete said, "It's gone!" Relief!

Now, experiencing a headache go like this is really no big deal but the evidence showed me that at least minor healing was possible when I prayed. Was that a pure coincidence? Headaches can suddenly disappear. It's unusual – they normally fade over time but it could happen every now and then. The fact that it happened exactly as I prayed makes it a bit more of a coincidence. I would say "the Lord healed him" but it certainly is not in what I would call the miracle category.

More provision

After we had married and I had finished at university, Lizzie and I moved back to Rhodesia, where I started teaching science at Churchill Boys High School in Salisbury (Harare). Understanding the need for tithing, we made sure we paid it each month into the church. But life was a struggle (what has changed?). Once, with three weeks to go until the end of the month, we had $80 left. We still owed $50 for our tithe, leaving us with $30. Out of that, we knew our petrol would cost $19 (there was petrol rationing during sanctions so we knew exactly what our costs were), leaving us with $11. Out of the $11, we would have to pay a maid who washed and ironed our clothes $13, leaving us with minus $2. The cost of living then was much less than it is now but, by anyone's reckoning, you would struggle to buy three weeks' food on minus $2. Lizzie said that if we held our tithe over, we might just be able to make it.

We had prayed only a couple of days before and asked God to increase our faith and this seemed to me suspiciously like God wanting to teach us something. So I said we would pay our tithe if it was the last $50 we had. I asked Lizzie not to request others to pray, not to mention it to anyone because I didn't even want people to know about our need in case they felt they should give us something. If we received any money I wanted to know it was God at work. She agreed. On the Monday, we were going to our home group meeting and we steadfastly kept quiet about our need. No one said anything. We drove home and shortly afterwards there was a call from my mother saying that a friend of hers, Theresa, had just gone to the UK and visited my aunt in Edinburgh. She had given her £100 to give to me, so she had written to my mother to tell her. My mother said, "We will send you $100 tomorrow and then the rest when Theresa gets back". God had come up trumps! I had expected $50 and he provided us with $100.

There were so many "coincidences" here that I really don't think it is too far-fetched to suggest that God was at work. Our faith increased, through experimentation and taking risks.

And this provision is the experience of many Christians (such as George Muller, mentioned earlier) who live the life of faith by obeying the challenge in Malachi 3:10 to *"Bring the full tithe into the storehouse, that there may be food in my house. And thereby put me to the test, says the Lord of hosts, if I will not open the windows of heaven for you and pour down for you a blessing until there is no more need."* You see, God is not keeping the ten percent we give him for himself as if he, the God of the Universe, had need – the original tithes and freewill offerings of livestock given by the people of Israel were given to the landless priests for their keep or eaten communally at the festivals, rich and poor alike, and the tithe many modern Christians pay now is to the local church to be used in its day-to-day work of mission and aid to the needy. This could be seen as an early example of socialist taxation designed to level the rich with the poor, as the offerings asked for in the original Jewish Temple were carefully graded according to the means of the giver – for example. Jesus' parents were poor and so only expected to bring a dove in thanksgiving for the birth of their firstborn son, rather than a bull or lamb.

The unreasonableness of faith

On p 221, Dawkins quotes Martin Luther saying, *"Reason is the greatest enemy that faith has,"*[160] and indeed there are viral images of

---

[160] "The God Delusion" page 221

churches in the USA who proudly display this slogan. Now I am not going to try and interpret Luther but I do know that we always have to be careful to interpret sayings fully in context and I do not know the context in which Luther said that, though I can guess. In order to try and illustrate what I would mean by such a statement, let's think about my last story.

The "reasonable" thing to do under the circumstances we were in would have been to withhold our tithe. It was "unreasonable" to think we could live for three weeks on minus $2! It certainly flew in the face of all evidence. But we had just prayed for more faith. Faith speaks of trust in a living God. By faith I believed God was testing (the Greek *elenchos*, you may remember) us to see if we would trust him. That's why I said we should not tell anyone else about it. I was prepared to have my faith tested. If we had asked anyone else to pray, they might have felt moved to give us some money. I didn't want that. I wanted to test it to see whether faith worked or not. What would have happened if we had done the reasonable thing? I suspect we would still have received the money but it would not have benefited us in the same way. When God told Abram he would have a son, it was unreasonable; it flew in the face of the biological evidence (and Abram knew that) but he chose to put his trust in God and God came up trumps. I suspect he would not have done so if Abram had not believed God.

Is this grandiosity on the part of God? No – the Christian understanding is that God wants us to trust him because when that trust is vindicated by God's provision, then this (like a long marriage) in turn strengthens our love and trust in God so that we can go on to experience even more blessing. In the cliché, "it's a personal relationship" – we aren't robots that are obliged to obey

God but God wants us to freely love and trust and, yes, obey him as the rightful Lord of the Universe – not a cruel tyrant. True love is strengthened through adversity against the rational odds. Why is this albeit emotional principle so hard for atheists to understand?

Interpreting everything by cold rationality is not always the answer. Reason would stop us doing all sorts of things that we should, perhaps, do if we only had the trust to do it. Maybe that's what Luther meant, and what Dawkins misunderstood.

On-going provision

We have had other instances of provision, like when we received, at exactly the right time, exactly the right amount of money we needed to buy a desperately needed fridge. There have been numerous times when we have prayed and have not received anything; there have been many other times when we have. There have been times when we have not prayed but have wondered how we were going to eat, and we've had people ring the bell and hand us a ready-cooked meal. Faith is not a formula; it's a relationship with a God who cares.

Of course, a big block in this line of thinking is the idea that as well as God wanting a loving and trusting relationship with us, he also happens to be *"immortal, invisible, the only wise God"*[161], How could this kind of God need our love? Well, consider the fact that God chose to come to us as a foetus in the womb of Mary, and deliberately, in the words of the 1980s Christian songwriter Graham Kendrick *"laid aside his majesty, gave up everything for me, suffered*

---

[161]   1 Timothy chapter 1, verse 17

at the hands of those you had created" by dying an excruciating death by crucifixion, described in the Bible as a substitutionary sacrifice – i.e. Jesus dying the death all humans deserve so that we might be set free.

What sane God would put himself through all that when he is presumably all powerful and could just snap his fingers and make everything right? In fact, why did God make Adam and Eve undergo a silly test that God presumably foreknew they would fail and then blame them for what was the fault of his own design? And indeed, why would God have designed evolution as a way to produce humans when it leads to so much needless loss of life and suffering, and produces people with free will evidently not to God's taste? Surely, given evolution, it's easier to believe God does not exist at all than that God would have deliberately set up such a wasteful and senselessly cruel situation?

This is where we get into waters that intellectuals find nonsensical, but which some Christian authors with the right scientific background have taken the trouble to think carefully through. Denis Alexander in his 2008 book *Creation or Evolution – do we have to choose?* reaches the conclusion (with many other thinkers) that creation might not be "perfectly good"[162] (or as Voltaire sneers, the best of all possible worlds) in a philosophical sense, but that the process of evolution of a carbon-based biological system made the natural world "fit for purpose" for producing beings with genuine, apparent free will.

---

[162] This concurs with the Genesis chapter 1 account where each stage is described as "good" and the last as "very good" but never as "perfect"

In a sense this might well have been the "only way" practicable for the actual God who made this universe, as opposed to all the theoretical Gods we might dream up, God seems very confident in his judgement, telling us that like clay we should not question the potter – I suppose another statement that a cynical atheist might take as evidence of hunger for power or as demanding unquestioning obedience.

Very much apposite now is the looming, and much discussed, question of the evidence for God's goodness in the face of all the suffering we see in the world. The word "theodicy" to describe this idea (succinctly but I fear rather opaquely to the non-intellectual) was coined by Gottfried Leibnitz in 1710 but this "problem of pain" was clearly a problem from the word go and most recently tackled by C.S. Lewis in the book of that name.

The book of Job is arguably the oldest book written in the Bible. It is, quite possibly, wisdom poetry rather than an actual event but tackles this problem as a story of suffering and the struggle the hero Job goes through with God and with his friends. It is a book that bears extensive study to try and understand, but briefly, the great enemy, Satan, sneers at the faith of the man Job when God holds Job up as an example of a righteous man. Satan cynically proposes that Job's faith is just cupboard-love – *"Does Job fear God for no reason? Have you not put a hedge around him and his house and all that he has, on every side? You have blessed the work of his hands, and his possessions have increased in the land. But stretch out your hand and touch all that he has, and he will curse you to your face. And the LORD said to Satan,*

Behold, all that he has is in your hand. Only against him do not stretch out your hand."[163]

Now to me, this is mind-blowing. How could God seriously expect us to worship him if we are suffering and not being rewarded for our faith in Him in a real and material way? The idea in Malachi chapter 3 verse 10 of God *"opening the windows of heaven"* to the person who "tests him" in bringing in the full tithe has been taken up enthusiastically by the so-called "health and wealth" evangelists who promise that if we only obey God's commands – in particular to donate to their ministry over and above the prescribed ten percent – then they can guarantee that God will bless us materially. Indeed this would seem to be a reasonably accurate conclusion of Malachi chapter 3 verse 10.

But the Job story turns this idea completely on its head. Satan presumably thinks that the question of believing in God is a no-brainer if God behaves like the later Roman "household gods" and blesses the household where he is worshipped. Indeed there is a suggestion of this idea in the stories of the Ark of the Covenant. It brought pestilence to the Philistines when they captured it in 1 Samuel chapter 6, resulting in the Philistines immediately doing the right thing and returning the Ark to the Israelites, and then later on in 2 Samuel chapter 6 verse 11. the Ark resulted in blessing for the household of the gloriously named "Obededom the Gittite".

So in this paradigm (thought-pattern) of God rewarding obedience materially and punishing a lack of reverence, why then could God

---

[163] Job chapter 1, verses 9-12

consent to this bizarre test of Job's faith in such an apparently casual and callous way?

Strangely, in the book of Job, the answer is not really given, even after 42 chapters of argument and counter-argument between Job and his three friends (who reflect the dominant philosophy of the time and even used by some Christians today). His fourth friend who only appears on the scene toward the end of the book seems to have more insight than the others. When God finally speaks to Job, he gives him no answer but challenges him over his supposed knowledge *"Where were you when I laid the foundation of the earth? Tell me, if you have understanding."*[164] In four following chapters, God continues to challenge him but never tells him why he allowed him to suffer (though the reader knows).

Interestingly, though, it seems Job came to a far deeper understanding of and intimacy with God as a result of what he suffered. A proper philosophical answer to the meaning of suffering is never spelled out; the reader is left with questions – the sort of questions that have caused scholars over the centuries to try and fathom this book out. And yet it has been a book that has brought answers to people all through those centuries.

The fact of the matter is that when Christians suffer (some intolerably) in the world, through religious persecution or just plain bad medical or careers luck of the draw, a huge number cite Job as the one book of whose forty two chapters they can read and mull through (and sometimes learn from memory). It's a simple idea, isn't it, that ordinary people can grasp (very Hollywood as people might

---

[164] Job chapter 38, verse 4

sneer) – we are refined "like in a furnace" through persecution or other incidental suffering, and the crucial issue is whether we retain our faith in God's essential justice and mercy and goodness in the face of suffering.

What is the "evidence" for God in this situation? Should they be "reasonable" and conclude that their best bet is to believe in the God who can most materially (or emotionally) benefit them and therefore it would be wise to abandon ship in the face of suffering? Are such instances examples that the Abrahamic God is sadistic to his own people and therefore we should refuse to believe in him? No – just as most people accept the idea of faith in a friend being strengthened through adventurous trials through thick and thin in a Hollywood film, this is a classically simple idea akin to the idea in 1 Corinthians chapter 1 verse 23 that "the cross" (another word packing a lot of meaning) was a stumbling block to the Jews and foolishness to the Gentiles.

Back to the central idea – faith as God wants us to have it is tied in with all kinds of ideas of God stepping down to suffer alongside humans in the world that he had designed, wanting us to get to know Him as a person in every sense of the word but material, faith being strengthened through adversity (surely there is an inkling of this in the Darwinian observation of "survival of the fittest", but absolutely not in any kind of "Aryan master-race" sense).

However, it could be argued that all this is a psychological effect. We know the power of the human mind to believe falsehoods and that can cause desired results; feeling the comfort of God during immense suffering could very easily be some sort of placebo. Even headaches suddenly disappearing may be due to positive thinking and what proof have I got that those healings I saw in Pietermaritzburg were utterly genuine? Others may argue that "if it works, why knock it, even if it's not actually true". Personally, I am not happy with the latter reaction. If it is not true, I do not want to believe it. We need harder evidence if we are going to accept that faith has some substance.

Well, Christians claim to experience physical healing from disease and physical damage or disability on a massive scale across the world. There are many claims of people being raised from the dead and I have heard a first hand testimony from someone who claims to have died, as the result of being stung by a number of Box Jellyfish, and then been raised from the dead. I do not know of any similar claims from other religions because I do not move in their circles, but it would be interesting to hear of any documented cases. While I may not have experienced anything like that or like many other amazing healings that commonly take place around the world, I have experienced first hand people being healed when I have prayed for them and so I will share a few instances. Firstly, I knew some of those people who were healed in Pietermaritzburg personally and I know they didn't lie, so I am confident that those healings were genuine, but I was not involved in praying for them.

More healings

John was a man in his 60s who helped out by cleaning the church building in Finsbury Park, London where we worshipped after finishing at Bible College. The only problem was he had terrible arthritis in his knees and cleaning was sometimes agony. He had been to the doctors who had tried all sorts of remedies and it had got to the stage where they reckoned the only solution was to lift his knee caps, scrape the crystals off and put the knee caps back. He would then have to learn to walk again.

But we were having an evangelistic campaign coming up in the Hornsey Town Hall with a West Indian evangelist who also prayed for the sick. John prayed that God would heal him in this campaign but felt that God said, "No, I will not heal you in the campaign." John, typically, just accepted it with no complaint.

The Sunday evening before this campaign was due to start, I was leading the meeting. At one stage, I asked people to share anything for which they needed prayer and to pray together. This went on for a few minutes and I then suggested we could all pray together. John prayed from the back somewhere and actually thanked God for his pain! That did something to me. How could he do it? I prayed out loud for John's healing, hoping against hope that he would have some small improvement. Nothing happened for a moment.

Then, suddenly, there was a whole lot of clapping. I looked as John hugged Lizzie at the back of the meeting and then ran up the side across the front and down the middle, with his arms in the air, tears running down his face, saying over and over, "Thank you, Jesus! Thank you, Jesus!" I didn't know what had happened but he said he was standing there and, all of a sudden, a whoosh went through his body and every bit of pain disappeared!

A miracle? Well, I checked with a doctor who said arthritic pain can come and go but the crystals do not just go. John still had the crystals. He went to the doctor who was quite amazed but would not accept that he had been healed by God and told him to come back in a few weeks. When he returned after a few weeks the doctor discovered that the crystals had gone. I am still not going to claim that this was a miracle but I am convinced that it was God who did it.

Other healings

We have experienced God healing Lizzie instantaneously when she had her sacroiliac joint out causing her intense back pain – her leg silently lengthened in front of our eyes. I have known others' legs lengthening immediately as I have prayed for them. I don't know what was wrong in each case causing one leg to be shorter than the other as I never investigated – I was just pleased they were healed. However in one case – a lady in her twenties was complaining about the fact that she was having problems with her dancing as her right leg was shorter than the left. She had been to the doctor who said the only solution was to operate and shorten the left leg by cutting out a piece of the lower leg. She was not a Christian. As I prayed for her, her leg simply grew in front of our eyes. At her next dancing lesson the instructor immediately noticed the difference. She told a few others, including an atheist chemist, who just refused to believe it had happened.

This was not a case of a joint going back. Her leg actually grew. How likely is it that a leg on an adult will suddenly grow an inch or so in a couple of seconds? I have no doubt that, within the realms of chance, it is possible, even if it is millions to one against. What is the chance of that happening exactly as someone prays? I would suggest it is just about impossible. Was it a miracle of healing? I don't know. I am not going to claim it was, because I am not certain. I will leave it to your own judgment. But there is no doubt about the veracity of this.

We have seen numerous other healings. A man with an extremely painful leg suddenly had it completely released; two people in our church with cancer have been healed. Both also received medical treatment but neither of them was expected to live. One man had his bones riddled with cancer. The medical staff called him "the miracle man". He is still very much with us after many years and free from cancer. We have also had two people die of cancer but both accepted that they were going to die.

I would have to say that nine out of ten times when I pray I do not see any result but faith says I will keep on praying. If we are asking if prayer really works, then I don't know how you would properly test it. It's a bit like testing to see if marriage works. Besides this, I don't think we can say "prayer works" anyway. God works, yes. Prayer is asking him to work.

Now perhaps for some, this is still not enough evidence. I simply ask you to approach this with an open mind. Check out claimed healings on the internet – some will be wacky; some are well documented.

The nature of miracles – are they the suspension of natural law?

Some have claimed that because God created all things and formed natural law, he is perfectly able to suspend it when he chooses. That is a fairly reasonable view. However, the question is: does he suspend natural law? I believe that everything to do with matter, energy, force etc. has a scientific explanation – does that include miracles? What I am about to say is, I emphasize, purely my opinion. I welcome argument on it because I certainly do not have the answer.

The Bible tells us God is not the author of confusion (or chaos)[165]. So would he create even occasional confusion by suspending natural law? I don't believe he would. If a "miracle" has taken place, it must be within natural law, whether we understand the process or not. So how would Jesus have walked on water or multiplied a few fish and loaves to enable five thousand men (plus, I assume, roughly the same number of women and children) to be fed and have more left over than there was at the start? Many have suggested that the example of a little boy giving up his lunch inspired everyone to give but that is not what scripture says and the clear implication is that the multitude did not have enough to eat, so I reject that explanation. When it comes to walking on water, I am out of my depth (excuse the pun). I cannot answer but I still believe it happened (and that Peter did the same for a brief moment). I know Richard Dawkins and others will accuse me of having blind faith. That doesn't bother me. I still believe it happened. However, I also believe there must have been something scientific happening. Whether the surface tension of the water was temporarily changed or not, I have no idea. But something must have happened to prevent Jesus being up to his neck in water. Similarly, something very unusual but still scientific must have happened to the loaves and fishes without suspending the law of the conservation of matter. I really have no idea what it would be, but one thing is certain, neither of those things would happen under any normal circumstances. And it is also clear that

---

[165] 1 Corinthians chapter 14, verse 33

both had something to do with faith – the interaction of the human spirit with God.

Stephen Hawking and Leonard Mlodinov, in their *The Grand Design* say, "*We seem to be at a critical point in the history of science, in which we must alter our conception of goals and of what makes a physical theory acceptable. It appears that the fundamental numbers, and even the form, of the apparent laws of nature are not demanded by logic or physical principle. The parameters are free to take on many values and the laws to take on any form that leads to a self-consistent mathematical theory, and they do take on different values and different forms in different universes.*"[166]

I am not in any way arguing here for a multiverse but it seems that what we call "laws" may not be what they seem to be to us. It is well known that the consistency of understanding the behaviour of macro objects with understanding the behaviour of quantum particles has so far eluded us because somehow you need completely different perceptions of behaviour at the two levels.

A miracle, by definition, means something that happens that would not happen in the normal course of events. But what is normal? Could it be (I am only posing the question) that laws we would normally take for granted somehow behaved or took on apparently illogical or at least totally unexpected values when some miracles occurred? It might be that in some way impossible for us to understand, the sun really did appear to stand still on a day just over three thousand years ago and even to go "backwards" a few hundred years later. It's quite illogical to my mind and, I have no doubt, to yours. The chaos that

---

[166] http://www.math.columbia.edu/~woit/wordpress/?p=3141

would occur with the earth's rotation stopping and then restarting can only be imagined, but while all our normal existence seems to follow predictable patterns, maybe there are some occasions when the laws do not operate as we expect.

When it comes to miracles of healing, I feel slightly more confident, though only a little. Let's take the incident of a leg growing on an adult. As I said above, I cannot say that was a miracle, but it is massively unusual. Growth is normal in a child, but does not happen normally in adults. I knew a man in Rhodesia who had a car accident that caused damage to his thyroid gland which resulted in an over-production of thyroxin (the growth hormone). He suddenly started growing again and in a relatively short time had grown a few inches, but it was not normal and he became very ungainly.

Is it possible for a childhood kind of growth to happen in an adult in her twenties in one very specific part of the body? I am sure it must be but it does not normally happen. Is it possible for that growth to be thousands of times faster than normal? I see no reason why it should not be possible. That man grew inches within about 18 months; why could not growth be accelerated enormously? It is definitely not normal, but why can it not happen? Where did the matter come from? It could easily be supplied from within the body – but at an abnormal rate. Muscles can also be lengthened to accommodate the growth – much more easily than bone tissue.

But how about raising people from the dead? Well, it is certainly not the run-of-the-mill experience of most of us, but who is to say that life cannot come back into a dead body or that chemical processes cannot be reversed? Just because it is totally outside the experience of nearly everyone on this planet throughout its entire history does not mean it cannot happen. When there is an interaction of the human spirit with God, we cannot say what things are possible or not possible – and it can always be within (potentially) explicable scientific processes. Some people trust God – even when they have no scientific answer; others cannot think outside the "normal" scientific box.

Understanding trust

There is no formula to trusting God. Catherine Marshall relates the story of her own struggle with tuberculosis in her book, *Beyond Ourselves*. She was slowly dying of the disease but was, as a believer, praying for healing as were a number of her friends. But she steadily grew worse. She came to the conclusion that she just was not truly trusting God and was not properly believing. She decided that she was going to put all her trust in him and believe for healing. She subsequently had tests done and then waited for the doctor's call with news of the results.

When the phone at her hospital bed rang, it was the doctor who told her she was not much worse, but certainly there was no improvement. At that point, she almost despaired. She just gave up. She said to God that she was giving up on praying for healing. If he wanted her to live, she would live; if he wanted her to die, she would just die. Whatever he wanted, she would accept it. From that moment, she steadily improved and was completely healed. I have come across many other believers with a similar story to tell. I don't believe any scientific enquiry can really ever understand true faith.

What about unanswered prayer?

There are many Christians who insist that God always answers prayer – it's just that the answer is often "No!" That can seem very like a "get-out clause" so that you never have to explain failure. And I think it sometimes is just that. Is it that God is waiting for us to reach a certain state of heightened spirituality before he answers? Well that makes it dependent on us and that is quite contrary to what the gospel declares and it would have meant Job's friends were probably right in their assessment. The apostle James says that "*you do not have, because you do not ask. You ask and do not receive, because you ask wrongly, to spend it on your passions.*"[167]

So it would seem God does not answer some prayers or that he may say "no" on occasion. How about arthritic John in London asking God to heal him in the campaign and sensing God was saying "No"? God obviously intended to heal him *before* the campaign! Are those whose prayers are answered especially favoured while those whose prayers aren't answered second-class Christians? The fact is I would say, if we are being honest, most prayers remain, at least seemingly, unanswered.

Why trust him, then?

What if Catherine Marshall had in fact died? Well, of course the pat answer is that she would have "gone to heaven" – a subject I have not yet touched on for the huge can of worms it opens. Briefly, it's true that the reality of the resurrection is a cornerstone of Christian

---

[167] James chapter 4, verses 2b-3

belief, such that Paul can say with us in 1 Corinthians chapter 15 verse 19 that were Jesus to be proved not to have risen from the dead then our faith would be in vain. But this is not the reason why we should believe in God – he is not a sugar-daddy that we should abandon when the going gets tough. We should believe in God – in his essential goodness, so that we should trust him with the direction of our lives – anyway. Because the same God who revealed himself to Abraham and his descendants (including us) is, in fact, however you understand it or have evidence for this, the Lord of the universe before whom every knee will bow at the end of time, because that is who he is.

Whatever the next life may bring, we can't treat it like an automatic reward for obeying God in this life. As C.S. Lewis points out, the idea of heaven – or the life eternal – is an historically recent one only held by the Pharisee sect of the Jews in Jesus' day and not by the more intellectual Sadducees. Although we believe that there is an afterlife, atheists are quite right to point out that this should not be our primary motivation as if we need a carrot to do good. As the atheist Kurt Vonnegut put it, *"being a Humanist means trying to behave decently without expectation of rewards or punishment after you are dead"*[168], and many other atheists share this sentiment. To the mocker, Christians are pathetic as they only do good because they are afraid of hellfire not because they want to do good for its own sake.

So yes, hell is the big "elephant in the room". If God does not exist then we all snuff out when we die. If God exists then he sends the Christian to heaven (which the atheist Christopher Hitchens views

---

[168] http://americanhumanist.org/AHA/Frequently_Asked_Questions

as a "celestial North Korea", *"where all I get to do is praise the Dear Leader from dawn to dusk"*[169]. This is certainly the vision described both in Isaiah chapter 6 and in Revelation chapter 4, with the cherubim and seraphim (the angels of God's presence) and other indescribable "living creatures" calling out praise and so too the humans present (Isaiah himself in the first vision and the twenty-four elders "falling down before God's throne").

But surely the perception of this event is very different according to whether we have grown to love God personally through all the trials of life, or we have never had a proper encounter with God. Perhaps the argument in C.S. Lewis' *The Great Divorce* with its own unique picture of heaven and hell may help us here. Hell, according to Lewis, is the place to which previously non-believing humans will flee to escape the full glory of God in all its overwhelming and unimaginable light and splendour. Interestingly, along these lines, Hitchens adds to his quote above, *"I don't want this; it would be hell for me"*, backing up C.S. Lewis' picture.

But the every day reality of heaven as the next adventure starts is portrayed by John the apostle who saw the vision described in the book of Revelation. Here the reality of the next life, as detailed in the last two chapters of Revelation and possibly the only remotely reliable (however atheists understand that term) account of the next reality. And the vision is very simple and very modern: a garden city, laid out with glorious single crystals as the gates, with presumably the original Tree of Life now with the leaves "for the healing of the nations".

---

[169] http://www.atheistapologist.com/p/my-favorite-atheist-quotes.html

Are we now talking about some continuation of the work of the Spirit in the ordinary Christian's life, now able to reach its glorious purpose of creating at last the truly just and merciful and loving society that all people, very much including atheists, all long for? Who knows? The subject of the next life and in particular any sense of hierarchy in it, is a subject on which Jesus will not be drawn when his disciples are discussing what the future pecking order will be when Jesus comes into his glory. Instead, Jesus takes a child and says *"truly I say unto you, whoever does not receive the kingdom of God like a child shall not enter it."*[170] This is a statement that must make the blood of all self-respecting scientists boil, Christian or not. But it is an inescapable condition of entering into that perfect society, from which atheists would wish to remove the central figure of God.

If there is a hell, does that make God vicious?

How can a God of love be reconciled with suffering and particularly with commanding his people to destroy whole nations in their conquest of the land on the eastern border of the Mediterranean? Why would he even kill his own people when they chased after other gods? The Bible gives little explanation for this. It leaves us to try and fathom it out. In teaching, I try to get children to fathom things out for themselves, rather than giving them answers. That's an attempt to get them thinking in an adult way. God expects us to be adult and think things through, too.

The doctrine of hell is in a similar category to these Old Testament accounts. How can a loving God send people to hell (forever) just

---

[170] Mark chapter 10, verse 15

because they reject him? Surely he is bigger than this. Why can he not do something about it and just forgive them as Richard Dawkins suggests? He says, *"If God wanted to forgive our sins, why not just forgive them, without having himself tortured and executed in payment."*[171]

When I was growing up, there was a family two farms away from us. We knew them pretty well. There were four brothers and the youngest two were very close to my brother Rob and me in age. The third son is about two years older than I am. Three days before writing this I received an email to say that eight days ago, he and his daughter were walking their dogs on their farm when they were attacked by a gang, who raped his daughter, tied them both up with barbed wire and then axed them in the head – probably for no other reason than that his daughter in particular was trying to stop people illegally cutting down trees and causing destruction of the land by deforestation. He and his daughter were found a couple of hours later unconscious. She died after four days and he is struggling for his life[172]. The leader of the gang apparently phoned my late brother's father-in-law and boasted that they had just killed this man. I know there are far worse things that happen in the world but this is very close-to-home for me. No one can ever think this despicable behaviour is excusable no matter what the provocation. It cannot be said to be normal for anyone remotely human.

So, would we suggest that God should "just forgive" the people who did this? Should he just forgive all similar or worse atrocities? Quite frankly, if anyone thinks that, I find it obscene. Can you

---

[171] "The God Delusion" page 287
[172] He died two days after I wrote that paragraph

imagine the outcry if a judge just released a mass murderer and said he had decided he needed forgiveness and it didn't matter any more? Should Hitler, Stalin or Idi Amin just be forgiven? I find it quite extraordinary that anyone can think "just forgiving" is all right, particularly for such revolting and cowardly acts. Forgiveness cannot be other than an incredibly costly thing to do because justice must still be done. We rightly demand it. Wrong-doing must be punished. The only thing is, what do you call wrong-doing? Is the destruction of a family when a father walks out on his wife and children only a bit wrong? How about stealing and wrecking someone's life? Where do we stop? Do we have a point where we say that this sin is not bad enough to warrant punishment but a slightly worse one falls into the must-be-punished category? What would we think of a God who categorised sins like that? Do we just have the "seven deadly sins" (which have been invented by people anyway) as punishable and the rest just forgiven? Think about the implications of God "just forgiving" all sin when there is no repentance or remorse if that is what you think he should do.

The Roman Catholic doctrine of purgatory tries to get around this by suggesting that God sends people to a temporary place to be punished and cleansed before being allowed into heaven. That sounds a lot nicer but such a place is not mentioned in Scripture. I have to note here that there is considerable disagreement among Christians over the interpretation of the doctrine of hell. The majority of evangelical Christians believe hell is a state of eternal torment for all who reject Christ. Some have given considerable scriptural evidence to show that it is either not permanent or that hell is mainly a state experienced during this life.[173] I am not going to

---

[173] e.g. Rob Bell's book "Love Wins"

argue for any position here. I used to feel certain about it but, having read accounts that contradicted my beliefs effectively, the jury is out as far as I am concerned. I do, however, trust God to do what is right.

According to the apostle Paul, writing about the wanderings of the children of Israel in the desert, "*these things took place as examples for us, that we might not desire evil as they did.*"[174] That can be applied to everything in the Old Testament. What was God teaching us through all this conquest and killing?

I cannot give any full answer on this, but the Bible calls him a "jealous" God (something Dawkins understandably hates). However, this is not human jealousy. It is to do with a determination to get us to understand that he alone is worthy of our unreserved commitment because he deeply desires to bless his people. But sin prevents the reception of God's blessing.

In our modern view of life, we regard sin as just a bit naughty. It has come to mean slightly illicit pleasure. It is often associated with things like extra-marital sex or eating too many fatty cakes. So saying something is "sinful" is even used as an advertising gimmick (e.g. "naughty but nice!"). We don't tend to associate it with criminal behaviour like the atrocities I mentioned above. But the biblical concept of sin is anything at all that alienates us from God however good or bad that may be in our eyes. And, because God is love, he hates sin with a vengeance. Sin means, ultimately, permanent separation from him. That is described as death in the Bible. Sinners in the eyes of God are already dead. So the sin needs to die before God's life and love can be experienced.

---

[174] 1 Corinthians chapter 10, verse 6

In some way that I do not properly understand, God was demonstrating the terrible seriousness and consequences of sin when he destroyed nations and even put his own people to death. We are horrified at such actions because we do not appreciate how devastating sin is in God's economy. He then caused the intense suffering and death of his own son in order to bring us life and restore the relationship with us. Sin is so terrible that it has to be punished and God took the punishment himself. So justice was done. And it covered not only those utterly despicable sins like the brutal murder of the Elim missionaries and those people who attacked my ex-neighbour, but even, dear reader, your own indiscretions, to say nothing of more major things you may have done. God's forgiveness is costly and that is probably the understatement of the year. That is love. It is only when we begin to glimpse life from God's viewpoint that these things even start to make sense.

Did the cross itself cause the condemnation of *"remote future generations of Jews to pogroms and persecution as 'Christ-killers'* "[175]? I am not going to excuse this persecution in any way even though the first persecution was the other way round. That in no way makes it right. However, to suggest the death of Christ was responsible for this simply shows no understanding of what responsibility for actions entails. Those responsible for that persecution may have used the death of Christ as an excuse to persecute Jews, but that, again, is just sin. Did God know it would happen? Yes, he must have known. But would the answer be to forget the whole plan and leave us all to the consequences of our sin? I'll leave that to you to think through.

---

[175] "The God Delusion" page 287

Faith believes that God is good and that, even though the consequences of sin are terrible, God desires good for all people. Peter, the apostle, says that God does not want anyone to suffer those consequences but wants all to come to repentance – i.e. to know him. He bases this on the Old Testament (ostensibly the "fiercely unpleasant God" that Dawkins describes on page 58), where the prophet Ezekiel says, *"As I live, declares the Lord GOD, I have no pleasure in the death of the wicked, but that the wicked turn from his way and live."*[176]

Final thoughts on faith

What is it about faith that works? I really wish I could answer that question but I cannot. From the stories I have related above of my experiences, you could be led to believe that I think I have amazing faith but I know I haven't. Anyone who has been around in active Christian circles for a while will know that far more wonderful healings are experienced relatively commonly around the world. With the number of Christians there are around the world, I am certain these healings will be happening in numbers every single day. But they are rarely trumpeted abroad.

What I can say is that faith is not a formula. Faith itself cannot be subjected to empirical scientific tests. We may be able test the *results* of faith empirically. If a healing is claimed, medical experts can investigate asking questions about the likelihood of healing taking place at all or with no medical intervention. But faith itself is not a scientific phenomenon.

---

[176]   Ezekiel chapter 33, verse 11

I would suggest that if only a few cases are found where the likelihood of the healing taking place at all or with no medical intervention is virtually minimal, it would be strong evidence of the intervention of some other factor completely unknown to medicine – and that factor may be God.

I said above that it's not faith or prayer that heals – it is God. However, Jesus said, on a number of occasions, that a person's faith had made them whole. Clearly faith is an important element in healings. It seems obvious that he chooses to work when genuine faith is exercised but it is also obvious that he is not limited to or constrained by that.

Faith is not a commodity or system to be used. It is all based on a growing relationship with the God in whom a person trusts. It is dynamic. Jesus spoke of his disciples having "little faith", obviously wanting them to develop greater faith. As with many things, faith grows through trying and failing. Overcoming the fear of failure will usually lead to better results. We learn to trust others as we "test" them out; we learn to trust God and our relationship with him by trying and failing; learning from our failures and moving on. I seem to remember that was Edison's attitude in trying to produce a working light bulb. He is reported to have said "*I have not failed. I have just found 10,000 ways that won't work!*"[177] Like Roger Bannister visualising himself winning, maybe he "saw" a working light bulb long before it actually happened. Maybe he didn't. The point is he believed it must be possible and persisted until he found the answer. That is a kind of faith, whether he had spiritual faith or not.

---

[177]   http://quoteinvestigator.com/2012/07/31/edison-lot-results/

Faith in God implies a realisation of your own weakness or inability. To most people, that is counter-intuitive. Surely, we should be encouraging people to rely on themselves, not to think of themselves as being weak. Don't all the self-help books teach that? Well, I am not sure that they all do but what I have found is that when I feel weak, then it seems more likely that God will act; strangely, it's when I feel least like I have faith that he intervenes. Faith is not a feeling; it's a journey of discovery. Amazingly too, my confidence has grown as I have acknowledged my own weakness more.

So I, with many other Christians, would maintain that true faith is definitely *not* static. It is tested and tried and so grows and develops. It's not scientific testing but experimentation in life and it should develop character. Scientific knowledge is dynamic, too. But science knows nothing of the kind of testing I have described above. Science is nothing to do with a personal trust in a living personal God whom Christians report as interacting and communicating with them. That is where faith finds its dynamism. However, the first aspect of faith (belief) that I described is also dynamic. It should constantly be tested against evidence, both biblical and experiential, and, if it is found wanting in any way, it needs to be adjusted so that the believer moves on to further maturity in his/her relationship with God.

But the same can be achieved by positive mental attitude

It is also true that there is enormous power in the human mind for good or ill. Some people with a positive attitude overcome illnesses that should kill them and vice versa. Some of these people have no faith in God at all and attribute their eventual victory as a triumph of the strength of the indomitable human spirit. The "placebo" effect of a person receiving a powerless pill but believing it to be a wonder drug has anecdotal evidence the medical world over and should be looked at more carefully. Recently, neurologists have succeeded in enabling paraplegic patients, through electrodes in their brain, to communicate by electrical signals with computers and even apply the brake to cars.[178] Is the electrical power of the human mind the explanation for miracles of healing and not the intentional action of God?

Well, that is one possible idea, but it would need to be tested against the willpower of the person making the prayer. Do only the strong-minded pray successfully to God? I personally have seen a dog healed of cancer within 3 weeks when we prayed. The vet had said its leg would have to be amputated, but eventually a small growth was removed. I don't think it could be proved to be due to a positive attitude on the part of the dog. In addition, healing through positive attitudes normally takes a considerable time, whereas we often find instantaneous healing when faith is exercised in prayer.

Is this proof of God's existence?

Obviously my experience is not universal knock-down proof for the existence of God, but then none of the different bits of evidence pointing to the existence of an invisible supreme ruler of the universe have a way of being absolutely convincing to the determined sceptic. Dawkins says "faith heads" are immune to evidence. Probably true, but the same is very likely true of religious sceptics. Special pleading

---

[178] Science Daily, 29 June 2011

or not, it just boils down to the apparent fact that God simply does not want us to come to faith in him by only accepting knock-down scientific evidence. Why? Presumably because he really does value the kind of faith and character development that I have been trying to explain all through this chapter.

But, let's now leave the question of faith. We need to examine the whole question of morality as there are, we must face it, some really embarrassing bits of evidence to consider – not just in the Bible but in the behaviour of Christians (genuine or otherwise) through the whole of history. The fact that God seems to permit such embarrassing behaviour reflects directly on God's goodness which, you should have picked up by now, God really wants to demonstrate to us humans for some baffling reason. Dawkins perhaps rightly picks on this as the real Achilles heel of the Christian proposition of a perfectly good God who is in charge of this present universe we inhabit and this is something we should therefore take most seriously of all.

CHAPTER 10

The Character of God

It is in dealing with morality that Dawkins waxes most polemical. In the BBC discussion between Dawkins and McGrath[179], McGrath asked him why he was so angry. He seemed a little surprised as if it had not previously occurred to him but replied to the effect that he was angry at people being deceived into wrong thinking and not understanding the wonder of proper science. Having read his autobiography, he clearly was not force-fed religion at any stage. It seems that, although his parents were nothing like as militant as he is, they were not Christian believers and (quite rightly) stood up for him when one of his schools expressed concern over his "rebellious attitude".

I agree that forcing anyone (child or adult) into believing something they just don't believe is plainly wrong and I shall return to this in chapter 15. Personally, I don't think it is possible in reality to do that. You can make someone say they believe something but that does not mean they do. An example is the "conversion" to Islam of

---

179   This was recorded by the BBC but never aired for some reason; it can be found at: http://www.youtube.com/watch?v=3LGm0iWPC80

schoolgirls abducted in March 2014 by the Nigerian Boko Haram terrorist group. The abduction is abhorrent and the "conversion" is ridiculous. Such a statement can only be made by someone who is either singularly unintelligent and has no clue as to what faith is or someone who has an utterly evil agenda – or both.

Is YHWH (God) the character Dawkins describes?

We need to examine Dawkins' attitude to God himself – specifically the Judeo-Christian God, YHWH. Dawkins says:

> *The God of the Old Testament is arguably the most unpleasant character in all fiction: jealous and proud of it; a petty, unjust, unforgiving control-freak; a vindictive, bloodthirsty ethnic cleanser; a misogynistic, homophobic, racist, infanticidal, genocidal, filicidal, pestilential, megalomaniacal, sadomasochistic, capriciously malevolent bully.*[180]

You almost reel at this tirade of invective! I am not going to tackle each of these adjectives in turn; some of them are dealt with in other parts of the book and many like 'petty' are no more than straight-forward opinion. However, I need to deal with a few of them. Dawkins regards YHWH as fictional, of course, and I don't. If he is real, he is not going to be biting his metaphorical fingernails over these accusations, though he would be concerned at the effect on Richard Dawkins. I feel a bit silly trying to defend the God of the universe; he doesn't need me to do it! But I am concerned at

---

[180] "The God Delusion" page 51

people believing what Dawkins says without looking at any counter argument.

The image that Dawkins has of God is of a being who is said to thrive on the slavish adulation of his little creations and regularly orders them into literally suicidal missions with the false promise of a "better life" after death. Of course we need to add the rider that Dawkins would say this is a construct of the manipulative and cynical "priests" of Israel (or perhaps of Medina), But the point is that Dawkins says that such a God-proposition, is too amoral to be worthy of the allegiance of freethinking human beings.

The most succinct expression is in a recently circulated photo of a crazily staring pigeon with the caption, *"I refuse to believe in a God who preaches racism, sexism, homophobia and ignorance – and then sends me to hell if I'm 'bad'."*[181] This attack on the core of the Christian message of the "good news" is fast becoming the main line of attack of the social media arm of the Richard Dawkins Foundation for Reason and Science.

I would say this is exacerbated by the Christian tendency to want to concede any moral imperfection in ordinary Christians past or conveniently "abroad" and embarrassment coupled with a lack of deep understanding of the scriptures making any kind of robust defence of the goodness of the God of the Bible difficult. However, that caption portrays an image of God that I certainly do not recognise. I could not believe in that sort of God either. To suggest that the Bible teaches that is a gross misunderstanding at best and a deliberate distortion at worst.

---

[181] memegenerator.net/instance/12280095

He charges him with misogyny and this is a very common charge. Of course, there is nowhere where God is said to hate women but we do find passages where, for example, a greater sacrifice has to be given for the dedication of a boy than a girl and many similar Old Testament laws. That would appear to put a greater value on men than women. Similarly, in the New Testament, we find Paul making statements like *"I do not permit a woman to teach or to exercise authority over a man; rather she is to remain quiet."*[182] and stressing that a wife should submit to the authority of her husband.

Understandably, many women take exception to this kind of seeming male dominance. In my ignorance of feminine feelings over this, I produced a piece of teaching called *What is Man?* as part of my *Laying Deep Foundations*[183] series. I meant it entirely generically, but when presenting it to some educators from a Church of England background, I was taken to task over my use of the term by the women represented there.[184]

Many churches literalise this and in some Brethren assemblies, women are not allowed to say anything (not even to pray) in a meeting. We could go into numerous examples of this in both the Old and New Testaments. But concentrating only on these passages will give a very distorted idea of a biblical attitude to women.

---

[182] 1 Timothy chapter 2, verse 12

[183] http://www.amazon.com/What-Man-Laying-Deep-Foundations-ebook/dp/B005MQNYZK/ or http://www.amazon.co.uk/What-Man-Laying-Deep-Foundations-ebook/dp/B005MQNYZK/

[184] One problem is that in English, we have one word for meaning "mankind" and for a male person. In Greek, in which the New Testament was written, *anthropos* is used for man generically and *aner* (long *e*) for a male, so there was no confusion.

I cannot claim a massive knowledge of Middle-eastern cultures in biblical times, but I am sure that, in keeping with most of the world around them, they were times of very distinct male dominance. That was certainly true of the Israelites. And yet, there are several prominent women featured with one of them, Deborah, leading the nation.[185] We find Esther as a heroine during the exile of the Jews recorded in the book of Esther and another whole book about a Moabitess (with whom the Israelites were often at war) called Ruth who was an ancestor of Jesus. I very much doubt if this would have been normal in any of the cultures around. God called and used these women (and others) in the same way as he might have used men.

In the New Testament, we find Jesus being exceedingly counter-cultural. In John chapter 4, he is recorded as talking with a Samaritan woman. Jews had no dealings with Samaritans and it was absolutely not the "done thing" for a man to speak to a strange woman. His acceptance of women was demonstrated over and over again. Granted, all his closest disciples were men (women were not seen at the time as being able to be rabbis), but there was a large number of women among the extended group. In John chapter 11, verse 5 in the passage where Jesus is recorded as raising Lazarus from the dead, it says, *"Now Jesus loved Martha and her sister and Lazarus."* How unusual for the women to be mentioned first!

Then in the book of Acts, we find a husband and wife team of Bible teachers, When they are first mentioned, Aquila, the husband is mentioned first (we normally stick to that convention even today) but they are mentioned in two more verses and in both, Priscilla is

---

[185]   Judges chapters 4 & 5

mentioned before her husband. It seems she was probably the better teacher and took a lead role in teaching Apollo (a man) who later became one of Paul's prominent co-workers.[186] Priscilla and Aquila were good friends of Paul. Surely he must have known they were going against his instructions if he meant his statement to Timothy for women not to teach to be a general binding instruction for all time.

In addition, in 1 Corinthians chapter 11, Paul discusses the issue of submission of women and says women should have their heads covered while praying (in the meetings). Surely that also goes against his instruction to Timothy. Was he perhaps addressing a particular situation when he wrote to Timothy? That seems highly probable. He didn't know his letters would be recognised as scripture and misused by later generations.

The issue of submission is a "biggie" for some because of the negative connotation of servility. But that is in no way what submission means. In fact, submission is speaking about an attitude of love and husbands are called to love their wives as Christ loves the church. Loving means considering someone else's needs before your own; seeking to affirm and support them and desire the best for them. That is very similar to submission. Authority in the Bible is never seen as "lording it over" another. In fact church leaders are specifically told not to do that with those in their care.

I can quite understand someone concluding that God is misogynistic but that conclusion can only be from a reading of scripture that involves no in-depth understanding at all. It results from picking

---

[186] Acts chapter 18, verses 18 & 25-26

certain passages and ignoring others. We all know that is not the right way to evaluate anything.

Related to misogyny is another prejudice – racism. Is God racist? I deal with some of this when discussing the killing of the Amalekites below but we need to look at it in general terms here. God clearly tells his people not to mix with the other nations, not to have anything to do with their gods, not to intermarry and so on. Surely this is racist. It was this kind of attitude that was partly responsible for the development of apartheid. The attitude of Jews in Jesus' time to Gentiles was that they were all unclean, not to be touched and were sometimes called "dogs". Eating with Gentiles was forbidden – the exclusive Brethren today are very similar – they will not even eat with ordinary Brethren.

This apparent racism has to be seen against the background of the Old Testament. In spite of the fact that God had told the two nations of Israel and Judah not to mix with these other nations, they disobeyed him. The result was that they got into the vilest practices – like child sacrifice. Such was their depravity that God eventually brought first the Assyrians against the nation of Israel and then the Babylonians against the nation of Judah and they were both taken into exile. Israel ended up being absorbed into other nations but Judah (now called Jews) returned to the land much chastened. They were determined to ensure this never happened again and to obey God to the letter. That is why they developed such a killingly burdensome legalistic system and avoided contact with Gentiles like the plague. The pendulum swung to the opposite side.

However, if you look at God's promises to Abraham, you find that he said, *"In you will all the families of the earth be blessed."*[187] His offspring were originally supposed to be a blessing to others but they would not be so by taking on their vile practices. They had to be separate from that kind of activity – a bit difficult if you mix with people doing that kind of thing and their mixing resulted in pollution. When the Law was first given, the children of Israel were told not to do harm to any stranger (foreigner) living among them; in fact they were told *"you shall love him as yourself."*[188] So, instead of being a blessing and perhaps demonstrating a better way to live, they descended to the depths of the other nations.

But God's original intention was for them to be a blessing. In telling them not to mix with other nations, he was not being racist, just practical – and yes, to the extent of wiping out whole nations who would lead them into the horrible practices associated with their religions. God was not literally jealous of Baal but belief in this god/idol had the most devastating effect on its followers. I don't think we can equate this with natural selection, but if we think the violence of natural selection is perfectly all right, then this is no worse. I am not advocating this as being excusable on those grounds, by the way. I am saying that those who think purely in terms of natural selection are on shaky ground objecting to the slaughter by the Israelites that took place in those days.

Fast forward to the New Testament and we find Jesus apparently showing prejudice. *"It is not right to take the children's bread and throw it to the dogs,"*[189] referring to a Canaanite woman who had appealed

---

187 Genesis chapter 12, verse 3
188 Leviticus chapter 19, verses 33-34
189 Matthew chapter 15, verse 26

to him for help. However, when she responded by showing faith, he immediately helped her. I think he was challenging her to respond in faith and also, in a way, challenging others who were present. I mentioned above about his speaking to the Samaritan woman. That and his parable of the Good Samaritan were distinct indications of a non-racist attitude that challenged the Jews to the core.

Peter was still racist even after Jesus had ascended to heaven. He is recorded in Acts chapter 10 as having a vision of a sheet with all sorts of unclean animals descending and being told to kill and eat. He objected that nothing unclean had passed his lips (typical Jewish attitude of the time). God responded by saying he was not to call anything unclean that God called clean. He awoke and realised that God was referring to the Gentiles when some of them arrived and asked him to come and help a Roman centurion. Actually, later on he refused to eat with the Gentiles when there were Jews present and Paul had to rebuke him for his racist attitude.

So, far from being racist, God is reaching out to absolutely every person, no matter what their gender, race, nationality, colour, creed, age or any other factor that usually divides us. I can, with complete confidence, state that every person is welcome to him and is equal in his eyes.

I could go through the rest of Dawkins' long diatribe and show him to have misunderstood but I see no point. I deal a bit with homosexuality below but I need to return to one of his chief bugbears – teaching children to believe in God.

Children and belief

The likelihood of children ending up with a similar belief to that of their parents is quite high. Dawkins has shared with his readers his love for his daughter. Surely he would be upset if she decided to believe in God? It is natural for parents to want to share with their children their view of the truth and what the world is all about if they genuinely believe this to be true and therefore to the ultimate gain of their children. That is perfectly normal and, as a principle, is hard to fault.

The difference is that Dawkins says that while atheism is morally neutral (believing that there is probably no God because the atheist feels he or she has not sufficient evidence for God), belief in the Abrahamic God is inherently evil because of the evil that Dawkins sees in individual Christians and also in the perceived oppression that the Christian organisational church has exerted in history over what he feels are gullible believers.

Why did God permit the church at times to become so corrupt and oppressive as to give rise to, for example, the Inquisition with its witch-burnings? Why are fat-cat televangelists allowed to cream off the hard-won earnings of their admiring followers? What about the Crusades when the ostensibly laudable object of saving the mother city of Jerusalem from the "infidel" smack so obviously of material and geographical greed on the part of the European kings of England, France and Spain? And what about Christianity today when beneath the veneer of parish respectability, paedophile priests have not only been allowed to operate but have been positively protected in the interests of the reputation of the Church.

Once this cultural reverse-witch hunt has started, it seems there is no stopping the current revelations: nuns who bullied the prostitutes whom they "saved" into honest labour in the workhouse; slavery being revealed as ordained by God (ignoring the Christian motivation of Gladstone to abolish it).

We Christians are fair game and with each fresh revelation we groan complacently as we mutter things about original sin and the impossibility of total perfection of character in this life. Most recently of all, the twenty first century concept of "homophobia" has been used to hound the simple-minded fool who takes Leviticus and the writings of Paul, and the writer of Revelation, seriously, using the fact that Jesus never mentioned homosexuality as "proof" that the concept was cultural and therefore changeable like the Levitical food laws.

Obviously Jesus loves all sinners enough to die for each of them, but can we really second-guess what is the best way to live our lives? In a way I feel disappointed with Dawkins for jumping onto the anti-homophobia bandwagon by stating explicitly that atheism has no problem with homosexuality, Can he speak generally for atheists on this subject? As my friend Christina Biggs points out, surely if Dawkins had been honest he might have given a nod to the obvious scientific truth that if we all became exclusively homosexual tomorrow the human race would die out in a single generation. We might be near technologically to producing embryos from same-sex cells, but with the likely monetary cost to society (at least at the moment) it's hardly a sensible tactic for the human race as a whole to take.

Some Christians insist that homosexuality is anti-biblical; others equally strongly feel it is a legitimate expression of love. It's not the purpose of this book to argue one or the other but let's remember the well-known command from Jesus to "*judge not that you be not judged.*" Surely expressing love towards others whether or not you agree with them or their lifestyle is a "Christian" response.

The assumption on the part of many atheists (and certainly on the part of Richard Dawkins) is that religion should be removed and the world would be a far better place for it. John Lennon expressed this in his song *Imagine* where he paints a picture of a world where there was no belief in heaven or hell, no countries (presumably a one-world government) and no religion, no possessions, greed or hunger – just a brotherhood of man with everyone sharing. Dawkins speaks glowingly of the song (in the context of criticising some Christians for changing it). But the assumption in this is that it is religion, belief in heaven and hell, possessions and division into countries that is the cause of disharmony. But is it? Is it possible that it is something inherent in human nature that causes the evil we see – if we are honest – in every one of us?

CHAPTER 11

Is Monotheism the "Great Unmentionable Evil"?

In recent years there has been considerable media exposure of child abuse perpetrated by people in churches and children's homes run by churches. It has been mainly by Roman Catholics but is by no means limited to them. There can be no excuse for such behaviour.

However, many people brought up in my generation would find the statement that monotheism is *"the great unmentionable evil"* incredulous. One objection to becoming a Christian was that people thought they were "not good enough". It would not really have been thought possible to call Christianity evil. When I was at Bible College, I was asked in my second term to run a tiny little church in Dorking. We put on film evenings for children, thinking parents would be quite happy to let their children come along but many of them were not. In my naïveté I was amazed at this. Now, having experienced how manipulating some church leaders can be and with the recent scandals, I quite understand it.

No doubt Dawkins has all the above in mind as he attacks religion and calls it evil. But he also goes far beyond this. He quotes Gore Vidal: "*The great unmentionable evil at the center of our culture is monotheism. From a barbaric Bronze Age text known as the Old Testament, three anti-human religions have evolved – Judaism, Christianity, and Islam. These are sky-god religions. They are, literally, patriarchal – God is the Omnipotent Father – hence the loathing of women for 2,000 years in those countries afflicted by the sky-god and his earthly male delegates.*"[190]

"Anti-human religions" evolving from a "barbaric" Bronze Age text. "Sky-god religions"; "loathing of women for 2000 years" and so on. Evocative stuff indeed! Apart from the inaccuracy of saying Islam regards God as the Omnipotent Father (Muslims totally reject the concept of God as father), is this evidence-based? Certainly none is given, unless you accept Dawkins' highly subjective interpretation of these three religions as being "evidence". Listen to what he says:

> *The oldest of the three Abrahamic religions, and the clear ancestor of the other two, is Judaism: originally a tribal cult of a single fiercely unpleasant God, morbidly obsessed with sexual restrictions, with the smell of charred flesh, with his own superiority over rival gods and with the exclusiveness of his chosen desert tribe.*[191]

Now, I can understand how someone, after a cursory look at the Old Testament, could come up with this interpretation but it is clearly a "view" because it is seen very differently by Jews and Christians

---

190   "The God Delusion" page 58
191   Ibid.

(and, I imagine, by Muslims). Surely the people who have "seen it through" in attested personal relationship with God might be more expert on God's ways and means and motivations than people who insist on viewing faith solely from external appearances based on their presuppositions.

Yes, he does regard Christianity as a "*less ruthlessly monotheistic sect of Judaism*,"[192] though Islam is one that reverts to the uncompromising monotheism of the Jewish original and that also adds a powerful ideology of military conquest to spread the faith. I suppose I should be grateful to him for treating Christianity more kindly but he goes on to speak of the Crusades and Christianity also being spread by the sword.

I cannot get away with saying that this is all nonsense. He has a strong point. Israel was involved in conquering numerous other tribes in Canaan after they emerged from slavery in Egypt. And God told them to do it!

But I have tried to tackle this question in chapter 10. Other authors speak of the way in which Israel is a kind of parable of what God means about purity and what the Bible terms as "holiness" – the idea that God wants his people to come away from collaboration and compromise with the despicable activities of the surrounding nations like the child sacrifice mentioned in 2 Samuel. Obviously the genocide God ordered of these barbaric tribes is not very humane, but in the interests of forging an at least temporary showcase of a good and just society with its pinnacle in the beginning of the reign of Solomon, maybe it was "the only way" to then demonstrate the

---

[192]   Ibid.

necessity for sending his only Son as a sacrifice for the sins of the world. Surely if there was an efficient way to produce a good society even with a bit of judicious euthanasia, God would have taken that route rather than the literally suicidal one of going in person to sort mankind out. Could we see the whole of the history recorded in the Bible "logbook" as a kind of demonstration of the necessity for God to die in the place of mankind who rebelled against him?

I am not going to comment much on Islam, mainly because, as a non-Muslim, I don't feel properly qualified to do so. I am aware that there are conflicts of view among Muslims on the place of violence in their religion. Some believe the Qur'an clearly teaches violent jihad against non-Muslims; others insist it does not; that jihad is purely a personal battle against evil.

But yes, the history of Christianity after the death of Jesus is perhaps equally steeped in violence. The crusades of the 11th to 13th centuries were to me, a most horrible distortion of Christianity. They were most likely fought for political reasons: to try and regain access to Jerusalem and stop the spread of Islam by the Seljuk Turks. Granted, they were sparked partly by the destruction of Christian "holy" sites and by the persecution of Christians but I personally cannot imagine how anyone could be a genuine Christian and do such a thing.

But C.S. Lewis has attempted to answer even this hot chestnut, by saying that at the very least, the dedication of the individual Crusaders could be genuine and that sometimes, just as in the Old Testament and arguably as recently as World War Two, physical violence, conducted with decorum in the "rules of war" can even be seen to be a glorious thing, Certainly if there is no life after death it becomes the most horrible cruelty to pretend otherwise to the hapless soldier (and Muslim suicide bomber), but again, can we really double-guess God's opinion on this? Even Jesus, who spoke of leaving his peace with the disciples, talks in terms of the end times being a period of "the sword" with brother set against brother.

However, this participation in what is essentially evil is not limited to the times of the crusades. There are "Christians" crusading still. The Westboro Baptist Church in America, that I mentioned before, is an example of hate-filled attitudes against everyone they consider to be homosexual or anyone who has the temerity to stand up for them. Homosexuals are not their only target, either. They hate Jews, Muslims, Roman Catholics, the media and an enormous list of whole countries – probably virtually every political leader in the world. In their defence, I must add that I am not aware of them indulging in physical violence but their utterances are pretty inflammatory.

However, if you were looking at examples of Christianity, knowing nothing about it, and came across this vile filth (and, believe me, what they say is filth), you could be excused for thinking that it represented the general attitude of Christians to homosexuals, especially if you looked no further. I would hope, however, that you would look further and find that this is a complete distortion even though they appear to be evangelical Christians. Their entire emphasis is on what God hates, not on the love of God, which is emphasised by virtually all Christians. This may well be an illustration of what Jesus was talking about when he said, "*why do you see the speck that is in your brother's eye, but do not notice the log that is in your own eye?*"[193] The book of Proverbs declares, *"Hate is a cause of violent acts but all errors are covered up by love."*[194]

As I said before, surely the better course is to love people whether you agree with their lifestyle or not. This "church" is not an illustration of Christian attitudes. Surely Dawkins *cannot* genuinely believe that this is the kind of morality inspired by religious faith or that it represents in any way normal behaviour among Christians and yet, amazingly, he uses it to insinuate that this is the case.

Interestingly though, while Dawkins feels that sexual abuse of children is clearly evil especially if it results in physical harm, he seems to think that teaching them religious doctrine is far worse abuse. He mentions how a Roman Catholic girl had been fondled by a priest at the age of seven, but had also been told a friend who had died had gone to hell because she was a Protestant and she felt, as an adult, that the latter was far worse abuse.[195]

Now, that may well be true and we know psychological abuse can not only last a lifetime but affect future generations. I would agree with the fact that much church teaching has and probably still does cause damage. It would not surprise me if I found some teaching I had given had hurt someone. Going through life never hurting anyone is virtually impossible, no matter how pure our motives may be. And lots of church doctrine has been hurtful. I could think of the legalistic teaching in some churches today and say it is harmful. There can be no doubt that we have all hurt someone unless we have lived our lives in total seclusion.

---

193   Matthew chapter 7, verse 3
194   Proverbs chapter 10, verse 12 (BBE)
195   "The God Delusion" page 356

Dawkins talks about the "exclusive brethren" and their harmful teaching. I believe he is right. They are an example of an ultra-legalistic group which is a travesty of the gospel of grace taught by Jesus and the apostles. People get things wrong; we all get aspects of our beliefs wrong, atheist or believer. I would certainly not defend the Roman Catholic teaching mentioned above nor would I defend the Protestant equivalent. It is harmful and it is wrong. But that is not what the Bible teaches. It does include all sorts of things that are very hard to understand as I have mentioned above, but a lot of denominationally biased teaching is found absolutely nowhere in the Bible and we need to be aware of that before jumping to conclusions.

Persecution of Christians

But Jesus is clear about one thing: quite apart from the violence that Christians may indulge in wrongly or justifiably, one thing is predictable: Christians will be persecuted, sometimes to the death, and this persecution has got worse and not better with time. When he sent the twelve disciples out to heal, he told them:

> I am sending you out like sheep among wolves. Therefore be as shrewd as snakes and as innocent as doves. Be on your guard against men; they will hand you over to the local councils and flog you in their synagogues. On my account you will be brought before governors and kings as witnesses to them and to the Gentiles. But when they arrest you, do not worry about what to say or how to say it. At that time you will be given what to say, for it will not be you speaking, but the Spirit of your Father speaking through you.

Brother will betray brother to death, and a father his child; children will rebel against their parents and have them put to death. All men will hate you because of me, but he who stands firm to the end will be saved.

Do not be afraid of those who kill the body but cannot kill the soul. Rather, be afraid of the One who can destroy both soul and body in hell. Do not suppose that I have come to bring peace to the earth. I did not come to bring peace, but a sword. For I have come to turn a man against his father, a daughter against her mother, a daughter-in-law against her mother-in-law – a man's enemies will be the members of his own household. Anyone who loves his father or mother more than me is not worthy of me; anyone who loves his son or daughter more than me is not worthy of me; and anyone who does not take his cross and follow me is not worthy of me.

Whoever finds his life will lose it, and whoever loses his life for my sake will find it.[196]

This is, indeed, hard to understand. Jesus, who came to bring peace, seems to be saying he brings a sword and that he will turn members of families against each other. I think it could be said there is some hyperbole reflected in the Bible, but an understanding of the radical message Jesus brought would show that this conflict will be a consequence of people turning to follow him and the reactions of those in their families and outside them.

---

[196] Matthew chapter 10, verses 16 - 39

Jesus does not say we should take up arms against our fellow human, rather that the followers of Jesus will be persecuted by the enemies of God in the terrestrial future. And regrettably this is what I think we can see happening – not just in words in the media but in violence against Christian believers in countries all over the world. I'm not saying we should take this violence against Christians as proof of Christian innocence and in vindication of Christian faith – to Jesus it is a simple fact that we will be persecuted and that by warning us of this we are not to be discouraged but to hold on tight in our faith.

Moral codes

When it comes to moral codes, I must say I agree with Dawkins on a large number of issues. It doesn't take much intelligence to realise that the vast majority of people in the world would subscribe to a moral code that had some broad agreement. Virtually everyone of any religion or none would agree that murder, theft, rape etc. are utterly wrong. No one really likes a cheat or a con-artist. Not even con-artists like being conned. Apart from a few grossly perverted individuals, no one wants to see children abused physically, mentally or sexually.

Richard Dawkins, I think, is quite correct when he insists that Britain is not a Christian country and that the proportion of Christians is completely different from what the census would indicate. I am not sure how we could have a very accurate assessment of actual numbers of "committed" Christians, which, in my view, is the only genuine type of Christian. I think he would agree with me on that. But how do you frame a question to determine those kinds of data? In fact, I don't believe Britain has ever been a "Christian" country, though, in the past, being a "Christian" was probably a far more acceptable thing than it is now.

Novels such as Jane Austen's expose the hypocrisy that ran right at the root of "respectable" church-attending, middle class society. Charles Dickens was the most vehement of the whistle-blowers, exposing the scam of the work-houses and the perhaps invisible humiliation to which the prosperous subjected their less-well-endowed fellow humans. High moral codes have never been the exclusive domain of Christians.

Dawkins' view of the morality of religions

As I said, I am going to concentrate particularly on Christian matters as I do not feel qualified to speak on behalf of others and it is largely Christianity that Dawkins attacks so vehemently as that is the religion he knows best, having been brought up in a "church-going" society.

Despite the horror stories of the barbarities ordered by "Christian" generals in the crusades and the witch-hunts and burnings of the Inquisition, I would still say that anyone with any modicum of knowledge about the sweep of social history and of what the Christian church has done over the centuries would read chapters 6 to 9 of Dawkins' book and find their mouth dropping open at the stream of accusations he makes and his total lack of recognition of the massive amount of good that has emerged from the work of the church, particularly in Britain but also in many other parts of the world. I get the distinct impression that he is motivated entirely by his emotions here rather than by any objectivity.

One point I do find interesting is that he describes as "unchristian" the attitudes of some Christians who nastily attack those they perceive as their enemies.[197] If he feels that religion is so evil, why does he describe bad attitudes as "unchristian"? Without overtly acknowledging it, he clearly has some idea equating "Christian" with having a good attitude. And indeed Dawkins said in 2006 in the social media and on the website of his Foundation for Reason and Science, that he views the actual person of Jesus and his teachings as very laudable. There is a post on the old Richard Dawkins Foundation site[198] where he says that he himself would wear a T-shirt with "Atheists for Jesus" printed on it! It's just the Christian Church that Dawkins accuses of being so evil.

The fact is that Christians have been the drivers behind a mass of initiatives (notably the abolition of slavery by Gladstone and then the abolition of the workhouse in 1929 demonstrably the work of Christian activists) to bring about better conditions in society for those who have had no voice over centuries and still work today to do the same. I would say those people have been motivated to do what they have done because of their realisation of the love of God for others and have found that love moving them to action.

The most famous examples of modern times are Mother Teresa in Calcutta and Nelson Mandela (whose mother was a devout Christian) in South Africa with his attitude of forgiveness to those who had oppressed him so cruelly. However, there are many charities doing a whole lot of wonderful work and you probably don't even

---

197 "The God Delusion" page 241
198 old.richarddawkins.net/articles/20-atheists-for-jesus

know they are Christian – because they just serve others without saying they have any church connections.

Altruism

Richard Dawkins, as an evolutionary biologist, expounds the hypothesis, especially in *The Selfish Gene*, that altruism is genetically based. He says:

> *There are circumstances – not particularly rare – in which genes ensure their own selfish survival by influencing organisms to behave altruistically. Those circumstances are now fairly well understood and they fall into two main categories. A gene that programs individual organisms to favour their genetic kin is statistically likely to benefit copies of itself. Such a gene's frequency can increase in the gene pool to the point where kin altruism becomes the norm. Being good to one's own children is the obvious example, but it is not the only one. Bees, wasps, ants, termites and, to a lesser extent, certain vertebrates such as naked mole rats, meerkats and acorn woodpeckers, have evolved societies in which elder siblings care for younger siblings (with whom they are likely to share the genes for doing the caring). In general, as my late colleague W. D. Hamilton showed, animals tend to care for, defend, share resources with, warn of danger, or otherwise show altruism towards close kin because*

of the statistical likelihood that kin will share copies of the same genes.[199]

Now, in many ways, I am sure he is correct in this – there is no doubt animals (including humans) will vigorously protect their offspring and symbiotic relationships are very common in numerous types of organism. Personally, I would not call this altruism. However, I am convinced that genuine altruism is demonstrated and not only by humans. There have been documented cases of dolphins protecting humans stranded at sea. Perhaps this is due to some genetic quirk, but dolphins are extraordinarily intelligent animals that often have an affinity with humans and I feel there is quite a likelihood of their displaying behaviour and actions that may have an altruistic element to them.

His view that every single action we carry out is something to do with gaining a selective advantage, I feel, is simply an unrealistic verdict on the recorded actions of countless people, believers or not, through history.

In *The God Delusion* he classifies four types of altruism: "kin altruism" mentioned above, "reciprocal altruism" – a sort of "I'll scratch your back; you scratch mine" illustrated in nature by symbiotic relationships, a desire for a "reputation for generosity" and "conspicuous generosity" whereby the person (or animal) being generous gains a higher status in the society. He suggests the "Good Samaritan" tendencies within people might be a misfiring of a

---

[199] "The God Delusion" page 247

beneficial (to the individual) tendency to help others unrelated in any way and feel sympathy for others[200].

I am convinced that altruism is far more than that. People put their lives at risk to save others totally unrelated to them or even to save an animal unknown to them. No, I don't think you can explain all this by natural selection and the self-interest of those molecules called genes as it just does not fit the historical evidence. And the belief that this is in fact the underlying reality I find a deeply cynical and untenable attitude that would simply not stand the test of time in a real situation, whether in a marriage or in society as a whole. How does Dawkins arrive at the conclusion that this must be the real "truth" of all human relationships when our feelings so obviously aspire and sometimes attain to really kind, decent and forgiving behaviour?

I am sure many Christians have experienced the phenomenon of being given a gift (not in any sort of Secret Santa situation) completely and utterly anonymously. Many of them will have been the benefactor. The giver does not want to be identified and usually never is. How do we categorise that? Trying to attribute this to some genetic quirk I find offensive. I don't believe any of Dawkins' types of altruism are actually altruism at all – even by definition. If that is all he knows, I feel extremely sorry for him!

But let's go on and look at the question of atheism - is it evil or is it morally just as good as Christianity - or better?

---

[200] Ibid. page 252

CHAPTER 12

Atheism, Ethics and Evil

The evils of atheism

I would never claim that atheism **causes** someone to be evil. I have many atheist friends and colleagues and some of them I hold in very high regard. They are fine examples of humanity. I value their opinions and I highly value them as people. They have a high moral code.

Dawkins does not suggest that all atheists are good, either, to his credit. He discusses Hitler and Stalin. I feel his assessment of Hitler is probably quite good. He explains that he was sometimes seen as a "Christian" and sometimes as an atheist. With many other Christians I would say he most certainly was not a Christian, whatever he claimed, although he called himself a Roman Catholic. I think we could say without much controversy that he was a straight-forward megalomaniac, concerned only with himself and used everyone for his own perverted ends. He was, according to accounts of his former followers, clinically mad, being irrationally suspicious of everyone near him and trusting no-one and in the end committing the ultimate act of despair in suicide. I can't believe that someone with any awe of God could justify the actions attributed to Hitler, even though he used the apparently anti-Semitic passages in the gospels to justify his genocide of the Jews. That is entirely typical of people like that. His character had nothing whatsoever to do with being either a Roman Catholic or an atheist.

Dawkins admits that Stalin was an atheist but said his atheism had nothing to do with his being evil. There were, undoubtedly, aspects to Stalin's character that were similar to Hitler's but I believe there was also some idealism in him. He was a Marxist and Marx decried religion, saying it was "the opium of the masses". Communism (a form of Marxism) was militantly atheistic (and still is in places where it rules, e.g. in China). I cannot think of any system that has been more brutal in modern times in persecuting believers of all types as well as political adversaries and it has done so with a clearly stated atheistic agenda. However, that of course does not mean that atheism itself *causes* evil. Countless atheists are perfectly decent people who would never dream of perpetrating such atrocities. To claim that religion *causes* evil is equally misguided.

Dawkins' discussion on morality

Dawkins' verdict on a number of studies on morality and responsibility comparing the views of atheists and believers is that, *"the main conclusion of Hauser and Singer's study was that there is no statistically significant difference between atheists and religious believers in making these judgements. This seems compatible with the view, which I and many others hold, that we do not need God in order to be good – or evil.*"[201] It's worth noting here that he also suggests that religion *causes* people to become evil – a slight contradiction of this statement and, as I said above, as misguided as saying that atheism *causes* people to become evil.

On page 262, Dawkins quotes Sam Harris in his "Letter to a Christian", who shows crime statistics from the various states of the USA. These statistics demonstrate that "Red" states (Republican) on the whole have a considerably higher crime rate than do the "Blue" states (Democrat). Harris comments that *"while political party affiliation in the United States is not a perfect indicator of religiosity, it is no secret that the 'red [Republican] states' are primarily red due to the overwhelming influence of conservative Christians."* This would seem to back up Dawkins' claim mentioned in chapter 9 that atheism makes for a healthier mind. Harris is right to point out that political affiliation is not a perfect indicator of religiosity, but with the statistics quoted, I think it is of some significance. But what significance?[202]

Republicans, if they are Christians, tend to be "conservative". Conservatism (politically and to some extent religiously) tends to emphasise the individual, whereas liberalism and socialism tend to emphasise society. While it is only partially true, I think we could say that people who are politically conservative are more likely to be "out for themselves" than those who are politically liberal. Christianity emphasises individual responsibility and also a caring society.

---

[201] "The God Delusion" page 258

[202] It is possible to show that there is a close relationship of divorce statistics with eating certain foods but clearly there is absolutely no real correlation!

Individual Christians may tend toward one side or the other and not realise the importance of both. Democrat Christians will see the importance of caring for others; Republicans are more likely to see the importance of standing on your own feet and not sponging off others. I would think people who emphasise the individual are more likely to think of themselves rather than others and that, in some people, could make them more likely to commit crime.

Dawkins even suggests the figures could be due to greater intelligence on the part of atheists! There is no evidence here that it is Christians (conservative or liberal) who are committing these crimes so I think to draw any conclusion from this is spurious to say the least. Personally I would say the likelihood of a genuine committed Christian committing crimes is very low. Of course there is a likelihood of a criminal (especially a petty criminal) having a lower intelligence than average but if that is the case, they probably are not going to think too deeply about morality or anything else and they are every bit as likely to be unthinkingly Christian or unthinkingly atheist. Dawkins seems to ignore (or be blind to) the fact that atheism is not limited to intelligent people. There are bound to be countless people who do not believe there is a god but would not label themselves as atheist.

There may well be some who would call themselves Christian committing these crimes. Can we therefore blame Christianity (or Christ) for making them more likely to commit crime? That is, quite frankly, a ridiculous notion. It's tantamount to blaming someone's death on a medicine that was supposed to heal them but to which their body did not respond or that they did not take properly.

There is an idea (is this a meme?) doing the rounds that religious belief somehow takes the real virtue out of decent and kind, even sacrificial behaviour, as all the motives are put down to self-interest in a cushy place in the afterlife – the famous "pie in the sky when you die".[203]

Actually, Dawkins has somewhat confused ethics with morals but leaving that aside, I would very largely agree with him over the following though I disagree with the spirit with which he views it. He quotes someone (I know not who) in saying, *"if there is no God, why be good?"* and challenges this with, *"do you really mean to tell me the only reason you try to be good is to gain God's approval and reward, or to avoid his disapproval and punishment? That's not morality, that's just sucking up, apple-polishing, looking over your shoulder at the great surveillance camera in the sky, or the still small wiretap inside your head, monitoring your every move, even your every base thought."*[204]

I believe he is absolutely right to question such a complacent attitude. And, sadly, there are possibly millions of Christians who are motivated to do good simply because they are afraid of being bad. That was precisely the Pharisaical attitude that Jesus condemned. And I will say that he is more perceptive in this than are the many Christians who think that way. The apostle Paul found this to be one of the major problems in the churches in Galatia and he wrote at length about it. I believe legalism, as this is called, is actually an affront to the grace of God. Dawkins has got this right.

---

[203] Incredibly to modern ears, this exact phrase originates from the actual wording of a line in a 1911 Salvation Army hymn "In the Sweet Bye and Bye" but forever after parodied mercilessly by anyone who hated the "charity" of the Salvation Army or any Christian church.

[204] "The God Delusion" page 259

I believe he is also right in pointing out that the ethics of atheists can be just as good as those of Christians. He says this shows you do not need God to be good. But there is another way of looking at this. The Bible actually teaches us that mankind was created "in the image of God", i.e. reflecting his nature, so we should not be surprised if we find similar ethics among atheists and Christians and indeed amongst the majority of people of all persuasions.

When Calvin spoke of the "total depravity of man", he was using it in a theological sense. I don't believe he was saying that man without God is utterly given over to evil; that all non-Christians are the most terrible criminally-minded brutes imaginable. Calvin was an intelligent man. He had eyes and could see what people were like. Rather, he was saying that, because of sin, people have no means within them to make themselves acceptable to God. There is nothing that we could bring to him to say, "This makes me worthy of being accepted".

The only thing that a Christian can rely on to rescue them when in front of God's judgement seat is "the cross of Christ" – to rely only on the proposition that by Jesus dying and rising to life he had overturned death and made clear the way back to God. Emphatically, a Christian is not relying on decent actions, however well motivated: the true Christian will recognise that all our apparent righteousness in the words of Isaiah chapter 64 verse 6, foreseeing this day, "*is like filthy rags*." Read the rest of that chapter of Isaiah for a very fair exposition of the role of Jesus, the "Lamb of God", in bringing this about. "*By his stripes we are healed*" is the very succinct phrase for this concept used earlier in Isaiah chapter 53 verse 5 and set to music by Handel in his "Messiah", however insulted our pride may be at the necessity for such an abject stance.

So, while Dawkins' attempt to prove that "we do not need God to be good" has some truth to it, he has actually missed the point.

Ethics and morality

In his discussions of the similarities of Christians' and atheists' views on ethics (which he terms morals), Dawkins goes into details on what would be the right thing to do under all sorts of circumstances[205]. He concludes that the similarities can be attributed to our Darwinian past rather than to religion, but as I said above, it is something we should expect from what the Bible says as well. Ethics is a massive subject and Dawkins only mentions a hypothetical moral dilemma posed by Harvard biologist Marc Hauser following a line of thought suggested by moral philosophers. This is a common way to tackle ethical discussions and has certain similarities to the deliberations of Jewish teachers in formulating the "traditions of the elders" prescribing and proscribing how Jews should behave in all sorts of circumstances, designed to ensure they did not break the Mosaic Law.

This approach was what was castigated by Jesus as it failed to tackle the real issues of righteousness that, he said, were what was really at the heart of the Law – love, mercy and justice.

---

[205] Ibid. pages 254-258

No one gets it right all the time

As I said above, virtually every reasonable person on this planet would broadly agree on basic ethics. I should imagine (I am not going to assume it) that Richard Dawkins would agree that adultery is wrong. Most people would. But how many have committed adultery? We agree it is wrong to steal but how many of us have taken something from our work place or gone off sick when we're not? We hate anyone lying to us but how squeaky clean are we ourselves?

Even if we pass the ethical test, the Bible is not really concerned about a system of morals or ethics or of externally "right" behaviour. It is concerned about inward righteousness and purity of the heart – the intentions, the inadvertent judgement and above all hypocrisy, the mismatch between words, thoughts and actions excellently explained by James, the half-brother of Jesus himself. This might seem to be unfairly picky of God – after all, how are we to tell what people are thinking and why would we care so long as others behave decently in society and keep their noses clean? But as we will see, God is the ultimate perfectionist – Jesus said, "*be perfect even as your heavenly Father is perfect.*"[206] Why is this necessary for a reasonably well-functioning society?

---

[206] Matthew chapter 5, verse 48

CHAPTER 13

Morality, Ethics and Righteousness

Why is law necessary?

As we all agree on basic ethics, we would expect to find a world where peace and justice reign and there is no need for laws, wouldn't we? But we don't.

When my children were very small, they occasionally would not eat their food. I sometimes used a tactic that I am sure many parents have used. I would tell them *not* to eat their food because I wanted it. For a while the tactic worked until they worked out my duplicity.

The Israelites were given the Law. They had a moral code but they also had a problem. They could not keep it. We all know the story. Having a notice that says, "KEEP OFF THE GRASS" guarantees that someone will disobey it. So why have the notice? Because law is still needed. Without it, chaos would reign.

I believe Dawkins is absolutely right to say that we should all do the right thing anyway and should not need rules to tell us. However, much of the Mosaic Law was given for the right governing of a society that was supposed to be operating in obedience to God. I say "supposed to be" because it is patently obvious that they failed to live up to that standard. That is not an indication, however, that the Law was not needed; it shows how necessary law is.

In the book of Judges chapters 6 and 21, it says that there was no king in Israel (and so no law, presumably) and "*everyone did that which was right in their own eyes.*" If you read those chapters, you will see that neither of those were very happy times. Some pretty horrible things happened, even though people thought they were doing what was right. Of course, having a king was still no guarantee. Some of them ruled just to suit themselves. They ignored the laws God had given the nation through Moses. Our modern laws, though originally based around those same laws, have now digressed massively from them. We may think that many of them are nonsense, but I cannot imagine many people agreeing that none of them are needed.

Laws are needed not for those who obey them but for those who don't.

Freedom, maturity and law

The apostle Paul, writing to believers in Galatia, says "*so then, the law has become our guardian until Christ came, in order that we might be justified by faith.*"[207] Other versions say the law is our "schoolmaster"

---

[207] Galatians chapter 3, verse 24 ESV

to lead us to Christ. The schoolmaster in those days was the one who would take a naughty truant by the ear and make him/her go to school. This gives me the distinct impression that the law was meant for those who had not come to maturity – a maturity that is only achieved through faith. It had the purpose of showing the Israelites what God's strict requirements were but also of showing them that they were incapable of keeping them in their own strength.

Atheists make quite a big deal about atheism being the mature attitude, relying on evidence, particularly scientific evidence and having left behind the childish concepts of a god. Religious faith is seen as belonging to the less mature times before we had scientific explanations; it occupied the gaps in our knowledge but the gaps are constantly closing, so the time has come to discard this along with belief in fairies.

Stages of development

When I was doing my teaching diploma, I studied, for one tutorial presentation, the question of moral development in children. Having searched the internet, I think the name of the author of one excellent book I read was N.J. Bull. The book was called *Moral Development* and Bull set out the stages of development as:

1. Anomy[208] – "no law". This is the small child stage, where there is zero understanding of morality – just a realisation of parental love,

---

[208] The "nomy" part of each of these words is from the Greek "nomos" = law.

2. Heteronomy – "law from outside". Parents start to impose rules and the child may or may not understand the reasons for them, but they just have to obey,

3. Socionomy – "law from others" – e.g. peer group. The child (probably a teenager) does things to please peers or society,

4. Autonomy – "law from within". Generally the adult stage, where a person lives with the conviction of their own heart having thought through why they act in certain ways; they may or may not have their parents' values but if they have, the values will now be their own.

As I looked at this, it struck me that this paralleled the development of Israel. The stages equated to:

(1) Abraham and the unconditional covenant,

(2) Moses and the covenant of law,

(3) occupation of the land and the time of the kings when they followed more and more the ways of the surrounding nations and

(4) the new covenant in Christ.

Evidence for all of this can be found in the Old Testament, including of course the foreshadowing and prophesies of the new covenant. How likely is it that we would find this in this ancient writing produced by many authors over more than two thousand years? Possible, but highly improbable if this was simply made up.

Many people when they grow up actually stay in the third stage (socionomy). This is true of some Christians, of some believers in other faiths and of some atheists. A concentration on saying "most people believe 'x'" as in "the vast majority of top scientists are atheists" could indicate that someone is basing the validity of their belief on what others believe. While it may be useful in knowing that what you believe is shared by others who are sensible in their considerations, that is hardly an indication of maturity. The truth is never determined by a majority vote.

If you are an atheist and you take exception to this, I am sorry to offend you but you seriously need to consider what you say. Socionomy is, indeed, an advance over heteronomy but it is not full maturity. I imagine many stuck in stage 3 think they have arrived and are mature because they have moved beyond stages 1 & 2.

Now, I am not implying that all atheists are stuck in the third stage. Some hold their belief purely from their own conviction. However, I know virtually no atheist who really appreciates that Christian believers can, and often do, have a mature autonomous faith. All those I have come across erroneously think that Christian faith represents stages 1 or 2. And that is simply untrue.

Similarly, Christians who base their beliefs on the utterances of their favourite preacher or author are immature. There is nothing wrong with this in the early part of the Christian life because you need teaching from others as a child needs teaching. However, unless it progresses to belief that is your own conviction, where the opinions of others are useful for checking and informing your own thinking, then you stay in an immature stage of thinking.

As I pointed out in the Introduction, I went through a quasi-atheist stage – in my struggle to come to terms with a god who was clearly "not there" from any sort of scientific viewpoint. However, as I grew up, I was able to look beyond and understand that, while my childish belief was completely inadequate and science could, potentially, explain everything to do with matter etc., yet God was nothing like I had imagined or had struggled to understand. I grew up more than my "young man" phase and discovered an understanding of God that was much more coherent than anything I thought I had worked out in that quasi-atheist phase. What I have now is not determined by anyone else's belief of whatever persuasion. It is "mine".

Do we do what we know is right?

Getting back to morality and our inability to do what we really know is right, I have to say this is still a difficult concept to believe in such a civilised society as ours in Western Europe where the majority of children are still brought up in a loving home and therefore tend to be fairly well behaved citizens, save the occasional "little" indulgences. But the story is very different in broken homes – somehow the infidelity of one or both parents has rebounded on the children and as a result these young people can become unpredictable in their actions, The predominantly children's "riots" between 6th and 11th August 2011 in many cities in the UK sent shockwaves through middle-class society as even the sons and daughters of the well-off were "carried away" and committed theft and arson that their parents could never have dreamed possible.

I do wonder if the perceived predominance of black teenagers in the violence is related to that most shameful of episodes in British history of enslaving the African tribes-people whom their leaders cynically sold to the colonialists, leading to a deep sense of de-humanisation and lack of value. Yet this has not prevented the explosion of Christianity in Africa and the Caribbean, where the "negro spirituals" have identified with the Israelites in slavery in Egypt and positively embraced the promise of heaven to the oppressed. There has always in the Bible been the utter determination of God to lift the oppressed and to cast down the proud in heart.

It seems insulting to self-respecting intellectuals, but in fact as the privileged class we really do start at a disadvantage with God and, to use a biblical injunction, need to humble ourselves that we might be lifted. Is this humility anathema to atheists?

Can Christians claim to be morally better than non-believers?

When I first went to Bible College, I expected to find a bunch of people dedicated to God, showing love to one another, serving each other and keen to serve the surrounding community. I thought I would be going into an atmosphere where other people's good attitudes would rub off on me. Imagine my shock when I discovered they were just like me and no better than many who would not claim any belief in God. The sad fact is that many (probably the majority of) Christians do not seem to discover the fact that they cannot be good in their own strength. So they battle on and fail.

The problem with a view of Christian life that is focussed on our deeds and an over-concern about our spiritual health is that it is feeding exactly what is the problem – an emphasis on self. It doesn't work. So how is it possible to say that Christians are better than anyone else?

I and many others would say that is missing the point. As far as morals are concerned, I would want to see if a person becomes (and continues to become) a better person if they genuinely commit (unpalatable though that word may be to some people) their life to Christ. There are many who claim to be "Christians" because they were brought up in a "churchy" way but who have never made a whole-hearted commitment to Christ. I would only expect to see a transformed life in the case of those Christians who are truly committed to him – i.e. they hand over their lives to him and cease striving to appear good. And, sadly, I don't think they make up the majority of those who call themselves Christians.

When I look at my own life, if I am no different in my attitudes (affecting my thoughts, words and deeds) from the way I was a year ago, I have not been following Christ. And if I don't change for the better over the next year, it will mean I have been sitting back, and will probably have gone backwards. The Christian life is either dynamic or it is dead. It means having a transformed life, or perhaps I should say a being-transformed life.

As I said earlier, I agree with Richard Dawkins that a large number of people in Britain who say they are Christians are, in fact, not.

The apostle John, in his gospel, said "*but to all who did receive him, who believed in his name, he gave the right to become children of God, who were born, not of blood nor of the will of the flesh nor of the will of man but of God.*"[209] This strongly suggests to me that the only thing that truly makes someone a Christian is if they have "received" Christ. It has nothing to do with being born into a Christian family

---

[209] John chapter 1, verse 12-13 (ESV)

(not of blood); it's not to do with working it out. The will of the flesh, I think, refers to our minds, which are sometimes called the "flesh" in the New Testament, meaning a mind unaffected by Christ.

Being a Christian has nothing to do with what someone else wants for you (the will of man). It is to do with an encounter with God. Judging whether or not someone is a Christian is, therefore, a difficult matter. It certainly cannot be determined by a census. Ultimately only God and the person concerned really know the truth of the matter.

Having said that, I quite understand those who are not Christians looking indiscriminately at those who say they are, observing their morality and judging it to be either no better or worse than anyone else. Of course, a great many of these people are probably not Christians at all. Some people "become Christians" because they feel it might further their opportunities or gain them favour with a particular person. Some may simply want to belong to a nice group of people. Others may have a more sinister reason.

Christians and child abuse

So, how about the abuse of children I mentioned earlier? A natural conclusion one can come to from this is that the Roman Catholic religion somehow *causes* a person to start abusing children. But is this the truth? The vast majority of RC priests do **not** abuse children. I believe that the requirement for RC priests to be single and celibate is wrong. It is based on a misunderstanding of the position of priests in the church and in relation to Christ and it is completely unbiblical although I do understand the argument that it frees them to give more attention to those in their care (and the apostle Paul spoke of the advantage of not marrying so that the believer could be "all-out" for God[210]). But I am not trying to argue that point here. What I am saying is that this requirement gives opportunity to some men who have paedophilic tendencies to get into a position where they are trusted and can indulge their warped fantasies freely. It does not *cause* them to abuse children.

If we were going to assume that Roman Catholicism causes priests to abuse children, we would also have to assume that the teaching profession does the same simply because there have been a number of cases of sexual abuse by teachers. That assumption is obviously stupid.

Once this kind of behaviour becomes rife, the tendency of the leaders of the church is to try and bury the behaviour and keep it secret at all costs, believing that it is in the greater interest that the reputation of the Church is maintained rather than having any real respect for a transcendent God from whom nothing is hidden. As a result the deception starts to ensnare everyone and the real victims are, of course, the children. Clearly this is wrong – very wrong, but belief in God cannot be blamed for such wrong-doing. Rather it is sin that has not been addressed in those responsible.

It may be true that a person's "faith" has failed to change their actions in any way but that is only because they have failed to respond in a genuine way to the grace (a small word with a wealth

---

[210] 1 Corinthians chapter 7, verses 32 & 33

of meaning) of God. Faith only works if you respond to God's grace. As a poster I saw recently said, "Dreams only work if you do!"

If we were to assume that religion causes evil, we would have to conclude that atheism is about the worst cause of evil ever, having witnessed the desperate evils of communist governments over a long period of time.

However, I have already argued that atheism does not *cause* people to become evil, even if it is sometimes the motivation for their specific evil. People do evil because there is a tendency within each one of us to do what we actually know is wrong. The Christian theological term for this is "sin". You may choose to call it something else (e.g. moral weakness) but that makes no difference to the existence of this tendency within every human being on this planet.

CHAPTER 14

Sin and that Offensive Transforming Cross

The offence of the cross

On page 285 of *The God Delusion*, Dawkins describes the cross as:

> *A new sadomasochism whose viciousness even the Old Testament barely exceeds. It is, when you think about it, remarkable that a religion should adopt an instrument of torture and execution as its sacred symbol, often worn around the neck. Lenny Bruce rightly quipped that 'If Jesus had been killed twenty years ago, Catholic school children would be wearing little electric chairs around their necks instead of crosses'. But the theology and punishment-theory behind it is even worse.*

He continues with the theology of "original sin" and protests that it is a philosophy that condemns every child even before it is born and saying that original sin is unfair and it is God taking offence at something people do while naked (quoting Sam Harris). He also protests that the Christian focus is overwhelmingly on "sin sin sin sin sin sin sin".

Now it would be easy for me to say he has misunderstood the Christian doctrine on sin and on original sin because he certainly has but he is quite right to point out the horror of the cross and to question why the church majors so much on it.

Lenny Bruce makes a very valid point apart from the fact that an electric chair would never have been chosen as the instrument of execution for Jesus had he been murdered in modern times. It would be far too humane and so would the gas chamber, firing squad or almost any other method used today. The cross was not only an instrument of execution; it was designed to kill its victims in the most excruciating way they could imagine, prolonging death sometimes by days with the victim becoming increasingly agonised.

And when you consider that not a single sin is recorded against Jesus, that he was killed for political reasons and because of jealousy on the part of the Jewish hierarchy, his death becomes at least one of the most heinous crimes ever committed in history. I do not mean it was the worst in scale (the holocaust of six million Jews murdered by the Nazis makes almost anything else pale into insignificance in comparison) but as far as pain and injustice is concerned, it is hard to top the atrocity of the cross.

So why do Christians make such a lot of this horrible thing? Why do we see it displayed on most church buildings and in fact in Roman Catholic buildings find an image of Christ on that cross? Why would so many (Christians and non-Christians) wear the symbol round their necks? Why remember it with bread and wine representing his body and blood on a regular basis? Quite frankly, if the cross does not mean what Christians believe it to mean, then this is the most tasteless and horrific thing to do,

What *does* the cross mean?

Although I hesitate to do so, I feel I have to give some sort of answer to this. I hesitate because I cannot give any semblance of a scientific answer or reason and I cannot give any reason that I think will satisfy any atheist. When it comes to understanding creation, I can happily say that Genesis and science portray different and apparently contradictory views of the same thing but I can't do that when it comes to the cross. But I must have a go at trying to say something about it as it is such a "biggie" for so many.

In Galatians chapter 5 verse 11, Paul speaks of the "*offence of the cross*" and in 1 Corinthians chapter 1 verse 18, he says, "*the preaching of the cross is to them that perish foolishness.*" "Foolishness"? I would say it is more than foolishness – it's downright horror. But, ironically, that means if I succeed in explaining this satisfactorily to an atheist, I will have failed!

I have already mentioned this verse to show that atheists cannot understand the cross and I believe that is true, but I will try at least to explain Christian thinking on the cross and then to explain a little more about sin in the next section. It also means I will have to explain the clause "*to them that perish*", which will no doubt cause further offence. As it is not my aim to cause offence and this is not the thrust of the book, I don't want to get bogged down in this but I shall have to deal with it.

Sacrifice is central to the whole Bible. Abraham's near sacrifice of his son Isaac was not massively abnormal. It was the normal way of making a covenant in his time among all the tribes in the Middle East. Animals would be killed to represent the utter seriousness of the covenant into which two parties were entering. In Genesis chapter 22 verse 8, when Isaac asks his father where the lamb is for the burnt offering, Abraham replied, *"My son, God will provide himself the lamb..."* There is considerable evidence to show that the literal meaning of this is that God himself would be the lamb.

How this has come into the text I don't know and I doubt if Abraham had the slightest idea of what he was saying and the writer could not have known either but it could be seen as a prophecy to do with a descendant of Isaac (yes, I know, it could be pure coincidence). Another interesting thing is that it was very likely the same mountain on which Jesus was sacrificed nearly two thousand years later (yes, I know, that could also be pure coincidence).

Under Moses, a whole system of sacrifice was introduced. Numbers of animals were slaughtered every single day. All of this was for the forgiveness and removal of sin and because sin is a continuous problem, sacrifice had to be continuous. It was terrible and we would rightly recoil at the horror of this. The animals were completely innocent. Loving animals as I do (and I don't mean in a cuddly bunny sort of way), I find this utterly offensive. It is totally unjust but at the time, it would not have been seen in that light.

I am not of the opinion, either, that this is all made up as some modern theologians may suggest. I believe it happened. It all fits with the culture of the day. About this, the New Testament says *"without the shedding of blood, there is no forgiveness of sin."*[211] So it is not passed off in this somewhat more enlightened era as something we have sort of grown out of.

The sacrifice of a man

There are other suggestions in the Old Testament that a man would be sacrificed (this is in spite of the condemnation of child sacrifice to gods like Molech). Isaiah chapter 53 is a classic example. According to Jewish theologians, this is speaking about the suffering of Israel, but it so closely parallels Jesus' death, it is uncanny. I will not quote the chapter here, but I really suggest you read it and find out for yourself (yes, I know, this chapter could also be pure coincidence).

Psalm 22 (the first verse of which was uttered by Jesus shortly before he died) is another that has uncanny parallels with the suffering of Jesus. David could not have known that when he wrote it although he was no doubt expressing just what he felt (yes, I know that could also be pure coincidence).

Then in Zechariah chapter 12 verse 10, God says *"they shall look upon me whom they have pierced."* Of course, that's probably again pure coincidence. But Zechariah says in chapter 11, *"And I say unto them: 'If good in your eyes, give my hire, and if not, forbear;' and they weigh out my hire – thirty silverlings. And Jehovah saith unto me, 'Cast it unto the potter;' the goodly price that I have been prized at by them, and I take the thirty silverlings, and cast them to the house of Jehovah,*

---

[211] Hebrews chapter 9, verse 22

unto the potter."[212] Judas was paid 30 pieces of silver to betray Jesus and then regretted it deeply, so took the money and threw it into the treasury of the temple (after the authorities refused to accept it back). It was then used to buy the Potter's Field in which to bury strangers. No doubt that is all pure coincidence, too.

I could go on showing other places in the Old Testament where there are indications of a man coming to suffer and that this suffering would, in some way, be redemptive. No doubt, all these books were just cobbled together and they just happen to have all these strange (apparent) predictions that just happened to be fulfilled. There are many many other "coincidences" I could mention.

But that still doesn't answer the problem we have over the cross. It does seem to indicate that it may not have been an accident but was planned by someone (apart from just the authorities at the time). The Isaiah passage suggests that YHWH himself laid it all on this man who bears a close resemblance to Christ. How can any loving father do that to his son?

What we have seen is that there is a continuous theme running through both Old and New Testaments of sacrifice being necessary for the forgiveness of sin. In the Old, continuous sacrifice was necessary. This ceased temporarily during the exile of the Jews in Babylon and was re-instituted when they returned to Jerusalem and re-built the temple. It was still being practised when Jesus was born. Not many years after his death (and resurrection), Jerusalem was attacked by the Romans and brought almost to rubble and the

---

[212] Zechariah chapter 11, verses 12 & 13 (Young's Literal Translation 1898)

temple was destroyed. As sacrifice had to take place in the temple, it then stopped – and has never been started again.

According to Christian theology, Jesus' sacrifice was "once for all"[213] and so no further sacrifice is ever necessary (a huge sigh of relief for the animals!). His sacrifice ended the necessity for further shedding of blood as he had taken all the sin of the world upon himself for all time and it had been dealt the death blow – certainly as far as punishment was concerned.

How can this possibly be true? How can the death of one man mean I can be forgiven for all my sin – past, present and future? It's ridiculous – foolishness to say the least. Yes, it is and that is what Paul said it would be to them that perish. It cannot be understood by the natural mind – it's a mystery. There I go again, hiding behind the word "mystery" – anything I cannot explain is passed off as a mystery. Yes, I know, Richard, I'm a typical religious nut! Or am I? Maybe, it's just that you cannot understand it whereas I can and I cannot explain it to someone who has no frame of reference to understand it.

The thing is, it works. God satisfies his justice by punishing sin but piles it on himself (God provides *himself* the lamb). He pays the penalty himself and then lets me go free. I don't deserve it, I know, but he is merciful. Why can he not just forgive, if he is God. What's all the big deal about sin anyway? Why does he *"monitor our every base thought"* as Dawkins says?

---

[213] Romans chapter 6, verse 10; Hebrews chapter 7, verse 27; chapter 9, verse 26; chapter 10, verse 10

Anyone who asks that, I immediately know does not understand the horror of sin. Dawkins rightly recoils in horror at injustice (as any decent person would). Injustice is sin. We are incensed when someone gets off free because of a legal loophole and then does not face the justice and punishment that is their due. Why? Why should we not just say it's all right, don't do it again? Because we know that wrong-doing should be punished.

But what if our wrong-doing "doesn't hurt anyone else"? Well, if every action has a consequence, then really there is no such thing as a sin that does not hurt anyone else, even if that person is unaware of the hurt. As I hope I explained above, God does not have grades of sin. According to the book of Romans, if I have broken God's law, however minor my offence may be, I have broken it and that is that. God's total justice demands a penalty. But can't we just say sorry and start again? Well, let's look at the nature of sin.

What is the essence of sin?

I have concentrated a lot on sin above and will continue here (backing up Dawkins' claim about the emphasis Christians have), but before I continue, let me say that he may be right about some Christians, but actually the emphasis in the Bible is on being *released* from sin. Believers are called saints and ex-sinners (in spite of the fact that they obviously still do things wrong). Paul tells believers to focus their minds on things above, not things beneath; he tells them to think about things of good report and so on. The message of the New Testament is that we are taken out of our sin and into a new kingdom. But I still have to talk more about sin – sorry!

Having a good system of ethics has never made anyone good. It has not made me good and it has not made you good. I am not saying that to criticize you or myself. It's just a fact. The prophet Isaiah, in the chapter mentioned above, included the words *"all we like sheep have gone astray; we have turned each one to his own way."*[214] Paul, quoting Psalm 14 verse 3, agrees with this, saying, *"there is no one righteous; not even one."*[215]

That was the problem Israel had. They knew what was right. They had the Law. But in spite of the most amazing witness of the actions of God for them in the desert, they failed to keep that Law. It was not that they were particularly bad people. They were just people and people do wrong things. Babies aren't evil – they are just self-centred. But we still love them. As they grow up, we teach them to adjust their behaviour and they learn what is considered morally right – or we hope they do.

I suppose we could say that sin is putting *me* first all the time. Dawkins speaks of the "selfish gene" though of course he does not mean that literally but I suppose we could say that we are composed of a selfish nature at root. And then there's the problem that when I am aware of the wrong I do/have done, it makes me feel worse and has a tendency as well to make me feel "down" about myself and unable to cope fully with putting it right. Having to deal with guilt on top of this seemingly invincible enemy makes things doubly as hard.

---

[214]   Isaiah chapter 53, verse 6
[215]   Romans chapter 3, verse 10

We try to deal with this in various ways, putting the blame on our genes or on others for our faults ("it's all because I had an overbearing father") or saying we can just wash it away; what's done is done; forget it and move on, and countless other strategies. I am not decrying these strategies. They have their place in some circumstances but as far as I can tell, they don't fully deal with the problem. They don't make people better, though they make some feel a bit better about not reaching the standard they think they should.

Only righteous when we die?

Really, the only way we can completely overcome this horrible tendency within us is through death! That sounds pretty dramatic. But think about it. Dead people don't do anything wrong. They aren't in the least bit selfish. They never have wrong thoughts or wrong motives. They never say anything that will offend others. They don't steal, murder or commit adultery. They aren't ever jealous or envious. But that's hardly a viable solution, is it? I can't see it catching on.

But is it such a bad solution? What if I can receive forgiveness for what I have done and still tend to do? Hard to believe and accept, yes but what if I can? And then, what if I can *count* myself as dead? What if I can effectively give up all my rights to myself and come to the point of realising that my own rights and desires are not what is important any more?

In fact the New Testament writers state that death is the only way to overcome this tendency we call sin. Referring to the Old

Testament sacrificial system, the writer of the letter to the Hebrews says, *"without the shedding of blood, there is no forgiveness of sins"*[216] and the apostle Paul says *"so you must consider yourselves dead to sin and alive to God in Christ Jesus."*[217] The guilt that we feel is dealt with as well. As Christians, we believe that the penalty for our wrong-doing has been paid not through our own death but through the death of Christ.

This sounds pretty barbaric and Dawkins quotes Benjamin Franklin's tirade against Christianity, remarking, *"I almost shudder at the thought of alluding to the most fatal example of the abuses of grief which the history of mankind has preserved – the Cross. Consider what calamities that engine of grief has produced!"*[218] The crucifixion of Christ was certainly a barbaric act; a totally innocent man set up because of political intrigue, betrayed by one of his closest friends and put to death after a mockery of a trial in one of the cruellest ways ever devised by human beings.

However I cannot personally take Franklin seriously. He was a friend of Sir Francis Dashwood, who established the "Hellfire Club" and Franklin used to attend these very dubious meetings that apparently were fairly debauched quite apart from their habit of simply mocking all things Christian.

It is little wonder the crucifixion is misunderstood, but misunderstood it is. I don't blame anyone for thinking that someone believing in the efficacy of the cross is a fool. Indeed Jesus expected the "wise" not to understand his message either. He said *"I thank you Father...*

---

[216]   Hebrews chapter 9, verse 22
[217]   Romans chapter 6, verse 11
[218]   "The God Delusion" page 65

that you have hidden these things from the wise and understanding and revealed them to little children."[219] While the message of the cross has been abused by many and misunderstood by most, it has meant life for millions. Think of the words of Charles Wesley's famous hymn:

And can it be that I should gain
An interest in the Saviour's blood?
Died He for me, who caused His pain—
For me, who Him to death pursued?
Amazing love! How can it be,
That Thou, my God, shouldst die for me?

'Tis mystery all: th' Immortal dies!
Who can explore his strange design?
In vain the firstborn seraph tries
To sound the depths of love divine.
'Tis mercy all! Let earth adore;
Let angel minds inquire no more.

He left his Father's throne above
(so free, so infinite his grace!),
Emptied himself of all but love
And bled for Adam's helpless race.
'Tis mercy all, immense and free,
For O my God, it found out me!

Long my imprisoned spirit lay,
Fast bound in sin and nature's night;
Thine eye diffused a quickening ray;

---

[219] Luke chapter 10, verse 21

> *I woke, the dungeon flamed with light;*
> *My chains fell off, my heart was free.*
> *I rose, went forth and followed thee.*
>
> *No condemnation now I dread;*
> *Jesus, and all in him, is mine;*
> *Alive in him, my living Head*
> *And clothed in righteousness divine.*
> *Bold I approach th' eternal throne*
> *And claim the crown through Christ my own.*

Wesley was not just writing high-sounding words. He was poetically describing his experience and expressing what Christ had done for him.

Because some people have used the cross to justify violence does not mean that is the message of the cross; because others like Franklin think it is an engine of grief does not mean that view is therefore correct. Obviously some, like Wesley, have seen beyond the surface of the horror of the cross and realised that it represents "amazing love" on the part of a Deity whose creatures have rebelled against him but who, nevertheless, is prepared to pay the ultimate sacrifice himself on their behalf. And some like Isaac Watts can say:

> *When I survey the wondrous cross*
> *On which the Prince of glory died*
> *My richest gain I count but loss*
> *And pour contempt on all my pride.*

The cross levels us and lifts us up. It deals with our sin (and all have sinned) and removes our guilt. It means our debt (our penalty for sin) has been paid off, never to be brought up in accusation against us again because, as Christians believe, the punishment has been laid on someone who never deserved it but willingly took it on our behalf. God does not indulge in "double-jeopardy". But then the question arises – does just believing something like that make us automatically into morally upright people? And I have to answer very practically and say "No, it doesn't."

Dying to self?

Having your debts paid off is a most freeing feeling. But if that is all it is, it is not helpful. We then have to die ourselves – not physically but by giving ourselves up to another. Again, Paul says, "*he that is dead has been freed from sin.*"[220] He is not unrealistic, however. He is aware that this tendency called sin is a constant pull toward self-centredness. So "counting yourself dead" is not a one-off event but a constant exercise of putting yourself under God's authority.

I quite understand it if you think reckoning yourself to be dead is just a mind-game or a cop-out from facing the consequences of our actions. It is counter-intuitive. It's unreasonable. But Christians claim to have received a new frame of reference that you may not have received, so what I am saying may be touching on something that is currently meaningless to you. Millions have discovered that it works, however, and that it produces not only a "way out" but a genuine change of heart and continuous progress towards changed behaviour, thoughts and actions.

---

[220] Romans chapter 6, verse 7

It is well known that prison officers let preachers into jail because the prisoners who genuinely submit to Christ demonstrate permanent change in behaviour. Obviously, the prison officers could be thinking cynically that this is really a good form of mind-control to produce docile prisoners, but can we really be sure there is no reality of genuine heart-change and the capability to reform inwardly and therefore in genuine thought, speech and action?

I suppose I am starting to sound like the Director in *Brave New World* who conditions the "Delta" working-class babies to hate flowers and books with electric shocks. But the actual experience of Christians is of anything but alien mind-control. Andrew Sims points out, Christians tend to have a mature "internal locus of control" not a sort of external manipulation. Jesus promises true freedom of the will: "*the truth will set you free*"[221] and that really is the experience of those who are commonly known as "born-again Christians" – the overwhelming sensation of joy and light and release as many modern Christian songs try to express.

I believe we are all offered the means of becoming righteous. Whether or not we avail ourselves of it, it is still offered. It is an ongoing process that takes your whole life. But it is a gift. We cannot engineer it because if we struggle to become good, the concentration is still on self and that is precisely the difficulty we have – self constantly rearing its ugly head. Strictly speaking, everyone (not just Christians) has been offered the gift but there is a huge difference between being offered a gift and fully accepting it.

---

[221] John chapter 8, verse 32

Does it always work?

I believe there are many Christians who gladly accept the first part of this: the death and resurrection of Christ effecting the forgiveness of their sins and receiving new life. But then a number fail to grasp the second part: the necessity to die to their own efforts.

Instead, they "try to be good" and, as I said above, it does not work. It is only to the extent that we learn this lesson and understand that God, by his Holy Spirit, works within us and brings about righteous living that it works. I would not expect an atheist to be able to appreciate this at all. I can quite understand any non-believer classing all Christians together and judging Christian morality by what they see of any believer.

Who are "those that perish"?

But how about "*those who perish*" that I mentioned above? As I said above, everyone is offered this gift of life and it is effective for every person on this planet but we have to accept it. It is our choice. I have dealt with the problem of hell in chapter 9 and earlier in this chapter, so will not say more about it here but I have to say that *those who perish* does mean unbelievers (i.e. those who have not received Christ).

I would like to say it means something else but I can't. And it does mean that they perish. Is that annihilation or hell? I cannot be definite. Exactly what is meant by hell? Again, I cannot be definite. What I am sure of is that it means separation from God, the author of life. What I will say is I think it's better not to perish. Whether

I am right or wrong to believe that non-perishing is possible, I will leave you to judge, but the other thing to remember is that neither my opinion nor your opinion counts – it's what we ultimately find to be the truth that matters. And it may matter a great deal.

Why not just be good as other religions and even atheism require?

Virtually any religion will speak about the need to follow right principles, to live a good life and to help others. In many, it is your duty to do so. Most of them have a clear code of conduct and it is often hard to fault those codes. Atheists too, by and large, will have a clear sense of the necessity to be a moral person and to have high values.

However, no moral code, no system of ethics or religious principle can make anyone into a moral person. It makes no difference what religious rituals or exercises you follow. They don't work. Trying to keep the Ten Commandments doesn't work. Battling to follow Jesus' standards doesn't work. The answer lies, I am convinced in that small misunderstood and lamentably overused word "love" and its sister word "grace". The apostle John said, "*The law* (rules/moral codes) *came through Moses; grace and truth were realised* (made real) *through Jesus Christ.*"[222]

In Paul's first letter to the Corinthians chapter 13, he says, "*I may speak in different languages, whether human or even of angels. But if I don't have love, I am only a noisy bell or a ringing cymbal. I may have the*

---

[222] John Chapter 1, verse 17

gift of prophecy, I may understand all secrets and know everything there is to know, and I may have faith so great that I can move mountains. But even with all this, if I don't have love, I am nothing. I may give away everything I have to help others, and I may even give my body as an offering to be burned. But I gain nothing by doing all this if I don't have love."[223] Doing good deeds may be highly moral and beneficial to others. Having wonderful knowledge and understanding may make you highly acceptable to others.

But none of that counts with God. God knows the secrets of our hearts and he knows we fail because our hearts are not pure. Take all the goodness you can muster and subtract love – and you end up with nothing! And having that love means you have to receive it in the first place – and that unconditional love is received from God.

Stop trying to be good!

The point is, we cannot actually make ourselves righteous by our own efforts and yet so many religious people of every persuasion try to do so. Little wonder Dawkins and others criticize the thought that religion helps you to become good. The facts are that it doesn't. He is quite right.

It seems to defy logic to say that by ceasing to try being good and by receiving forgiveness and righteousness, it is possible to overcome this selfish tendency that afflicts everyone. But that is the contention of biblical teaching.

---

[223] 1 Corinthians chapter 13, verses 1-3 (Easy-to-Read Version)

Jesus did set impossibly high standards. Even if you lust after someone sexually, you have committed adultery; if you hate someone, you are guilty of murder. No one can possibly live by those standards. But, underneath all his teaching was the most vital message of all. We need him because we cannot do it ourselves.

He lived a perfect life but he also *"knew what was in man."*[224] There is a necessity for a radical encounter with God, resulting in a fundamental change in the inner man – what we call the heart. Outer (visible) righteousness results from the inner change. Still, we do not become totally morally perfect. I am far from it. But I trust in the grace of God to forgive me completely, give me his perfect righteousness and to continue to produce changes in me to become the person he desires. I can be completely relaxed in it even when I go wrong. And I can assure you, I do!

This is precisely the thing that is hard to understand for most people. It's not because it is too intellectually challenging. It's simply because our natural instinct is to be in control – to do it ourselves. Frank Sinatra summed it up excellently in his song *I did it my way.* Our natural instinct is to aim for achievement, collect skills, and become someone that the rest of the world will respect for our talents and character.

Having lived for years in Glastonbury and still being closely associated with the town, I see it in all the New Age religions that flourish there. All of them appeal to pride – increasing your spirituality, your sensitivity to this, that and the other. There are courses on how to become a goddess (pretty expensive, I may add; deity doesn't come

---

[224] John chapter 2, verse 25

cheap). Every one of them appeals to the pride of self-effort. When you analyse it, Dawkins does the same.

But it's impossible. Yes, we can patch ourselves up; we can put on an air of respectability; we can say nice things. None of it changes the heart. It's sin – that inevitable tendency in every single person that finds a way to promote self. That's why the investment bankers went wrong. It's sin. Sin sees an opportunity to enrich a person (even at the expense of damaging thousands of others) and follows the path. It may not be money; it can be all sorts of things that damage others while seeking to rise up.

As a human being, I have that tendency, and so do you. I can guarantee one hundred percent that you do not live up to your own standards. How do I know? Because it is true of every single person. The whole of humanity is born fatally flawed.

The only way we can ever achieve the impossibly high standard of biblical righteousness is by receiving it. As soon as I try to do it myself, I mess it up. God's standard is total purity and freedom of our motivations – lost to self so much that it simply doesn't occur to us to insist on our own interests but to be so caught up with his love that we cannot help loving others.

And this love is only available as a gift from God's Spirit as we invite him into our lives to take command. This is not tyranny – he does not invade us as a foreign force. Rather, his presence frees us from the drive to conform to what others want or even what we think we should be so that we can become fully ourselves. We remain uniquely ourselves but set free from that which would bind us. Living with someone you deeply admire will mean you become more like them;

living with God's Spirit changes our character to become more like him. Paul tells us that *"we all, with unveiled face, beholding the glory of the Lord, are being transformed into the same image from one degree of glory to another. For this comes from the Lord who is the Spirit."*[225]

The gospel actually means freedom for us to be authentically ourselves with no fear of what anyone else thinks – not even of what we ourselves think we "should" be. I really think that is good news. Just because some Christians never understand that does not invalidate its purpose or effectiveness.

Two types of morality

If you think of morality or human goodness, then what Dawkins says probably goes some way toward a decent standard. However, I think he is quite right to say that you do not have to be religious or have a belief in God in order to be a reasonably moral person.

But if you start looking at New Testament righteousness, rather than human goodness and morality, you find it is talking about something quite different. The Pharisees were regarded, as a group, as sticking absolutely to what was right according to their strict interpretation of Jewish Law. They were highly moral people – at least on the outside. The ordinary people looked up to them as wonderful examples. They trusted in themselves and relied on their own strength of character. There is a shadow of this in Dawkins' insistence that people can be righteous (he doesn't use that word) in their own strength. Of course, his beliefs are not the same as

---

[225] 2 Corinthians chapter 3, verse 18

the Pharisees but the principle is similar. But what did Jesus say? *"For I tell you, unless your righteousness exceeds that of the scribes and Pharisees, you will never enter the kingdom of heaven."*[226] What? How is it possible? Well, it isn't! That's the point.

New Testament righteousness is something completely different from human goodness and morality. It's not just in a different league; it's in another kingdom. If you are thinking, "What on earth is he talking about?", then I understand. I am referring to something completely outside your experience and understanding. While biblical righteousness may be similar to our normal concepts of morality, it is not the same thing. Christians speak of the "grace" of God. It's that grace that has been extended to us and enables us to see just around the corner – a corner that is out of sight to those who rely just on themselves and yet one that opens up vistas of which you cannot even dream until you begin to believe.

I would recommend Philip Yancey's book *What's so Amazing about Grace?* if you are interested in pursuing this further. Isaac Newton, a former slave trader who repented and ended up campaigning against that diabolical trade, wrote the hymn *Amazing Grace*. This gives you a glimpse of what grace is about – we start receiving it when we are what Jesus called being "born again"[227] and continue have it added "grace upon grace" as we get to know this amazing God's amazing grace.

---

[226] Matthew chapter 5, verse 20 ESV

[227] That term has been castigated and associated with a simplistic and literalist type of faith, but I am happy to agree with Jesus on this and having committed my own life to him, I have been "born again" along with "all the saints".

CHAPTER 15

Is Faith Bad for You?

On page 346, Richard Dawkins says, "*More generally (and this applies to Christianity no less than Islam), what is really pernicious is the practice of teaching children that faith is a virtue. Faith is an evil precisely because it requires no justification and brooks no argument.*"

Well, let me put my hand up and say I believe faith is a virtue (not the twisted version of faith he portrays but what the Bible teaches as faith).

He says that faith itself is evil because it requires no justification and brooks no argument. The same idea appears elsewhere in *The God Delusion*, too. I don't know what Bible Dawkins has read but I don't think it is the same one I have read. I have come across plenty of passages telling people to teach their children the way of the Lord and so on but have never come across one saying it never needs any justification and there should be no argument. I may be wrong, of course, and would be very pleased if Richard or anyone else would point me to those passages.

That is, most decidedly, NOT the way I have taught my children; in fact it has been quite the opposite and I have been thrilled when they question me. I am also thrilled when adults, for whom I have pastoral responsibility, start to question and argue (I don't mean antagonistically) with what I have said. I want people to think for themselves, otherwise what they believe has no validity or value. Making a statement like Richard Dawkins' above, which is based on the observation of the way some people see their faith and then generalising it, is not in any way reliable and is highly likely to be untrue.

In chapter 9, he describes the teaching of faith to children as child abuse. He cites the case of Edgardo Mortara who was taken from his Jewish parents in Bologna in 1858 because his illiterate Roman Catholic carer, Anna Morisi, had baptised him earlier. He blames this on the 'religious mind' and he is quite right. But it is a complete perversion of Christian teaching and therefore actually has no force of argument.

Besides, if we are going to blame religion as such for this instead of people with completely unbiblical ideas about baptism (I agree with Dawkins over the stupidity of thinking some water administered without any agreement on the part of that child could have the slightest effect) and who have no regard for family, then strictly speaking we must blame atheism for the actions in communist USSR, where children were used to inform on their parents. Teachers would pleasantly ask children if they ever put their hands together (in a typical praying posture) at home. If they said they did, their parents were liable to be arrested and the children taken into care. But perhaps that is not abuse because they were simply preventing those children from being indoctrinated by their parents!

If the cases he mentions are abuse by religion, then these were abuse by atheism. But, once again, I would say that while atheists did abuse these children, it was not specifically atheism itself that caused it and so it was also not Christianity that caused the abuse of Edgardo and others. It was caused by some so-called Christians acting completely wrongly and in contradiction to the spirit of true Christian conduct.

"Abuse" is a pretty strong word, especially in light of all the real child abuse that has come to light in recent years of the type that I mentioned in chapter 13. This is, of course, perfectly reasonable if it is in fact true that God is no more than a man-made myth with no objective reality. It is also reasonable if belief in God is in fact, as he claims, a real psychiatric delusion with negative consequences on human behaviour, leading to people behaving literally as mad with its attendant violent and disturbing behaviour.

Faith and self-control

Professor Andrew Sims, former president of the Royal College of Psychiatrists, explains that faith is actually shown to be good for people and that it fits very well with the human need to belong, producing robust mental health. This eminent psychiatrist, retired now but one-time President of the Royal College of Psychiatrists, has the clear conviction that faith is healthy. Mature faith involves an *internal locus of control*, in spite of the fact that the attention of faith is external (on God). Having self-control is good for you. An internal locus of control is associated with maturity of attitude and I find this reflected in the book of Jeremiah when he says:

Behold, the days are coming, declares the LORD, when I will make a new covenant with the house of Israel and the house of Judah, not like the covenant that I made with their fathers on the day when I took them by the hand to bring them out of the land of Egypt, my covenant that they broke, though I was their husband, declares the LORD. But this is the covenant that I will make with the house of Israel after those days, declares the LORD: **I will put my law within them, and I will write it on their hearts.** *And I will be their God, and they shall be my people.* **And no longer shall each one teach his neighbour and each his brother, saying, 'Know the LORD,' for they shall all know me, from the least of them to the greatest, declares the LORD.** *For I will forgive their iniquity, and I will remember their sin no more.*[228]

So, far from true religion being an external control, it seems it is to be very much a control from within (the "heart"). This is Bull's stage 4 – the autonomous stage of development I mentioned earlier.

As I grew up, I gained my own values, not my parents' though clearly they had influenced the way I thought. As a Christian, I think I can demonstrate that I increasingly follow what are my own inner convictions, not what someone else tells me I ought to do. Of course, living in this "fellowship" with God is still acknowledging God's authority in my life, but I would maintain that God gently works within to bring me to the perfection he has already given me.

---

[228] Jeremiah chapter 31, verses 31-34

Are we good because it is good for us?

I have already discussed altruism and said how I feel Dawkins' analysis (purely based on genetics and selective advantage) is a very inadequate view and in fact does not constitute altruism at all. But do people do good just because it gives them some other advantage or it is "good for the soul" as some people say?

The description of the devil's strategies portrayed by Lewis in *The Screwtape Letters* is taken largely from the book of Job, where Satan is seen as cynically implying that Job is only faithful to God because he knows it will benefit him and that human beings are merely objects of fun to be manipulated. And this is increasingly the view taken by the New Atheists of religious believers' motivation for doing good.

In 1956, Jim Elliot and four friends attempted to reach the Huaorani Indians in the rainforest of Ecuador in order to show them the love of God. These people were a wild savage tribe of head-hunters known as Aucas ("savages"), utterly suspicious of anyone from outside and at war even with others in their tribe. They managed to make contact and arranged to meet with some of them on the shore of the Amazon River. When their plane landed, another bunch of Huaoranis leaped out and butchered them.

Jim's widow Elisabeth, who wrote the book *Through Gates of Splendor* about this episode, and some other women very close to these men, undoubtedly deeply, deeply hurt, decided that they had to continue to reach out to the Huaoranis. They made contact and met up with them. The Huaoranis could not understand such love and accepted them. I hope you can see that has nothing to do with a moral code or system of ethics. It indicates hearts that have been deeply touched with love; a love deeper and more powerful than the hurt that was inflicted upon them by those Huaoranis.

You don't act in that irrational way because you have worked out a system of ethics to determine what would be right in certain circumstances. You do it because your heart has been radically changed by something far more powerful than your own reason.

This is only one of countless examples of what I would consider genuine altruism. It is in no way confined to Christians either. It may be true that we can explain all sorts of behaviour in genetic terms and relate it to selection pressures, but I am convinced that goodness, let alone righteousness is something way beyond that.

Religion and war

I feel I need to say something about this before we leave this chapter simply because Richard Dawkins makes so much of it. And the thing is, in many ways he is right. Arguments over religion have caused the most terrible amount of conflict historically. Christianity is certainly not exempt as we all know from Northern Ireland and many other parts of the world. Muslim conflict is almost legendary and there is no major religion that can claim no part in conflict.

His assessment of violence on the part of the "American Taliban" has a lot of truth to it, too. I have made the point that killing or attacking anyone because you dislike what they do is the very opposite of the spirit of Christ. When I see the attitude of much of the Christian right in the USA, I am relieved that they are not in power.

However, my feeling is that many of these people are not really committed Christians. I am not going to judge the members of other religions in this because I am not qualified to do so. As far as Christians are concerned, all I can say is that you cannot blame Christianity or Christ for the actions and attitudes of people who display the opposite of his teachings. It is not his fault that anyone uses scripture to justify their wrong-doing (Dawkins adequately makes a similar point about Hitler).

Dawkins says no one has ever waged a war in the name of atheism[229]. He is probably right. But atheists still wage war. And as I mentioned before, communism must be the most brutal system in practice in modern times.

The "religion" of communism is deeply atheistic; it is paranoid in its hatred of all religions and has done everything it can to eradicate them wherever it holds sway. Its atheism has got to be one of its major motivations in this abhorrent oppression. It has been claimed that Stalin wanted to murder twenty million Jews in the USSR[230]. I am not sure that there were as many as that to murder, but it would represent genocide on a massive scale. The same report says that his Jewish commissars murdered about fifty million non-Jews. This man was an avowed atheist and while I will not say his atheism as such was responsible for his whole motivation, it has to have motivated the whole communist system of the USSR.

Maybe we can say this is not war because it was not one state against another (nor is the Northern Ireland conflict), but it is worse than

---

229   "The God Delusion" page 315
230   http://globalfire.tv/nj/03en/history/stalin.htm

most wars – with a brutal dictator obliterating vast swathes of his own people. It is disingenuous either to ignore this or to pretend his atheism was an entirely separate issue.

I met a man in Rhodesia called Ndabaningi Musa. He was a diminutive fellow but fearless. He had been recruited to engage in terror long before the main troubles started there. He led a gang of men to petrol-bomb a Christian rally at Glamis Stadium at the then Salisbury showground. Why did they want to do that specifically? Partly because most of the people there were white but also because they hated Christianity. Musa, however, listened to the sermon and was converted. The planned petrol-bombing never took place. He then went around the tribal areas reaching out to the "freedom" fighters but he had a price on his head. They wanted him dead because he was a Christian. These men were trained mainly in Communist China or the USSR and were (probably unthinkingly) atheist.

Some of those fighters murdered the Elim missionaries, including a friend of ours, at Dawkins' and my old school, Eagle. Why? Because they were Christian and were educating children to be peaceable. The militant atheistic mindset hates spirituality with a vengeance and those people were brainwashed by atheists to hate Christians. A journalist school friend of mine reported on the atrocity and said it was the most brutal and foul murder he had ever seen, involving rape and mutilation, even of a baby, and that no one would ever want to see that sort of sight.[231]

---

[231] I am happy to report, though, that I have subsequently heard that all but one of those men became Christians and many of them are now pastors (such is the power of the gospel)

I still maintain that atheism itself does not *cause* evil. It is people who do so. Although atheism itself does not produce conflict (but some atheists do), so Christianity does not produce conflict (but some Christians do). I don't blame atheism as a belief for communist brutality. Dawkins cannot do so in regard to Christianity. I really think Richard Dawkins knowingly went a bit "over the top" on this one.

Conclusion

To sum up on the whole question of morality, I would like to say that I agree with Dawkins in his assessment of ethics. There will be a huge overlap of belief between Christians and atheists and with those of all sorts of other religions. That simply supports the Christian belief that all mankind have been made in the image of God, i.e. with a reflection of his character. An atheist can be highly moral but cannot, however, have what the Bible calls "righteousness".

When it comes to righteousness, then, the gospel provides a means of receiving and living in real inward purity of heart – the biblical concept of righteousness, which is found nowhere else. Righteousness is received; morality is developed. I would say (with a certain hesitation because I know there will be reactions from people of different religions) that it's not found in any other religion, not even in Judaism and certainly not in atheism. That does *not* imply that Christians are morally perfect. It is patently obvious that they aren't. But the means is available and, if people avail themselves of the opportunity, they become righteous in a measurable sense.

While every Christian receives the gift of Christ's righteousness, no Christian on this planet reaches that perfect moral standard in this life but every one is a work in progress – a work we believe will only be completed after this life is ended and we are in the actual presence of God – described in the book of Revelation as "the new heaven and new earth".

CHAPTER 16

Purpose in Science and Faith

It is often said that science can only deal with processes, hypotheses, theories, laws and so on, and knows nothing of purpose, while faith deals with purposes. It is put slightly differently sometimes in saying that science deals with the 'how's of life while theology deals with the 'why's. While there is some truth in this, it is not entirely true.

Dawkins deals with this and speaks some truth when he says:

> *What on Earth is a why question? Not every English sentence beginning with the word 'why' is a legitimate question. Why are unicorns hollow? Some questions simply do not deserve an answer. What is the colour of abstraction? What is the smell of hope? The fact that a question can be phrased in a grammatically correct English sentence doesn't make it meaningful, or entitle it to our serious attention. Nor, even if the question is*

a real one, does the fact that science cannot answer it
imply that religion can.[232]

Of course there are non-legitimate 'why' questions but theology does not (or should not) attempt to ask or answer them. In addition, while science can answer many 'why' questions, there are some it cannot and there are also many questions to which there can be different answers, depending on what aspect the questioner is after. He is also right to say that the inability of science to answer some 'why' questions does not imply that religion can. However, it is not logical to assume, therefore, that religion cannot answer many of them.

We need to understand questions before we answer them, too. A friend was driving her small son to school one morning and he asked her, "Mummy, does Jesus eat bacon?" She thought – he was Jewish so probably never had bacon – and so started explaining that Jews believe pork is unclean and so he probably never had it, but that according the New Testament, we can eat all foods, so he would not mind bacon – no doubt quite true. He replied, "That's good because I had bacon for breakfast and, if he is in my tummy, I hope he likes it!"

The other thing is that theology does not pretend to have the answers to all questions. It asks questions and seeks answers. I hope to show here that faith / theology finds a different dimension of answers to questions than does science. Both disciplines are correct; both ask questions; both seek answers but they are on completely different levels.

---

[232] "The God Delusion" page 80

When I was at school, we always had to write up every practical (especially in chemistry and physics), starting with the "Aim" of the practical. I have continued to teach children to do this or to state a prediction for their practical. Scientific investigations are very much purposeful endeavours. We may not always be able to predict the results of investigations but we have a very definite aim in carrying out investigations. Science has a purpose to discover the material truth of the universe.

However, to attribute purpose to the objects of scientific study is another matter. A pride of lions may well have a very definite purpose when it goes out hunting and, instinctively, they often work to a plan. They have evolved tactics that make them one of the most efficient mammalian predators having "discovered" that co-operation results in less expenditure of energy for a greater return. However, I really cannot imagine a pride of lions having a conference to work out the best tactics – with an appreciation of the specific purpose of the conference. I hasten to add that I don't literally mean they "discovered" anything – the lions that co-operated survived better than the ones that operated solo as they evolved. Those lions that hunted less efficiently or less collaboratively tended to produce fewer offspring.

To suggest that evolution itself is purpose-driven is scientific nonsense. Fishes did not develop lungs in order to invade the land; birds did not grow wings in order to fly, although some scientists may use that language. I believe Chris Packham, a rationalist presenter of "Spring Watch" on BBC TV, was speaking about a particular butterfly and said it was designed to survive. He does not actually believe someone designed this butterfly or that there was some purpose driving its evolution to design it in some particular way. It's just a way of saying something that fits in with the human perception of reality, like speaking of the sun rising and setting.

A purpose-driven process is said to be teleological; i.e. that there is an end or a purpose in view. Science, as a general rule, has no place for such thinking. But it is strange that creatures that are apparently part of and a product of a purposeless universe are capable of having a concept of purpose. It's strange that we can plan with a purpose. Why do we need to find purpose if there is none?

Just because science has to disregard this type of "purpose" does not logically mean that there is, therefore, no purpose in the universe. Science does not have all the answers to existence. It is only part of our understanding; one angle on the totality of existence.

Science and the explanation of purpose

In Dawkins' view, teleology is the thinking of children. He says:

> Bloom also suggests that we are innately predisposed to be creationists. Natural selection 'makes no intuitive sense'. Children are especially likely to assign purpose to everything, as the psychologist Deborah Keleman tells us in her article 'Are children "intuitive theists"?' Clouds are 'for raining'. Pointy rocks are 'so that animals could scratch on them when they get itchy'. The assignment of purpose to everything is called

*teleology. Children are native teleologists, and many
never grow out of it.*[233]

While I would agree that children are naturally teleologists, is it
therefore true that having a sense of teleology means someone is still
childish? Such logic is faulty.

Michael Shermer takes a somewhat different line in his book "The
Believing Brain". The blurb about this book on the Skeptic website
states:

> *We can't help believing. Our brains evolved to connect
> the dots of our world into meaningful patterns that
> explain why things happen. These meaningful patterns
> become beliefs. Once beliefs are formed the brain
> begins to look for and find confirmatory evidence
> in support of those beliefs, which adds an emotional
> boost of further confidence in the beliefs and thereby
> accelerates the process of reinforcing them, and round
> and round the process goes in a positive feedback loop
> of belief confirmation.*[234]

As I said in chapter 1, the scientific mind has to find explanations
for everything and here we have an illustration of that in Michael
Shermer. He has to explain why smart people believe in non-smart
concepts as he puts it. He is, himself, trying to connect the dots into
what is, for him, a meaningful pattern, and this has become for him
a belief about how religious beliefs are formed! It is just as true of

---

[233] "The God Delusion" page 210
[234] http://shop.skeptic.com/merchant.mvc?&Screen=PROD&
Store_Code=SS&Product_Code=b144HB

an atheist as a Christian. Shermer has a need to connect the dots in order to explain why, in his view, people believe nonsense. That is in order to make it fit with his world-view. But can he guarantee that his world-view is actually correct in the first place?

This is also the contention of Eugene Curry writing an article, *The Disbelieving Michael Shermer: A Review Essay of Michael Shermer's* **The Believing Brain**. He states that Shermer's evaluation of Francis Collins' conversion to Christ was that it was due to *"an emotional trigger"*, whereas his own conversion to atheism was facilitated initially by an *"intellectual consideration."*[235] This brilliantly illustrates the arrogance of New Atheist thinking.

It is automatically assumed that atheistic thinking is superior to religious thinking. It is entirely rational, whereas believers are irrational. His views are exempt from the wrong patterns that have evolved in the rest of the human race because he has become an atheist. According to Curry, he relies very much on evolutionary psychology that tries to explain absolutely every phenomenon of human psychology in evolutionary terms. Evolutionary psychology itself is not highly regarded as science because it cannot rely on empirical experimentation and verification.

Having said that, once again I think Shermer is at least partly right. There is a clear tendency within us to reject evidence that belies what we believe and to major on evidence that supports our beliefs. That is true of everyone, not only religious believers.

---

[235] Eugene A Curry, "The Disbelieving Michael Shermer: A Review Essay of Michael Shermer's *The Believing Brain*", Journal of the International Society of Christian Apologetics, Vol 5 No 1 April 2012

However, I would want to ask further questions. If the dots do not actually form meaningful patterns and the meaningful patterns we form in our minds are purely illusions, then why would we have evolved to form them? Maybe it's a by-product of some other aspect of our evolution. But why would scientists be trying to find the theory of everything? Surely a theory of everything would, in the end, be something that joins every single dot into a meaningful pattern – ultimately a pattern that is an illusion and is, therefore, completely pointless!

Science itself is a process of trying to join the dots and make meaningful patterns. Why pursue it if it is actually an illusion? Why try to find cohesive theories of anything? Why do I have a need to imagine there is a purpose to my life? Why not just live, reproduce successfully and then die? Why go through all the worry of trying to make my life worthwhile?

An Appetite for Wonder

Dawkins' biography is entitled, *An Appetite for Wonder*. It's great to have an appetite for wonder – I wish more Christians had. But what selective advantage does such an appetite give someone? What purpose can be served biologically by a mind like that? Are such people liable to produce more children – probably the reverse is true! What was the biological purpose in Fred Hoyle studying astrophysics as he did? Why are Brian Cox's presentations on astronomy so popular (apart from the fact that a lot of women find him attractive) and why do so many find the heavens enthralling? Why bother with any sort of scientific enquiry or artistic expression?

Maybe we can say it is simply the by-product of human intelligence. But human intelligence is massively more powerful than it needs to be for our biological survival. Saying there is no purpose in the universe or life is purely an opinion and nothing more. And if there is any purpose in life, science does not really have the means of explaining it to us.

Are we just biological machines?

Richard Dawkins, in exploring the difficulty of understanding just who or what we are, says:

> *A wave seems to move horizontally across the open sea, but the molecules of water move vertically. Similarly, sound waves may travel from speaker to listener, but the molecules of air don't; that would be a wind, not a sound. Steve Grand points out that you and I are more like waves than permanent 'things'. He invites his reader to think ... "of an experience from your childhood. Something you remember clearly, something you can see, feel, maybe even smell, as if you were really there. After all, you really were there, weren't you? How else would you remember it? But here is the bombshell: you **weren't** there. Not a single atom that is in your body today was there when that event took place... Matter flows from place to place and momentarily comes together to be you. Whatever you are, therefore, you are not the stuff of which you are made. If that doesn't make the hair stand up on the*

11

*back of your neck, read it again until it does, because
it is important".*[236]

"You are not the stuff you are made of!" Indeed, we're not – in a way, and yet in another, we are, even if it is temporary. But what we really are endures all the changes in the molecules of which we are made. So it was I as a child who lived on that farm in Rhodesia; it was you who was born on your particular birthday. Who you really are endures and lasts. What am I? What are you? Why can I not say that the essence of who I am is something beyond my physical makeup, even though all my thought processes may be explained in terms of chemical reactions; what I am is something beyond even my psychological make-up, my character, because if my character changes radically through some dramatic event, I will still be "me". You would still be "you".

What is wrong with calling that essence our soul? Just because we cannot point to its position, does not mean that it is not there. I cannot understand how someone can quote that with such approval and yet not have "eyes to see and ears to hear" and be able to look beyond the scientific box and see around the corner. There are aspects of life that could be better explained outside scientific concepts.

Possibly, in trying to understand purpose, we need to look beyond science and see if there are some answers.

---

[236] "The God Delusion" page 415

The concept of purpose

Atheistic thinking, imagining that science is all that is needed to explain life, would say that the universe is purposeless. You cannot have a teleological view of the universe.

Interestingly, I was listening to two Hindus on BBC Radio 4 and they were saying that in Hindu thought, there is no teleology in the universe; it has no purpose. One of them said the expansion and contraction of the universe is like God breathing in and out or opening and closing his eyes. I am certain they did not mean that literally, but it was a poetic way of putting it.

This is also believed by Theosophists and is termed "Involution/ Evolution". It is nothing to do with organic evolution, but to do with there being an *"infinite number of universes in an infinite cycle of births, deaths and rebirths."*[237] When you think about it, they are expressing in a poetic way what some scientists (mainly atheistic) postulated about a constantly expanding/contracting universe (Big Bang followed by Big Crunch) as a way of getting away from having to agree with the universe having a definite beginning.

They all believe, essentially, in the same or at least a very similar thing – a purposeless constant universe. While this says more about Hinduism and Theosophy being atheistic than atheism being religious, if we insist that Hindus believe in a god, then I feel we can legitimately say that some forms of atheism have a belief in a god-like theory even though there is clearly no belief in a "god entity". I

---

[237] McCandless, David, "Information is Beautiful" page 47 – source Wikipedia, New Scientist

would not class all atheists in the same category but I think the New Atheists may well be.

Getting back to our current theme, theism contends that the universe is not purposeless. In spite of the rationalist or freethinker claiming that our seeing purpose in the universe is an illusion created by minds that are more at ease with seeing purpose in events, they still need to answer the questions I posed above.

The fact is that we do need to see purpose in events. A baby dies or some other family tragedy occurs. One of the first questions is often, "Why did this have to happen?" I lost my brother Rob as a result of a car accident in 1988. All sorts of 'why' questions went through my mind. I still don't know why he died. Yes, I know the medical reasons – I'm not stupid but I can see no purpose in his death. He was literally one of the top cattle farmers in Zimbabwe and left a young wife and three very small children. His death was a loss to the country and a terrible loss to his family and friends. I can rationalise and say that he would have been horrified and heart-broken at the rape of the country that has taken place in recent years and is better off not having had to experience it but that is not a reason for his death. I cannot say there must be a purpose but there is a human need to find purpose.

God's purposes in our lives

Dawkins mentions Abraham's test when YHWH told him to sacrifice his son Isaac. He cites it as showing how totally unreasonable YHWH is (or is made out to be because Dawkins regards him as fiction anyway). I quite understand that view if we only look at this incident superficially. But it misses the point entirely. How can I really know whether I trust God or not, unless I am put in a position where that trust is tested?

It has happened to me – thankfully not in quite such a dramatic way. Having had my trust tested on numerous occasions, I can say I am grateful to God for putting me through the experiences although I never liked them at the time. I am sure Abraham was, too, once the test was over. There was a purpose in what God did and, in many instances in my life (not all), I can see the purpose in why I have had to go through certain experiences. I have been changed as a result.

Do our lives have a purpose?

I would imagine Richard Dawkins sees the purpose of his life, apart from scientific research, as being to enlighten those unfortunate people who believe in the fairy-story of religious doctrines, so that they realise they are trusting in a complete myth and that they follow his lead in giving it all up.[238] He says "*if this book works as I intend* (his purpose), *religious readers who open it will be atheists when they put it down.*"[239] But why have a purpose at all when the universe has no purpose? Why not just go with the flow and let things happen? We can say, with a fair degree of certainty, that Richard Dawkins considers his life to have at least one purpose. It is, however, a little

---

[238] I am sure a number of people will be influenced by him in losing their faith but I came across a young lady from Cambridge University who read his book, recognised the weakness of his arguments and decided she needed to investigate the Christian faith – and ended up becoming a Christian!

[239] "The God Delusion" page 27

ironic that his purpose is, when you think about it, to show people that there is no purpose.

The Bible makes outrageous statements, e.g. saying that believers are "called" and "chosen" – chosen even *before* the foundation of the cosmos.[240] What? How is it possible for us to be chosen before there was even the slightest inkling of our existence, when the chance of any individual coming into being is so tenuous as to be utterly impossible to predict, especially before the Big Bang had even happened? As I said earlier, we cannot easily speak about "*before* the Big Bang" if time started *with* the Big Bang.

I am pretty sure the apostle Paul knew just how preposterous his statement was when he spoke of being chosen before the foundation of the cosmos. He was a highly intelligent and educated man but it seems he had seen something most people could not even imagine. He goes on in this verse to say that we were chosen that we should be holy and blameless before him (God). He clearly reckoned that God had a purpose in choosing us.

Paul, moreover, saw his own calling by God to have a distinct purpose, as he explained to King Agrippa when on trial before him, He claims that Jesus spoke to him, saying, "*I have appeared to you for this purpose, to appoint you as a servant and witness to the things in which you have seen me and to those in which I will appear to you, delivering you from your people and from the Gentiles – to whom I am sending you to open their eyes, so that they may turn from darkness to light and from the power of Satan to God, that they may receive forgiveness of sins and a place among those who are sanctified by faith in*

---

[240] Ephesians chapter 1, verse 4

me.[241] He was called to be an apostle and an apostle had a specific function or purpose.

Jesus himself also clearly saw that his life on earth had a purpose – a purpose beyond teaching. He stated that he came to give his life for the forgiveness of sins. There was obviously far more to his life than that but the point is that *everyone* is seen as having a purpose.

Is science, therefore, wrong to reject teleology?

I do not actually have a problem with science refusing to accept a teleological view of the universe. It is not scientific to attribute purpose to processes or to animal instincts. The problem as I see it is that some people think that science has the only truly valid explanation for all things and as teleology is not scientific, attributing purpose to anything is, at best, an erroneous construct of the mind.

I hope I have shown that science is properly limited in its scope and cannot consider purpose, except as an interpretation, like the purpose of a predator in going hunting. But the fact that science cannot include it does not negate purpose in the universe.

My purely biological function is the procreation and nurturing of children until they can successfully repeat the process and perpetuate my genes. Having fulfilled my part in that, I could say that my function has been completed and I might as well just die. Matt Ridley makes this clear on pages 201 and 202 in his book *Genome*, where he shows that natural selection will weed out genes

---

[241] Acts chapter 26, verses 16-18

that cause damage in an organism during its reproductive phase but it has nothing to act upon with genes that cause damage after that phase is over because the organism has ceased to produce any offspring. Organisms have a sort of built-in obsolescence and in most, death will follow not long after the reproductive usefulness of that individual has ceased.

But I have no difficulty at all in believing that I can do more in the time I have left that will, I hope, be of benefit to others. It will not help perpetuate my genes but my purpose in life, I am convinced, is far more than my biological function. It could be argued that no one normally wants to die, so my conviction that I still have a purpose in living is purely wishful thinking. But, in that case, why do I not, like a butterfly, just die once I have reproduced and fulfilled my biological function?

I don't think the majority of people would disagree with the notion that older people can still be very useful members of society and can contribute, usually in some invaluable way, to those who are younger. They can perform a useful *function*. But function is not quite the same thing as purpose. Function has more of a sense of immediacy about it; it has a slightly mechanistic suggestion, as in "what is the function of the eye?" Purpose has a more distant final sense about it. We are thinking more about the overall effect of a life once it has come to an end, which is a teleological perspective. It is asking questions like: "Why am I here? Why am I alive at this moment in the history of the universe?"

Science can only answer, "You just happen to be alive now; there is no other reason than that." And, in fact, that would be perfectly true. Attempting to suggest some teleological reason would be scientific nonsense. It would be quite wrong of me, as a believer, to take issue with someone who looks at this question scientifically and gives an answer like that. Science cannot and should not give any type of metaphysical answer to the question "Why am I here?"

But faith can!

Because faith is looking at the same question in a completely different light, it is looking at answers that lie outside the realm of science. Believers need to understand the wonder and the limitations of science and stop fighting what they sometimes see as a contrary view to theirs. It's not contrary; it's just looking from a completely different angle. And there's nothing wrong with that angle. As a believer, I am able to incorporate and understand a scientific approach and, at the same time, see things from a spiritual perspective, without compromising either.

Christians (and I suspect most theists) believe that every person has a purpose, whether or not they know it. That is true of believers or non-believers. Sometimes that purpose may be difficult to determine but nobody is just a purposeless accident. While I include short-term purposes, I am thinking more of the overall purpose of someone's life. It even includes monsters like Hitler, Stalin and Amin as well as current megalomaniacs.

The purpose of creation

Viewed from the angle of faith, the universe is not purposeless, either. The Bible says, "*for by him all things were made, in heaven and on earth, things seen and things unseen, authorities, lords, rulers, and powers; all things were made by him and for him.*"[242] This is a totally non-scientific statement but that does not mean it isn't true. It is stating that Christ is responsible for creation (it doesn't say how) and that creation is there *for* him. Looked at from one viewpoint, it would be excusable to think it is saying the universe is there as his "toy" but that is only because of our limited understanding.

A Christian faith position would say that the ultimate purpose of the existence of the universe is that it is there "for" Christ; it is there for God. God created all things for himself. That seems like a very selfish reason from a human standpoint. But look at it this way: if God is love as the apostle John says, then he needs someone/something to love. The love that exists between the Persons of the Godhead is fine; God is infinite. But his very infinity means his love is inexhaustible; it too is infinite. Infinite love may flow within the Godhead but his love knows no bounds and he could create a universe (or maybe a multiverse) on which to lavish his love without diminishing the love between Father, Son and Spirit. Actually, true love is selfless, in that it lavishes all on the beloved. That is how God loves us.

An illustration of purpose

I think a good illustration of what I mean is a "Magic Eye" or stereogram picture. These are the pictures that are composed of a roughly repeating pattern. However, if you look through the picture (allowing your eyes to relax so that they are not looking directly at the pattern), and allow different parts of the pattern to coincide

---

[242] Colossians chapter 1, verse 16 (CEV)

or merge with each other, suddenly a 3-D image emerges which is probably nothing to do with the pattern but is composed of parts of the pattern.

Now the 3-D image is not actually there – it's an image that is formed by your mind and the effect of overlapping parts of the pattern. Obviously a scientist can explain what is happening to cause the image to appear, but the point is it is not real. Strictly speaking, the only thing that is "real" is the pattern. There is nothing more to it than that. I can imagine someone who is unable to "get it" saying that those who claim they can are only imagining it and it is nonsense. But the *whole purpose* of creating the pattern is to display the 3-D image. That is what makes the pattern meaningful. So, the image *is* there – it's just hidden to those who do not have "eyes to see".

In a similar way, I believe that the purpose of this universe is to display the nature of the God who created it – even though, from a scientific ("real"[243]) view, he is not there – but he *is* there – unseen to those who are unable to "get it". Jesus said, *"Having eyes do you not see, and having ears do you not hear?"*[244] Unless you are able to look "through" the seen and see something else behind it all, you will constantly think those who do are just imagining nonsense. Faith has to look beyond.

---

[243]   i.e. is measurable - matter, energy, force etc.
[244]   Mark chapter 8, verse 18

CHAPTER 17

Awe and Wonder and the Purpose of the Universe

Richard Dawkins has a great sense of awe at life and existence. Look at this that he wrote in his book, *The Ancestor's Tale* on page 506:

> *If, as returning host, I reflect on the whole pilgrimage of which I have been a grateful part, my overwhelming reaction is one of amazement. Amazement not only at the extravaganza of details we have seen; amazement, too, at the very fact that there are any such details to be had at all, on any planet. The universe could so easily have remained lifeless and simple, just physics and chemistry... The fact that it did not – the fact that life evolved out of nearly nothing, some 10 billion years after the universe evolved out of literally nothing – is a fact so staggering that I would be mad to attempt words to do it justice. And even that is not the end of the matter. Not only did evolution happen: it eventually led to beings capable of comprehending*

the process, and even of comprehending the process by which they comprehend it.

Yes, he is quite right. I find that staggering as well. How can this happen? But it did. I would add that the Bible states we are made in the image of God and if he created all things, then it is not surprising that we evolved to learn and have an appreciation of how he did it. But Dawkins goes on:

> *..... It is not pride in my book but reverence for life itself that encourages me to say, if you want a justification for the latter, open the former anywhere at random...*
>
> *Not only is life on this planet amazing and deeply satisfying, to all whose senses have become dulled by familiarity: the very fact that we have evolved the brain power to understand our evolutionary genesis redoubles the amazement and compounds the satisfaction.*
>
> *'Pilgrimage' implies piety and reverence. I have not had occasion here to mention my impatience with traditional piety, and my disdain for reverence where the object is anything supernatural. But I make no secret of them. It is not because I wish to limit or circumscribe reverence; not because I want to reduce or downgrade the true reverence with which we are moved to celebrate the universe, once we understand it properly. 'On the contrary' would be an understatement. My objection to supernatural beliefs is precisely that they miserably fail to do justice to the sublime grandeur of the real*

world. They represent a narrowing-down from reality,
an impoverishment of what the real world has to offer.

Although he is not expressing faith here, Dawkins is certainly expressing something of what I would hope faith would include. He may not recognize that this is the case but I sincerely believe faith must, if it is any good, result in this kind of reverence and even more so. Indeed, he continues:

> *I suspect that many who would call themselves religious*
> *would find themselves agreeing with me. To them I*
> *would only quote a favourite remark I overheard at a*
> *scientific conference. A distinguished elder statesman*
> *of my subject was having a long argument with a*
> *colleague. As the altercation came to an end, he*
> *twinkled and said, "You know, we really do agree. It's*
> *just that you say it wrong!"*[245]

I find myself rising to this wonder, this amazement. The universe is mind-blowing and causes us, if we allow it, to be filled with reverence and awe. Life, in its stupendous complexity, is even more amazing. It speaks to me and causes me to be lifted up. Of course, I mean that it speaks to me in a poetic way by making me look beyond the cold facts and see something else than simply biological life. Can we, however, say that the universe "speaks" to us? Is it legitimate to talk of reverence and awe, whether in a religious sense or not? I am sure it is.

---

[245]   Dawkins, Richard, "The Ancestor's Tale" page 506

The purpose of the whole creation

When Jesus entered Jerusalem on Palm Sunday, the people were shouting out praises to him. The Pharisees got pretty annoyed. It seemed the people imagined he was the Messiah. However, Jesus rebuked the Pharisees and said something quite extraordinary. He said if the people did not praise him, the very stones would cry out. I think this was more than mere hyperbole. Psalm 148, which I will repeat here, suggests that the entire creation is there to praise God:

(I can read this in two ways. I can read it like Christopher Hitchens as more evidence of the North Korean "Dear Leader" mentality or I can read it as it is meant to be read. God does not need our praise. He is not a megalomaniac with a diseased mind needing to be falsely adulated all the time. But we need to appreciate all he has done. Gratitude is the best attitude for living life. Turning your attention off yourself onto something greater is healthy. Can I suggest you read it as it was meant rather than as Hitchens would imagine).

> *Praise the LORD! Praise the LORD from the heavens;*
> *   praise him in the heights!*
> *Praise him, all his angels; praise him, all his hosts!*
> *Praise him, sun and moon, praise him, all you shining*
> *   stars!*
> *Praise him, you highest heavens, and you waters above*
> *   the heavens!*
> *Let them praise the name of the LORD! For he*
> *   commanded and they were created.*
> *And he established them forever and ever; he gave a*
> *   decree, and it shall not pass away.*

Praise the LORD from the earth, you great sea
creatures and all deeps,
fire and hail, snow and mist, stormy wind fulfilling
his word!
Mountains and all hills, fruit trees and all cedars!
Beasts and all livestock, creeping things and flying
birds!
Kings of the earth and all peoples, princes and all rulers
of the earth!
Young men and maidens together, old men and
children!
Let them praise the name of the LORD, for his name
alone is exalted; his majesty is above earth and
heaven.
He has raised up a horn for his people, praise for all his
saints, for the people of Israel who are near to him.
Praise the LORD! (English Standard Version).

Of course this is poetry, not literal. The psalms are all poetry. And poetry uses imagery to portray truth. That's the point: it is portraying truth. And the psalmist clearly gives a picture of the whole of creation praising God; even heavenly bodies and clouds. Just because we think of praise as being vocal does not mean that that is all there is to it. And – is this not expressing in some way something similar to what Dawkins was trying to express in his book? Maybe we could say, "You know we really do agree. It's just that you say it completely differently!"

According to the Bible then, the ultimate purpose of creation is to exist for the praise of the God who created it. This universe, so vast that it is really impossible for anyone to properly take in its incredible wonder, is not purposeless. I appreciate that to some readers this will seem like pure nonsense. It has nothing whatever to do with science. The very idea of trees praising sounds ludicrous, let alone inanimate objects like stars.

But maybe the praise the Bible speaks of in this context is something totally different from what we can imagine. And I cannot imagine what it means myself. However, truth does not depend on my imagination or knowledge or on yours.

I do believe that appreciating the science of the universe vastly enhances our appreciation of its beauty, and it enhances my wonder of the God who created it. When I think that he is infinite and the universe is finite (even though it seems infinite); when I realise that this God put in place everything needed to produce such an amazingly intricate system, (incorporating vast sub-systems), I can only lift up my heart in praise.

I cannot imagine we will ever come to the end of scientific discovery. Our constantly increasing knowledge only leads to more questions but that will never lead us to the purpose of the whole thing. It will only show us how it works. It is only as we are prepared to step around the corner and look from a completely different perspective that our mouths will drop open and we can declare, "Oh, so that's what it's all about!"

We don't believe there is purpose behind existence just because we are more comfortable with that view. That would be nonsense. As far as I am aware no other animal has that need, though of course I can't be certain of that. Why would we have evolved to have that need? Is it a product of some quirky result of natural selection or is it because we were created different from other animals not only in our body shape and intelligence but perhaps we have what the Bible calls "the breath of life" – a potential for understanding a totally different dimension from that which is sensed purely by our brains and bodies? Is there something around the corner waiting to be discovered? Is our mechanistic scientific view of the universe all there is? Has the fact that we can potentially explain every mechanism in this universe disproved the existence of any other dimension or can we explore it scientifically while at the same time glimpsing another dimension, another kingdom where meaning comes to light?

Is it at this point where we have to say science and faith have such different views of the universe that they are fundamentally separate; science looking at process and faith at purpose? My strong conviction is that this is not true and we need to go on to examine the possibility of the compatibility of science and faith in the next chapter.

CHAPTER 18

Are Science and Faith Incompatible?

Dawkins would (almost) definitely say yes. He states, *"nevertheless, there is something utterly special about the hypothesis of ultimate design, and equally special about the only known alternative: gradual evolution in the broad sense. They are close to being irreconcilably different."*[246]

It is certainly not just Richard Dawkins who strongly believes this. A very large number of people in the UK would say that science has disproved the Bible. I don't think as many would deny the historicity of Christ[247] but a fair few would.

Ben Fenton, writing in the "Daily Telegraph" of 27th November 2006, said, *"I've never been quite sure how Christians and other theists deal with evolution, as it seems to deal a rather severe blow to the need*

---

[246] "The God Delusion" page 85

[247] Dawkins insists Luke got his gospel wrong as the census was in AD6, but see the following sites for possible explanations of this: http://www.ankerberg.com/Articles/editors-choice/EC1205W3C.htm and http://www.biblehistory.net/newsletter/quirinius.htm

for a God. I mean, without creating the world, all He seems to have done since we became social beings a few thousand years is to referee the whole thing."

This betrays, again, a typical atheistic assumption that science can only have an atheistic interpretation when it actually can equally legitimately have a theistic or an atheistic interpretation, and it is interesting that a number of prominent scientists are evangelical Christian believers[248]. A 2009 poll estimated that as much as one in three of American scientists professed belief in God although it is hard to determine exactly what they mean by a belief in God.[249] But some of these are research scientists at the world's top universities. They are highly respected men and women in their different fields.

The percentage of believing scientists in the West grows to virtually one hundred percent Christian or at least believing in some sort of God when we look back in history to the pioneers of modern European science such as Newton, Descartes and Copernicus. Although Dawkins argues that this was because the only schools were then run by monks and this was the only way to get the equivalent of research grants, some have used the evident success of this modern European science to argue that it was the Christian

---

[248] Dawkins argues that their numbers are very small and he may be right. However, he quotes the findings of a study done by the Royal Society into the numbers of their fellows who are serious believers and it turned out to be about 4.8%. I would doubt if the percentage of genuine Christian believers in Britain is more than 5%, so this is very much in line with the general population, contrary to what he suggests. When I was at university, there seemed to be more serious believers in the Science faculty than in the Arts.

[249] http://www.pewforum.org/data/

worldview of a universe created by a purposeful God that gave the scientists the expectancy that they would be able to make sense of the universe and that it would obey repeatable and constant laws. I do want to stress, however, that these facts do not, of themselves, lend any legitimacy to a claim that God therefore exists.

In fact, the vast majority of these scientists would have ended up by developing scientific beliefs in the intelligibility and orderliness of the universe that were very close to those of Dawkins and other atheistic scientists.

Arguably, a Roman polytheist brought up on tales of the immoral and irrational and petty gods might well not have any reason to expect any kind of consistency in the behaviour of the universe – the poet Ovid in his series of allegorical poems *Metamorphoses*[250] envisaged the spiritual world as being a place where literally anything was possible and most of the time humans were the playthings of the Gods – rape being really quite routine! Clearly this would not lend confidence to any nascent scientist in ancient Greece or Rome (as they roughly shared the same mythology) as to any repeatable behaviour in the natural world – the very word "metamorphoses" speaks of unpredictable and strange transformations (most famously Narcissus turning, for no apparent reason apart from the whim of Zeus, into the flower of that name).

Is this a serious basis for observational and experimental science? This argument is not new. Although it doesn't really follow that atheism necessarily results in a similarly whimsical universe, there certainly is no guarantee (by the presence of a lawgiver and designer)

---

[250] en.wikipedia.org/wiki/Metamorphoses

that we can reasonably expect the universe to be intelligible to the mere blobs of protein and fat that we ostensibly are. Of course, the counter-argument could be that in fact we do observe repeatability in the universe and that our apparent "faith" that it will continue to be so is just the reasonable consequence of this empirical observation of continuity. But did I ever say you could win by rational argument alone?

Dawkins, in his conviction that there is no compatibility between science and a faith position, has quite a "downer" on modern believing scientists and other intellectuals, imagining that their reasonableness gives credibility to those who have sinister agendas – people like those he calls the American Taliban. For example, he speaks of C.S. Lewis *"who should have known better."*[251] I get the impression that he thinks they have very much let the side down and are traitors to the cause, rather like Muslim extremists who think ordinary non-violent Muslims are not being true to the Islamic faith. I am not saying his views are akin to those extremists, I hasten to add, but it is a bit ironic that this great promoter of radical free thinking gets annoyed with people who do not think like he does.

"Freethinking" – a myth?

I must say I am fascinated by the way language develops so that words mean something different from what they originally meant. An obvious example is the word "gay" which used to mean "happy" and was changed to mean "homosexual". Now, those of us involved in some UK schools find that teenagers are using the word to mean

---

[251] "The God Delusion" page 117

"disagreeable" or similar. So it has come to mean something almost opposite to its original meaning.

The word "freethinking" has come to be associated with atheism, going as far back as 1881 when *The Freethinker* magazine started. The implication is that people who believe in God cannot truly think for themselves. They are bound by dogma and have to believe certain things. Chris Barker, writing in *The Freethinker* defends Professor Richard Lynn who even suggests (as did Dawkins) that atheists are more intelligent than religious people.[252]

The Bible posits a different explanation of this observable phenomenon: that intellectual people have more self-respect than the ordinary person. Simply put, intellectual people, like the Greeks whom Paul encountered in Athens, have a tendency to rely on their own intellectual powers and to have a more jaded view of the enthusiasms of the common people, giving everything a "rational explanation" and being careful to show surprise or wonder at anything new.

Of course there are exceptions, of passionate and enthusiastic scientists who are almost incoherent with wonder at the beauty of the universe, as shown in the cartoons of the female biologist who coos in delight at the strange blobs of jelly that she is producing in her experiments. I have come across many scientists who share this infectious enthusiasm, both atheist and Christian.

---

[252] http://freethinker.co.uk/2012/05/26/atheists-are-more-intelligent-than-religious-people/

But when it comes to the matter of faith in an unrepeatable, non-material God who cannot be weighed or measured or in any way pinned down by human scientific means, one finds a baffling total incomprehensibility in these very likeable scientists. They say they would like to believe, they would love it if the story were true, but they just can't bring themselves to give assent to this proposition that they can't measure by their beloved scientific methods.

Is this simply what the Bible calls "pride"? This could be seen to be too condemnatory, as if they didn't want to concede a reality outside their control. In Paul's assessment of Greeks when he writes to the Christians of Corinth, he says the "gospel" is seen by the Greeks as merely "foolishness". Paul doesn't even seem to be embarrassed by this label, simply observing that the "*foolishness of God is wiser than the wisdom of man.*"[253]

In his third letter (called 2 Corinthians) to these believers, Paul gives another explanation for this inability to understand the gospel. He says "*in their case the god of this world has blinded the minds of the unbelievers, to keep them from seeing the light of the gospel of the glory of Christ, who is the image of God.*"[254] The "god of this world" is a reference to the devil or Satan who is portrayed as a deceiver. Now, the existence of a devil is largely regarded as a laughing matter by most people today but as C.S. Lewis pointed out in his *Screwtape Letters* the senior devil explains to his younger apprentice that one of the first strategies to employ is to convince his charge that they (the devils) do not exist.

---

[253] 1 Corinthians chapter 1, verse 25
[254] 2 Corinthians chapter 4, verse 4

(I remember hearing a story (probably fictional) of a wealthy worldly man who employed a naïve Christian as his personal servant. They got on well but the servant kept telling his master that he needed to believe otherwise "the devil would get him". The master simply said the devil never bothered him. One day he was out hunting pheasants and brought down two birds – one was virtually dead but the other one was only winged and was trying to take off. He sent his dog in and it went for the dying bird. "Stupid dog!" said the master, "Go for the other bird!" The servant said, "I have just realised why the devil doesn't bother you, sir!")

But, what I find fascinating about freethinking is that you have to be an atheist to be a freethinker. You are not allowed to believe in God and be a freethinker. Only those who believe in the non-existence of God can truly be classified as freethinkers. And that is free?

Did Alister McGrath or C.S. Lewis or Denis Alexander or Andrew Sims become less intelligent on realising that believing in God made more sense than their previous atheistic convictions? Did they give up their open enquiring minds? When you examine the use of terms like this, you realise that atheists can be just as coercive as the more extreme religious believers. They have simply hijacked a word. The problem is they then believe the propaganda it promotes without thinking about it.

Of course there are plenty of instances of forced religious belief. Many of the "Christian" cults that have sprung up in recent years use some type of coercion. There are numerous examples, particularly among the closed communities. Some of these have led to tragic results like the Jonestown massacres of 1978 and the case of David Koresh with his followers on a ranch near Waco in Texas in 1993.

These cults are actually anything but Christian but they are religious nonetheless. It is also very difficult for Jehovah's witnesses to leave their religion without being severely ostracised and castigated.

In spite of the Qur'an stating that *"there is no compulsion in religion"*[255], Muslims who convert to any other religion can be subjected to persecution and even death. However, strictly speaking, that is going against at least what this part of the Qur'an teaches. Not being familiar with the whole of this work, I cannot comment on whether or not there are verses commanding death for converts from Islam to other religions.

There is coercion among some Christians, too. But that is distinctly *not* biblical Christianity. The apostle Paul, arguing about whether or not to observe certain days above others, said, *"Let every man be convinced in his own mind."*[256] He may have been dealing with a limited issue but the principle still stands. It is quite wrong to insist on someone believing something they cannot genuinely believe. That's not belief; it's not faith. It is bondage. The gospel, on the other hand, is repeatedly stated in John's account to have as its purpose to "set people free". Are we to maintain an attitude of "ah, you say that, but I know better" when it comes to the person of Jesus who was, very few people deny at the very least, a model human being?

The truth is that not a single person on this planet is a completely free thinker. Some may be freer than others but no one is completely free. Every one of us has been influenced by our past, by our personality, by our parents, teachers, friends and many other people.

---

[255] Surah 2:256
[256] Romans chapter 14, verse 5

We have been influenced by our experiences. That influence can be positive, drawing us toward itself, or negative, driving us away. We are undoubtedly influenced by our genes. If you think you are truly a free thinker, independent of any kind of genetic, hormonal or psychological influence and independent of any consideration of what others think of you, then I suggest you think again and do an honest appraisal.

My younger daughter, Ruth, has studied for both her first degree in Natural Sciences and her Master of Research at Cambridge University before going on to a PhD. We have had numerous discussions on our journeys back and forth and in one of her Father's Day cards to me she said, "Thank you for the chats we have had and for challenging me to look at the world in different ways". I have tried to ensure that they all think for themselves and that they believe whatever they do because of their own convictions, not mine. My older daughter and son both questioned the veracity of the Christian faith that we taught them and we encouraged them to do so. My son spent some time having partly abandoned what we taught him in childhood. When he eventually came back, it was on his own conviction. We had been praying for him but we never battled to persuade him.

But we also have to ask the question: What guarantee of truth does free thinking give you anyway? Dawkins says, *"People of a theological bent are often chronically incapable of distinguishing what is true from what they would like to be true."*[257] This implies that theology somehow tends to cause an inability to discern truth from error while he, as an atheist, is equipped to do so.

---

[257] "The God Delusion" page 135

Does this view stack up? Anyone can be deceived, religious or not. Granted, being forced to think in any particular way is not good but if anyone thinks that they can come to their own conclusions uninfluenced, they have to be either extremely arrogant or extremely stupid. The whole of our knowledge and understanding has come about as the result of the cumulative thinking of billions of people down through the ages. Isn't it sensible to find the wisdom of others and learn from it? Even critics of the Bible agree that there is the most amazing wisdom contained within it if only one takes the time to explore it.

In today's world, where knowledge is highly prized, we seem to have lost our appreciation of wisdom. I exceeded my parents' level of education and ended up knowing and understanding more than they did about science. But they had had greater experience of life and greater wisdom than I had. I have found that some old African tribal elders may be totally uneducated but still have a wisdom born of experience that is of great benefit to others. It makes sense to learn from our predecessors not only their knowledge but their accumulated wisdom as well.

Looking at the world

But perhaps Dawkins is right. Perhaps there is only one valid explanation for the universe and life. Perhaps science supersedes everything else; maybe science will find the theory of everything, the end of the infinite regress and we will finally have something in which we can totally put our trust and in which every other theory finds its origin. Oh, sorry, that is beginning to sound awfully like finding God!

Is God a Super-Angel?

I cannot be sure of this but I believe I am right in saying that most atheists would have a very similar concept to that of Richard Dawkins, i.e. that Christians believe in God as an entity having a discrete existence (probably in a spiritual form like some kind of super-angel but still able to be examined by some sort of scientific instrument). If you are an atheist and that is not your view, then please accept my apologies. Angels are technically spirits created by God, and although God is also Spirit (i.e. non-material) the distinction is that God is not created by anyone, but has always existed before the origin of the observable universe and even now upholds and maintains the universe.

I do think that a good many Christians probably do believe in God as some sort of super-entity, but that is not a biblical concept.

Some Christians accuse scientists of a conspiracy to push evolution and that they withhold evidence against it. I cannot agree with that. It may be true of a few militant atheists but the vast majority of evolutionary biologists are simply trying to investigate the theory and refine it. There are many different variations on how it would have happened in specific instances. That does not mean there are different theories of evolution as some people suggest or that there is massive disagreement among scientists. Science progresses through disagreement, investigation, etc. We need to understand this and avoid giving the wrong impression about other people's motives.

I have to say that if God is like a super-angel and it is claimed that this kind of God is responsible for creating the universe approximately six thousand years ago over a six-day period, then call me an atheist (I wonder how many creationists will use that to try and discredit me).

Creationism and compatibility

There has been considerable effort expended to try and prove that the universe is only six thousand years old. This is, basically, a creationist approach to show the compatibility of science and faith but strictly on "creation science" grounds. However, if you consider simply that our home galaxy, the Milky Way is one hundred thousand light years across and we can see, by sophisticated instruments, across the other side, it means the light has been travelling for at least one hundred thousand years. And we are able to see billions of light years into the universe. That light has taken that long to reach us. It is difficult to maintain a young earth creationist stance when faced with that kind of evidence. Our nearest galaxy is Andromeda. It is 2.6 million light years away and has been known for a very long time by astronomers. If the universe was six thousand years old, we would not be able to see any other galaxy and most of the Milky Way would be invisible to us.

I hope I have already argued sufficiently that God is not an entity, however. So trying to argue for the non-existence of God assuming he is an entity is totally irrelevant. And that means that much of Dawkins' argument is irrelevant.

Atheists may object that I am simply putting God out of bounds for scientific investigation and that this proves nothing. They are right. But it is ridiculous to attack a view of God that is not held by your opponent, which is precisely what I find the New Atheists doing. So *they* prove nothing. They are simply stating that an imaginary God does not exist! Most Christians would agree.

In fact it can be argued that the modern scientific understanding of the immense age of the Universe, coupled with what many maintain to be the "reasonable presupposition" of a transcendent God-creator, in fact can deepen our awe of God. A God who is willing to watch over such a vast universe as it expands and evolves to increasing complexity over such long periods of time must be a very patient and all-seeing God!

Dr Christina Biggs pointed out to me that "*in fact, the universe is not inconceivably or infinitely vast, nor is it so ancient that Earth could be seen to be a mere freak of chance and a totally insignificant small mote in time and space.*"

I asked her to explain and she said that:

> *Our Sun, at 4.5 billion years of age and therefore about a third of the 13.82 billion years old Universe, is likely to be just a second-generation star. We know that for there to be the whole range of atomic elements present in our planet as in all the objects in the Solar System (including the Sun), that the Solar System must be itself formed from the dust of a dying supernova and therefore there must have been at least one "parent" star going through the whole lifecycle of a star from protostar to red giant to supernova, just to "cook" the elements at the intense heat necessary. But it seems to be a little, if ever, commented-on fact that our Solar System cannot, from its age, have more than about*

five short star life-cycles in its genealogy? Coupled with the fact of the very recent emergence of Homo sapiens in the process of the biological evolution on Earth, it almost seems too neat, that the Universe is only just old enough to have given rise to a species such as ours that has evolved through the natural evolutionary process! Could it be that evolution is in fact God's best chosen method of bringing about freely-thinking sentient beings with a sufficient complexity to appreciate in any depth the sheer interest of God's character with his humour, wisdom, joy, and of course, blazing love; that he is content to work with us but only really (as Lewis puts it) satisfied with what we could think of as "fully evolved", morally perfect humankind?

Ok, so can we find any real compatibility between science and faith? There is a deal of incompatibility when dealing with the doctrinal stances taken by some, but I hope I have shown that these positions are not necessarily "what Christians believe". I believe it necessary to state what I would personally judge to be the bare minimum of Christian belief and see if we can find some compatibility there. I will try to do that in the next chapter.

CHAPTER 19

Can we find any Compatibility?

What is essential Christian belief?

With the disagreement among Christians that exists over the "how" and the age of creation, I shall try and set out what I see as the bare minimum of Christian faith as far as God and creation is concerned. Let me say (before anyone misconstrues the above question) that by "essential" I do not mean any sort of compulsion. There are certain irreducible minima of belief that mark out someone as being a Christian. This cannot be compared with freethinking which merely suggests that people who do not subscribe to an atheistic belief system are not free. But it would be perfectly reasonable to say that if you believe in God you cannot be classed as an atheist. My mother was once asking a young lady about her mother and the lady said to her, "My mother doesn't believe in God but she is definitely a Christian!" The lack of logic is obvious!

So what are the basic Christian beliefs, stripped of denominational tenets or particular interpretations?

282

- Firstly, it is essential to believe in the existence of the self-existent (uncreated) transcendent and immanent God and only one God, eternal, immortal, infinite and invisible.
- Then, that this one God is manifested in three "Persons" – Father, Son and Holy Spirit. These three are not parts of God; each is fully God, of precisely the same nature.
- **Then, that this God created all things.** This is not necessarily creationism; that is an interpretation. **It is simply that the whole of creation came from absolutely nothing ("creatio ex nihilo" is the theological term) and all matter, time and space and every aspect of creation was created by God.** I say this even though the Hebrew word "bara" actually has more of a sense of fattened rather than created.
- Then, that the Son became fully man. He was not half-man, half-God but completely man and yet still God. Yes, he gave up his glory while on earth but he never ceased being God.
- Then, that he died on a cross and was raised from the dead, not resuscitated (brought back to life) but that he was raised with a different kind of body.
- Then, that his death & resurrection enable anyone who believes to be forgiven their sin and enter into a new life of following him. Following him is only possible because he has sent the Holy Spirit to live within believers.

Now, I imagine some people reading the above saying, "And you believe that?" Yes, I do. Just because you don't believe it does not make it untrue. Just because I do does not make it true. I am not stating these to try and convince you. You need to be convinced in your own mind (to borrow a biblical phrase).

I am simply stating Christian beliefs like this so that we have a basis on which to pursue further discussion in this chapter. I shall be concentrating on the aspect of belief about creation (in bold above) because that is where the whole issue of faith and science impinge on each other the most.

Genesis

The oft-quoted figure of six thousand years for the age of the Earth has a relatively simple and internally logical origin, if numerically inaccurate. Archbishop James Ussher (1581 – 1656) calculated the date of creation as being the night before Sunday 23rd October 4004 BC. This was done, no doubt, by calculating backwards taking into account the reigns of the various kings of Israel and Judah, the sequence of a combination of the two named genealogies of Jesus listed by two of the gospel "reporters", and the ages of the patriarchs listed in Genesis all the way back to Adam and Eve. This assumes the total accuracy of each age mentioned, thinking of years as our currently understood time of 365.26 sidereal days on average, without considering that the Hebrews saw genealogy differently from the way we see it today. So, they would say "son of" for anyone who was descended from a particular person. Jesus was called "son of David" even though there were numerous generations between them. It also assumes that wherever the word "day" is mentioned, it has to be understood as a literal twenty four hour day. It ignores the Hebrew language which was very "concrete" in its expression and so expressed abstract ideas in concrete language.

Looked at from our perspective now, this does seem a most extraordinary calculation but ever since then many Christians have taken that as being absolute and to this day a fairly sizeable proportion still believe it.

I am only describing here what people agree is the standard "six-day creationist " account for the record. As the aim of this book is to try and acknowledge Richard Dawkins' challenge to the Christian church in his pivotal work of *The God Delusion*, I am principally talking to scientists here, whether Christian or not.

Very few Christians with a good background or even general understanding of science take this hypothesis of a "six-day creation" followed by just six thousand years of history before the present day literally, as the scientific evidence for an Earth 4.5 billion years old and a universe 13.8 billion years old is so well-established as to be universally recognised. The vast age of the Universe is even accepted by the recent Intelligent Design movement, who would still insist that the development of biological life can be demonstrated to be designed rather than the product of random mutation plus natural selection and hence reject the current understanding of the process of evolution that is so widely accepted by the majority of biologists of both Christian faith or none.

If a "six-day creationist" reading this wants to argue with me, I am not going to rise to the bait and argue the toss about interpretations of Genesis or indeed about the possible change in the speed of light with time (which seems to be a currently popular theory). I would say only two things:

Firstly, why would God create a universe with an appearance of great age when it is only ten thousand years old or less? Why would he want to deceive us, especially when Paul says in the book of Romans *"for what can be known about God is plain to them, because God has shown it to them. For his invisible attributes, namely, his eternal power and divine nature, have been clearly perceived, ever since the creation of the world, in the things that have been made. So they are without excuse."*[258] To suggest that this is the case would suggest, at least to me, that God is a deceiver and so people would have an excuse for not believing him.

Most importantly, though, I believe that such a literalistic interpretation robs the Bible of one of its main purposes, which is not so much to inform as to stimulate and cause us to seek; to impart wisdom more than knowledge.

Secondly I would say, for which I am grateful to Ernest Lucas in *Can we believe Genesis today*, that the Genesis language about the cosmos is almost laughable in its naïveté until we realise the lack of resources the ancients had: for example, the word "firmament" in the Hebrew used to describe the sky is literally a metal dome with holes (the windows of heaven) in it for the rainwater to come through[259]. Again, the ancients did not enjoy the benefits of telescopes to tell them otherwise; so we should not sneer, but realise that maybe for God the important thing was not an "accurate" twenty first century description of his universe, but what the Hebrews understood about God's lordship over it – it has been pointed out that God making the "two lights in the sky" (the sun and moon) carefully avoided attributing any sense of deity to these created objects (in contrast to the beliefs of most religions around the Hebrews), and the throwaway *"and he also made the stars"* should bowl us over. According to some

---

[258]   Romans chapter 1, verses 19 & 20
[259]   http://en.wikipedia.org/wiki/Firmament

estimates, there could be as many as one hundred and seventy billion galaxies with the number of stars in each ranging from ten million to over one hundred trillion!

The "Big Bang"

We have already looked at the current theory about the origin of the universe (as we know it) – the Big Bang theory. It is based on the observable evidence that galaxies are generally moving away from each other, so the universe is constantly expanding. This has been extrapolated backwards to calculate that the universe is about 13.8 billion years old and that it must have originated as a singularity which suddenly "inflated" as astrophysicists would term it. As already mentioned, the current hypothesis is that there was "no space, no time, no universe". This has exercised my brain and, of course, it is something impossible to visualise – we have no point of reference or imagination. What was there? The singularity was really nothing and nothing became something. How? What caused it? There were no laws to govern it. As I was thinking about this, I happened to come, in my regular Bible reading, to John chapter 1, verses 1–3 where I read this statement (please note, I do not say "this explanation"): *In the beginning was the Word and the Word was with God and the Word was God. He was in the beginning with God. All things were made through him, and without him was not anything made that has been made."*

In my imagination I was transported 13.8 billion years back to the beginning. As I said before, one day we may be able to work out how something can come from absolutely nothing, but although I could not imagine in any way what the scene could be like, I saw, poetically, the answer to my question "What was there?" Scientists say nothing suddenly became something; Christians say God created all things *ex nihilo* (out of nothing). I really don't see a conflict or incompatibility. The Word was there; God was there. Words have creative power. And words convey information and meaning. Does that relate, in some way, to the laws of physics?

Matter was rapidly formed from the vast energy that was released and gas spread at mind-blowing speed so that within about 15 seconds the new universe was about the size of the solar system. That, by the way, is many times faster than the speed of light. This has continued ever since, with galaxies and nebulae forming and stars within them plus planets around some stars.

Breaking news in March 2014 of the discovery of gravitational waves or ripples in the structure of space-time from the oldest known light in the universe by researchers at the Harvard-Smithsonian Centre for Astrophysics suggests that the theory of an eternal pulsating universe is incorrect. If this finding is correct, the discovery of waves from the calculated time of the immediate birth of the universe is the strongest evidence yet found of a spectacularly rapid period of inflation immediately after the Big Bang.

But historically, readers may be surprised to learn that in fact the discovery of a definite point in time at which the universe came into being (or at least a point from which the universe was seen to expand) was unsavoury to the non-believing scientists of the time, who saw immediately that this was compatible with the idea of a God creating the universe from nothing. In its place, many respectable astrophysicists tried to push an idea – the "Steady-State theory" of an eternal universe that has always existed.

The observed expansion in all directions of the universe is deduced from the Doppler effect ("red-shift") in the wavelength of light produced by known elements in the stars, but the Steady-State theorists tried to reconcile this fact with their favoured theory by hypothesising that galaxies were continuously being created from nothing to fill the space made as the universe expanded so that the universe could be said to have always had the state of continuously expanding. Of course that would mean that if the universe had always been there (eternally) and had always been expanding, its size would be infinite. And, as far as we know, it isn't. This theory has now been all but discarded.

Compatibility?

Andrew Parker, in his *Genesis Enigma*, was staggered at how the authors could have written stuff that coincided so amazingly with our present understanding of origins, I have noticed something similar. What follows is an attempt to show that, in some ways, the Genesis account *does* reflect our current scientific understanding of the origins of the universe, the solar system, Earth and life on Earth. But I am, in no way, trying to show that this account parallels science.

If you accept, as I feel is reasonable, that the Genesis account is poetic (there is evidence that it was written in an ancient Hebraic poetic style[260]), then I feel we can examine it in a very different light. Even today, we speak of the sun rising and setting although

---

[260] Ancient Hebrew Research Center http://www.ancient-hebrew.org/23_ genesis_1.html

we know it doesn't. I don't have any problem in using those terms. They express a truth about the movement of Earth relative to the sun which is meaningful and helpful. We speak of the moon as full or new and of it waxing and waning, in spite of the fact that it doesn't change shape at all. But it seems to do so to us. The writers of the Bible were not trying to produce a modern scientific account of the origins of the universe. They were writing in a way that expressed what it would have been like to observe things happening had there been anyone on Earth to do so.

If we take the Hebrew word "bara" to mean "fattened", then the very first verse could be said to express something like the Big Bang Theory. I reckon "fattened" is quite descriptive of this possible gigantic on-going inflation. It becomes, "In the beginning, God *fattened* the heavens and the earth".

If the solar system evolved as is suggested, with gases around the sun slowly cooling and coalescing to form gaseous blobs which eventually formed planets under the influence of gravitational forces; then that some of these contracted and formed the rocky planets: Mercury, Venus, Earth and Mars, the biblical account actually fits somewhat with it. It says *"the earth was without form and void"*. Is this a description of a gaseous stage?

As it solidified, any water on a young extremely hot earth would have existed as a huge cloud of steam and vapour enveloping the hot rocky surface. As it cooled, some would have started to liquefy and remain on the surface, eventually forming seas (the waters above the firmament being separated from the waters below the firmament even though, as I have said, the firmament was thought of as a sort of metal dome). Light would have been visible after some time but no heavenly bodies would appear until there were breaks in the clouds, so the sun, moon and stars would not appear for a while. I am quite happy seeing it as a truthful poetic account of this process but it certainly isn't scientific.

The evolution of life

Both the Big Bang and evolution are highly emotive issues as far as a great many religious people are concerned, and not only among Christians. I have had (brief) discussions with a Muslim who was also utterly convinced that evolution was a lie. He was, no doubt, basing his belief on a literalistic interpretation of the Qur'an (which contains some similar accounts to the Hebrew scriptures).

I have a number of very close friends who believe firmly in a six-day creation six thousand years ago and that all species were created in forms very like those we see today. I respect them, even though I disagree with them. I would say, though, that the precise wording of the Genesis account is not the central issue.

Richard Dawkins has accurately put his finger on the central issue here: what does a full acceptance of evolution (random mutation and cold indifferent natural selection) say about the character and care of God for his world? Are we saying that everything we see around us is, in origin, the product of the "values" of randomness and purposeless lack of direction on the part of God?

Dawkins describes the evolutionary process excellently in his various books – e.g. *The Selfish Gene*, *The Ancestor's Tale* and *Climbing Mount Improbable*, where he shows the step-by-small-step series of unnoticeable changes over millions of years that get us to the amazing variety of biological species we see today. In *The Blind Watchmaker* he discusses what he calls "The Dawkins' Weasel" – a computerised program starting with random strings of characters (as if someone who had no idea what they were typing were using a typewriter) and continues line after line, but every time they hit a letter in the correct place, it "sticks" there. Generally speaking, after somewhere between forty to a hundred lines, the statement, "Methinks it is like a weasel" will appear. This illustrates how randomness can generate something meaningful (a functioning organism). The sticking of characters would represent mutations that are beneficial and so are retained.[261]

Does this view of the origins of life mean that, if there is a God, he is lazy? Do the principles of randomness, purposelessness and lack of direction in evolution lead us to conclude that God lacks inspiration and ideas? Or is he some sort of cosmic gamester throwing the dice and seeing what comes out? Is the appearance of design and acceptance that the universe must be designed the result of a philosophical laziness that refuses to acknowledge the need for a rigorous scientific approach to origins?

Dawkins' writing stands out for his appreciation of the beauty, elegance and ingeniousness of the system he studies. He excellently demonstrates the overwhelming evidence for the Darwinian understanding of evolution and explains it in clear succinct ways.

One of the big objections to evidence for evolution on the part of creationists is the supposed evolution of the eye. They point out that for the eye to function properly, everything about it would have to

---

[261] http://www.softwarematters.org/weasel.html

CAN WE FIND ANY COMPATIBILITY?

work all at once, and it would be impossible for all that to evolve together so that it was a fully functioning eye. He deals with this in some detail and shows how that is an erroneous assumption.

His conclusion over the creationist view of a God who just snaps his fingers and creates a ready-made universe in six twenty four hour periods and then gives it an appearance of age is that such a God is lazy and that such a scientific approach is lazy because it does not bother to try and find intelligent answers.

Actually, I agree! If God is behind absolutely everything, then to use God *as an explanation* for anything is, for a scientist, laziness. Either he does everything or he does nothing. Dawkins is quite right to attack the "God of the gaps" approach to science. It is just not good enough. Creationists need to think about that!

But surely a God who can create a universe with the amazing laws that govern it; that evolves over billions of years to produce the wonder that we observe, let alone what we still have to discover or the beauty and complexity of living systems that are self-adjusting and adapting must be anything but lazy! Dawkins attacks those theists who accept natural selection saying they do not have their consciousness raised but that "*They note that evolution by natural selection would be a very easy and neat way to achieve a world full of life. God wouldn't need to do anything at all.*"[262] I have never heard that thought from any theist and would count myself among those who fully accept evolution and natural selection.

---

[262] "The God Delusion" page 143

But what was God doing while the universe evolved over the 13.8 billion years we think it took? Was he just "twiddling his thumbs" (a picture – please don't take that literally) watching it unfold according to the laws he had set up. Is he a deistic absentee landlord just allowing things to happen and leaving no evidence whatever of his existence? Does he care nothing about what happens in the photosynthetic reactions going on inside a leaf as long as most leaves continue to photosynthesise?

Is he involved or not? If he isn't, we may as well forget him and just get on with life. As far as we are concerned, such a God to all intents and purposes might as well not exist. That sort of God is hardly necessary as any kind of serious explanation for the colossal variety of life we see. And if it is a matter of a God who snaps his fingers to create everything being a "lazy" kind of God as Dawkins suggests, then surely evolution has done away with the "need for a God" as Ben Fenton puts it.

As Andrew Parker observed, the creation accounts in Genesis bear extraordinary pointers to a possible evolutionary process. I pointed out in the Introduction and earlier in this chapter that I had seen similar pointers.

A summary view

To summarise what I believe is a reasonable view, I would say that God is intimately involved in absolutely everything, even though everything to do with matter, energy, force, etc. works according to laws and theories we already know and are continually discovering. Those laws were "thought out" by God in the first place and they represent his working and if we have "eyes to see" and "ears to hear", we will understand that he is revealed through them (yes, including the harshness of so much of existence).

I believe that behind this apparently cold indifferent universe, there is a God who is able to make *all things work together for good to those who love God, to those who are called according to His purpose.*[263] I believe, beyond that, that his desire is also for those who do not love him, for those who see no purpose in this indifferent universe. However, I do not think there is any incontrovertible evidence to support this as an argument. I believe he has deliberately made it hidden to those who do not want to believe. It is only those who are prepared to admit they may not have it all "sussed out" and are prepared to look around the corner who will begin to catch a glimpse of who is behind this extraordinary creation (the living and the non-living).

House or home

Houses are built of bricks or stones and mortar, of timber and roofing material. Homes are built on relationships, on belonging, on loving and being loved, on acceptance. You feel you can be yourself in your home; you don't have to pretend. We may say, "That is my house" or "That is my home". We may be talking about the same physical structure but there is a big difference between the two statements. You know exactly what I am saying. Science studies houses. Faith seeks and finds a home.

---

[263] Romans chapter 8, verse 28

Science looks at what is; what can be quantified; it looks at the structure and, sometimes, concludes that there is nothing else to it. There is nothing else to a house than the house. I can potentially know absolutely everything there is to know about a house. But if I neglect to see that its purpose is to be a home where people live and move and eat, where they relate to each other with all the joys and pains of those relationships, then I find I actually don't know what the house is all about. That is another dimension to the house that I would not have realised. A house can be a house without being a home. I need to see it very differently to see it as a home.

Finding the poetry

I love Alfred Tennyson's "The Eagle". Let me quote it here.

> *He clasps the crag with crooked hands;*
> *Close to the sun in lonely lands,*
> *Ring'd with the azure world, he stands.*
>
> *The wrinkled sea beneath him crawls;*
> *He watches from his mountain walls,*
> *And, like a thunderbolt, he falls.*

If we were to examine this scientifically, we would have to conclude that the whole thing is rubbish. Firstly, eagles don't have hands. Secondly, they are no nearer the sun than I am and, if I happen to be at a greater altitude than the eagle or if I am on the equator and the eagle in the Scottish highlands, it is further than I am. Then, we may be able to describe the sky as azure but the world isn't. And to describe an eagle as being ringed with the world is totally inaccurate. In the second verse, we could protest that the sea isn't actually wrinkled, though some may think of waves as wrinkles. The sea, strictly speaking, does not crawl. In fact the water particles stay pretty much in the same place as the waves pass by. In addition, mountains do not have walls and eagles do not fall like thunderbolts.

But, if I ignore the science, I find it still expresses the truth about this magnificent bird. It evokes in me a picture that causes awe which was Tennyson's intention. By understanding something of the science of eagles and reading the poem but not confusing the two, my appreciation is massively enhanced.

The biblical account of creation is the poetry behind the science. It is not supposed to be the science and we could pick all sorts of holes in it if viewed purely scientifically but it is the truth, and, as I hope I have shown, it is not incompatible with current scientific theory provided one understands that it is making statements that are not meant to be scientific. It is, actually, far more scientifically compatible than Tennyson's "Eagle" and yet, I am sure the vast majority of atheists would have no difficulty with Tennyson. That leads me to believe that the objection to the existence of God and insistence on such a scientific approach by some atheists has little to do with science and more to do with what they *want* to believe. It has less to do with an intellectual conviction and more to do with an emotional antipathy towards belief.

Can we not see that there may be another dimension to life beyond the obvious? Are we so proud of our intellectual ability that we fail to see that perhaps *"the foolishness of God is wiser than men"*[264]? The

---

[264] 1 Corinthians chapter 1, verse 25

more I learn, the more I realise how very little I know – and I really mean that in spite of it being a cliché. I am becoming more and more dubious about those who "have it all worked out". Jesus, it seemed, never sought to give people answers that resulted in no further questioning, but rather tried to get them to seek further, because it is only in seeking that we will find and once we cease seeking because we think we have the answer, we stop learning – and we are in danger of despising those who are still seeking because they have not found the answer as we have. Jesus sought seekers as those who would follow him.

Richard Dawkins is very moved by poetry. In his book *Unweaving the Rainbow* he speaks of ultimate meaning and the poetry of science and I think he is absolutely right. That poetry is not heard in a cold appreciation of facts but in seeing the wonder and beauty behind it; in appreciating the intricacy and exquisite interdependence of all things. You have to have a mentality that "looks beyond" the cold facts. You have to have an appetite for wonder as he so rightly expresses in the title of his autobiography. But who is to say we must stop there? Who is to say there is not another dimension, another poetic appreciation that goes beyond? I may be able to see beyond the facts of the refraction of light in a rainbow and drink in the beauty, but does that mean it cannot also speak to me of another glory? Do I have to stop with a limited human appreciation? Why do I have to conclude there is no more to it than that?

Richard Dawkins has very effectively demolished belief in the atheist concept of "God" – a God in which they imagine Christians believe, but actually a concept that is a figment of their own and his imagination, based on atheistic presuppositions about the universe. He has made some very valid points about the church and I am grateful to him for that. Christians would do well to take note of his criticisms, but I hope I have shown that he has completely failed to address his primary purpose in his book – to show that no God exists. I am totally confident that God is alive and well and is just as infinite and eternal as he has always been and always will be. No argument one way or the other will ever change the truth. As humans, we do not have the prerogative of deciding on the existence or non-existence of God.

It's about time we became honest and admitted that none of us has the full answer. I can learn much from others. I enjoy being challenged by those who have the humility to realise they do not have all the answers. I can learn much from them. I hope they can learn from me.

My appeal is to both Christians and atheists. Let's stop our entrenched attitudes; let Christians become honest over science and learn from it; let atheists open their minds to the fact that there could be another dimension they have not even dreamed of yet. Both sides of this silly debate would be enriched by listening to each other.

CHAPTER 20

Concluding thoughts

A call to work together

Richard P Feynman, the great physicist said, in 1956:

> *Western civilization, it seems to me, stands by two great heritages. One is the scientific spirit of adventure — the adventure into the unknown, an unknown which must be recognized as being unknown in order to be explored; the demand that the unanswerable mysteries of the universe remain unanswered; the attitude that all is uncertain; to summarize it – the humility of the intellect. The other great heritage is Christian ethics – the basis of action on love, the brotherhood of all men, the value of the individual – the humility of the spirit.*

> *These two heritages are logically, thoroughly consistent. But logic is not all; one needs one's heart to follow an idea. If people are going back to religion, what are they going back to? Is the modern church a place to give comfort to a man who doubts God – more,*

one who disbelieves in God? Is the modern church a place to give comfort and encouragement to the value of such doubts? So far, have we not drawn strength and comfort to maintain the one or the other of these consistent heritages in a way which attacks the values of the other? Is this unavoidable? How can we draw inspiration to support these two pillars of western civilization so that they may stand together in full vigor, mutually unafraid? Is this not the central problem of our time?[265]

Surely that is a better way of working than the acrimony that currently sadly exists, than the assumption that science and faith are diametrically opposed and can never co-exist; that one must win and the other lose. I would want to add to Feynman's summary of Christian ethics and say it is far more than ethics; it is a parallel journey with science; a journey of discovery and adventure, even though it is looking at it all from another angle. I genuinely need both.

Sir John Houghton, in his paper *Big Science Big God*, says, *"As humans we have two eyes to view the world. Their combined 'binocular' vision enables us to see depth in scenes that cannot be identified with either eye on its own. When we open together both our spiritual eye and our material eye, we will appreciate a depth and richness, the existence of which we could not have imagined."*[266]

---

[265] http://en.wikiquote.org/wiki/Richard_Feynman
[266] Houghton, Sir John, "Big Science Big God" page 10

Concluding thought: the glory of creation

I totally agree with Richard Dawkins that science is a fascinating wonder. Pursuing knowledge about the universe and everything in it can fill you with awe and Feynman wonderfully expresses that above.

Richard Dawkins' opinion is that science gives us a far bigger picture of the universe than does a religious view. He quotes Carl Sagan in *Pale Blue Dot* who asks, "*how is it that hardly any major religion has looked at science and concluded, 'This is better than we thought! The Universe is much bigger than our prophets said, grander, more subtle, more elegant'? Instead they say, 'No, no, no! My god is a little god, and I want him to stay that way.' A religion, old or new, that stressed the magnificence of the Universe as revealed by modern science might be able to draw forth reserves of reverence and awe hardly tapped by the conventional faiths.*"[267]

I look at this and cannot help agreeing with nearly all he says. Maybe a majority of Christians have a small God. I can't say. Sagan may well be inspirational in his writing as Dawkins suggests. But if he (or Richard Dawkins) thinks the God of the Bible "is a little god", he has sadly misread the Bible. How can something infinite ever be described as small. He is infinitesimally vast and yet infinitesimally small. Size is hardly an attribute that can applied to the infinite, either physically or metaphorically.

Richard Dawkins also quotes J.B.S. Haldane who wrote, "*Now my own suspicion is that the universe is not only queerer than we suppose*

---

[267] "The God Delusion" pages. 32-33.

but queerer than we can suppose...I suspect that there are more things in heaven and earth than are dreamed of, in any philosophy."[268] Like Dawkins, I rise to this but as a Christian, my response is "Amen"! It reminds me of the apostle Paul who said, *"But as the scriptures say, 'No one has ever seen, nor ear heard, no one has ever imagined what God has prepared for those who love him'.*"[269] He may have been thinking primarily of spiritual things, but why can it not include more? Why not include the utter wonder of the discovery of the universe and life? Actually, when I think about it, I have a huge amount in common with Dawkins and yet I can see the universe from another totally different angle and so I draw a very different conclusion from what I observe and understand.

You see, Christian faith is nothing to do with ritual or keeping certain days. It is nothing to do with following traditions and having particular "services" whatever that may mean. It isn't about any building however magnificent a building may be. It's not even about being moral or ethical or good, though that is clearly important for anyone, Christian or otherwise. It's nothing to do with believing certain dogmas, although all believing Christians will find they hold certain basic truths in common.

No, biblical Christianity is about finding a living, dynamic and active relationship; a relationship that constantly grows; a relationship that encompasses others; a relationship that causes increasing wonder in the Other but also in the creation. It is one where you know you have never arrived but are always drawing closer; where you are constantly hungry and thirsty for more and yet are satisfied; where

---

268 Ibid. page 407
269 1 Corinthians, chapter 2, verse 9

you are "poor in spirit" and yet rich in appreciation; where you may suffer but remain confident in him. Christian faith positively encourages us to walk in the "wide place"[270], to expand our thinking, to see beyond the horizon. A number of verses in the Old Testament referring to enlarging of borders or tents can be seen in the context of expansiveness of thinking, like the small passage stuck in the middle of the genealogies of 1 Chronicles called the prayer of Jabez that starts off, *"Oh that you would bless me indeed and enlarge my border..."*[271]

God's salvation (and I mean that in its broad sense) results in release into jubilant expression: *"You have turned for me my mourning into dancing; you have loosed my sackcloth and clothed me with gladness."*[272] Psalm 18 verse 19 says *"He brought me out into a spacious place; he rescued me because he delighted in me."* Really, the whole idea of salvation is about being brought into complete freedom rather than just being taken out of a hole.

In the New Testament, there are hints that a questioning seeking open attitude is the one that gets rewarded. I mentioned the reaction of the people who observed the phenomena at Pentecost, but we also find Jesus telling his disciples to ask, to seek and to knock and that they would then receive, find and the door would be opened.[273] In addition, in Mark chapter 3, where Jesus tells the parable of the sower, the disciples come to him privately and ask the meaning, so he tells them and says what would seem to be grossly unfair: *"To you has been given the secret of the kingdom of God, but for those*

---

270 e.g. Psalm 119, verse 45
271 1 Chronicles chapter 4, verse 10
272 Psalm 30, verse 11
273 Matthew chapter 7, verse 7

outside everything is in parables."[274] What? How is that fair? Well, the disciples were open and asked; the others just accepted it as a lesson in agriculture. Faith is to do with seeking and asking. Faith is rewarded; the others were not interested.

I believe faith teaches us that there is more to this universe than the totality of what science has given us or could ever hope to give us. When I look at the heavens I can say, *"The heavens declare the glory of God and the sky above proclaims his handiwork."*[275] I have to think beyond their seemingly infinite vastness and realise there is an Infinite that is greater. When I begin to listen to the poetry behind what I can see, my appreciation is immeasurably increased.

Of course, if I don't realise there is poetry behind it, I will never know what I am missing. My appreciation will end with the science, and I will probably be quite satisfied with that, as are most atheists. But once I have heard one stanza of that poetry, I will ever hunger for more because I will realise there is another dimension to our existence that can never be plumbed by science. I may well realise that I can begin even now to appreciate the things that have not entered into my mind hitherto because Paul actually goes on after writing the verse above to say, *"these things God has revealed to us through the Spirit. For the Spirit searches all things, even the depths of God."*[276] But here's the rub – you need to look around the corner before you can experience this. You may say this is rubbish – "prove to me there's a corner"! No, I can't prove it. It's up to you. If you refuse to seek, you won't find it. If you decide to risk it, you will. It's called faith!

---

[274] Mark chapter 4, verse 11

[275] Psalm 19, verse 1

[276] 1 Corinthians chapter 2, verse 10

A prime characteristic of a child-like (not childish) attitude is wonder. Wonder at the creation; wonder at life; wonder at those stars; wonder at a new animal; inquisitiveness and fascination at everything new. Life holds endless possibilities and excitement, un-jaded by negative experiences and dashed hopes. Wonder is an amazing capacity and I would like more of it; I hope you would, too. Richard Dawkins has maintained it in his life and in that way is still child-like. Another prime child-like characteristic is questioning. Always curious and wanting to know why! Is wonder and questioning something of what Jesus meant when he said, *"Truly, I say to you, whoever does not receive the kingdom of God like a child shall not enter it."*[277]

I have to enter into that dimension, that kingdom; I have to be re-born and then I can appreciate both science and faith. *I have to look around that corner.*

---

[277] Mark chapter 10, verse 15

APPENDIX A – THEISTIC EVOLUTION ORGANISATIONS & RESOURCES

Affiliation of Christian Geologists
www2.wheaton.edu/ACG/

Answers in Creation (Old Earth Ministries)
www.oldearth.org

Christians in Science
www.cis.org.uk

Biologos
biologos.org

Genesis Proclaimed Association
www.genesisproclaimed.org

Interdisciplinary Biblical Research Institute
www.ibri.org

Perspectives on Theistic Evolution
www.theisticevolution.org

Reasons to Believe
  www.reasons.org/

The American Scientific Affiliation (ASA)
  network.asa3.org

The Faraday Institute
  www.faraday.st-edmunds.cam.ac.uk

The Science and Religion Forum
  www.srforum.org/

APPENDIX B – CREATIONIST / THEISTIC EVOLUTIONIST FIGURES

In a survey done in 2006, the proportion of Christians believing in theistic evolution to those believing in special creation was 27%:55% with 13% accepting atheistic evolution[278]. That means 32.9% (twenty seven out of eighty two) of believers are non-fundamentalist. According to a Gallup poll, one third of Americans believe in theistic evolution, while forty six percent are creationists[279]. That gives a greater proportion (33:46 or forty two percent) but I will stick to the former figure.

A survey published in The Guardian on 2nd March 2009[280] which had been conducted to mark the two hundredth anniversary of Darwin's birth found that eighty percent of people in the UK disagree with creationism and seventeen percent do believe in it but, interestingly, *"under a third"* felt that a belief in creationism and evolution was

---

[278] http://www.religioustolerance.org/ev_public.htm
[279] http://www.gallup.com/poll/155003/hold-creationist-view-human-origins.aspx
[280] http://www.guardian.co.uk/world/2009/mar/02/charles-darwin-creationism-intelligent-design

possible[281]. That proportion (presumably about thirty percent) is across the whole belief spectrum, so it is difficult to determine how many of those would count themselves as Christians. However, the probability is that they would be predominantly Christian or believers in another religion and, in view of the fact that committed Christian believers[282] are almost certainly in the minority in the country, it would mean that a fairly high proportion of Christians would accept evolution as an explanation of creation.

However, the following observations are relevant:

- The survey was conducted by "Theos" on only 2,060 people, so is probably not highly reliable,
- I found a large number of references to this survey and they tended to emphasize different figures; some included twenty two percent who accepted ID as probable, but that seems inconsistent with the figure of eighty percent disagreeing with creationism even if the seventeen percent is included in the twenty two percent,
- As Theos is a Christian organisation, it is possible that there may be some bias (but then we would have to conclude the same in the case of a survey conducted by an atheist organisation).

---

[281] I could not determine how much "under" but it was presumably closer to 33% than 25%, so was probably around 30% or so.

[282] By "committed" Christian, I mean someone who has made a conscious decision to turn his/her life over to Christ and demonstrates that in life by following him; I would not regard someone who simply "attends church" as being committed. I remember hearing about a pig and a hen discussing their part in a human breakfast. The pig said, "The thing is, you are involved, but I am committed!"

I would conclude that we cannot draw anything definite from these figures but it does give some idea of how people in the UK think. According to this survey, it seems the majority of believers (of all types) would accept theistic evolution. Paul Woolley, director of Theos concludes: *"There are two lessons in particular that we can learn from Darwin. The first is that belief in God and evolution are compatible. Secondly, in a time when debates about evolution and religious belief can be aggressive and polarised, Charles Darwin remains an example of how to disagree without being disagreeable."* It would be good if more people were able to disagree without being disagreeable. I would love to see this debate being conducted along proper lines of consideration between all parties even if there is very strong disagreement.

Further study if you are interested:

Proportions of scientists believing in God/evolution etc.:

http://wiki.answers.com/Q/Approximately_what_percentage_of_recognized_Scientists_believes_in_Creation?#slide=1

Article on different beliefs on creation in Wikipedia (quite informative):

http://en.wikipedia.org/wiki/Creationism

BIBLIOGRAPHY

Abuelaish, Izzeldin "I Shall Not Hate" Bloomsbury London 2012

Adams, Douglas "The Hitchhiker's Guide to the Galaxy" Pan Books 1979

Alexander, Denis "Creation or Evolution – do we have to choose?" Monarch Books Oxford 2008

Allen, Robert (Consultant Editor) "Penguin English Dictionary" Penguin Books London 2002

Andrews, Edgar "Who Made God?" EP Books, Darlington 2009

Augustine, St. "The Literal Meaning of Genesis" Paulist Press, New York 1982

Aurelius, Marcus "Meditations" Kindle e-Books

Bell, Rob "Love Wins" Harper Collins, London 2012

Brooke, John Hedley "Natural law in the natural sciences: the origins of modern atheism?" from "Science & Christian Belief", vol 4. No. 2 (April 1990)

Collins, Francis "The Language of God" Free Press New York 2006

Coulson, C.A. "Science and Christian Belief" Oxford University Press, London 1955

Eareckson Tada, Joni "Joni: An Unforgettable Story" Zondervan, Grand Rapids 2001

Ehrman, Bart "Did Jesus Exist?" Harper Collins 2012

Elliot, Elisabeth "Through Gates of Splendor" Tyndale House Publishers 1986

Eugene A Curry "The Disbelieving Michael Shermer: A Review Essay of Michael Shermer's *The Believing Brain*", Journal of the International Society of Christian Apologetics, Vol 5 No 1 April 2012

Darwin, Charles "On the Origin of Species" Kindle e-book

Dawkins, Richard "An Appetite for Wonder" Transworld Publishers, London 2013

Dawkins, Richard "The Ancestor's Tale" Weidenfeld & Nicolson, London 2005

Dawkins, Richard "The God Delusion" Random House eBooks 2009

Dawkins, Richard "The Selfish Gene" Oxford University Press 1976

Dawkins, Richard "Unweaving the Rainbow" Penguin Books, London 2006

Houghton, Sir John "Big Science Big God" John Ray Initiative, Briefing Paper No. 15 University of Gloucestershire

Hawking, Stephen & Mlodinow, Leonard "The Grand Design" Bantam Press, London 2010

Holder, Rodney "Big Bang Big God" Lion Hudson, Oxford 2013

Huxley, Aldous "Brave New World" Vintage Books, London 2007

Koenig, Harold, McCullough, Michael & Larson, David "Handbook on Religion and Health" Oxford University Press 2001

Krauss, Lawrence "A Universe from Nothing?" Free Press, New York 2012

Le Fanu, James "Why Us?" Vintage Books, New York 2010

Lewis, C.S. "God in the Dock" Eerdmans, New York 1970

Lewis, C.S. "Mere Christianity" Collins, London 1952

Lewis, C.S. "Surprised by Joy" Geoffrey Bles, London 1955

Lewis, C.S. "The Four Loves" Harcourt, New York 1960

Lewis, C.S. "The Great Divorce" HarperCollins, New York 2001

Lewis, C.S. "The Lion, the Witch and the Wardrobe" Geoffrey Bles, London 1950

Lewis, C.S. "The Pilgrim's Regress" Eerdmans, USA 1958

Lewis, C.S. "The Problem of Pain" HarperCollins, New York 2001

Lucas, Ernest "Can we Believe Genesis Today?" Inter-Varsity Press 2001

Lyle, Jason & Chaffey, Tim "Old Earth Creationism on Trial" Master Books 2008

Marshall, Catherine "Beyond Ourselves" Hodder Christian Essential 1962

McCandless, David "Information is Beautiful" HarperCollins London 2009

McGrath, Alister & Joanna "The Dawkins Delusion" IVP Books Illinois 2007

McGrath, Alister "Dawkins' God, genes, memes and the meaning of life" Blackwell Publishing Oxford 2007

Morison, Frank. "Who moved the stone?" Authentic Media 2006

Morris, John "The Young Earth: The Real History of the Earth – Past, Present, and Future" Master Books 2007

Morris, Simon Conway "Life's Solution" Cambridge University Press 2004

Otis, John "Theistic Evolution: A Sinful Compromise" Triumphant Publications 2013

Paley, William "Natural Theology" Oxford University Press, 2008

Parker, Andrew "The Genesis Enigma" Doubleday 2009

Polkinghorne, John "The Anthropic Principle and the Science and Religion Debate" Faraday Institute for Science and Religion April 2007

Pullinger, Jackie "Chasing the Dragon" Hodder & Stoughton 1980

Ridley, Matt "Genome - the autobiography of a species in 23 chapters" Hodder Perennial, London 2000

Shermer, Michael "The Believing Brain" Robinson, London 2012

Sims, Andrew "Is Faith Delusion?" Continuum, London 2009

Strobel, Lee "The Case for Christ" Zondervan, Grand Rapids 1998

Topham, J.R. "Teleology and the concept of Natural Law" from "Science & Christian Belief" vol 1. No. 2 (October 1989)

Vine, WE "Vine's Expository Dictionary of New Testament Words" MacDonald Publishing Company McLean, Virginia

Yancey, Philip "What's So Amazing About Grace?" Zondervan, Grand Rapids 1997

The Penguin English Dictionary Penguin Books Ltd., London 2001

References to any online works are acknowledged only on the relevant pages